Every army must know the rules of engagement in order to be effective in warfare. The same is true for the twenty-first-century church. This book is a must for those who are on the front line, and I heartily endorse it to God's elite forces.

The strategies in this book are written by one of God's present-day generals who is committed to leading the saints to victory.

—Apostle John Eckhardt

Cindy Trimm has spiritual insight that is invariably unique and profound. The kingdom principles expounded in this book provide the power tools needed to change regions dominated by tyrannical, diabolical demonic systems. The systematic methodologies explained here will make an indelible impression and develop the generational dominance of God's people in a kingdom environment. After reading *The Rules of Engagement*, I am convinced that any person and ministry involved in transforming nations for the future need this resource as a catalyst for change and development. The systems and dimensions described herein will be engraved in the minds of every reader, everywhere. This book is an essential read.

—Bishop Tudor Bismark
Jabula—New Life Ministries

In a world where the enemy is out to distract and deceive as many as he can, even the very elect, this work is extremely timely. When it comes to spiritual warfare, it is clear to me that in this early part of the twenty-first century, Cindy Trimm is one of God's generals. She has done extensive research on this subject that has been impacting lives around the world. This latest work is a compilation of three books and is a powerful tool for persons in preparation for spiritual warfare as well as those already engaged in spiritual warfare. Cindy Trimm shares a wealth of information, instruction, and principles in this book that, if applied, will equip you for victory over the enemy in every area of your life. This book is indeed a training manual for the believer and a must-read for those who wish to walk in victory.

—Bishop Neil C. Ellis, Cmg, DD, JP
Senior Pastor/teacher, Mt. Tabor Full Gospel Baptist Church

Great insight on allowing the kingdom to work in you. An excellent resource for your personal and ministry library.

—Apostle Ron Carpenter
Redemption World Outreach Center

Cindy Trimm documents Scripture in a masterful way and exposes the strategies and tactics brought against us by the forces of evil. The principles expounded upon in this book will cause life-changing victories in Christ.

—Pastor Marion Meares
Evangel Cathedral

Cindy Trimm, a prophet, a pastor, a writer, and a humanitarian has helped to shape the lives of many of God's powerful leaders, including myself, through insightful, prophetic teachings on prayer. This book is a weapon with a double-edged sword to help you to strategize how to mightily pull down every stronghold in your life. I highly recommend it! Read it and win!

—Judy Jacobs
His Song Ministries
International Psalmist, Author, Teacher, and Worship Leader

I was once told that the greatest teachers are those who were the greatest students. Cindy Trimm had to have been that exceptional student absorbing every ounce of wisdom, knowledge, and understanding that was available. Hearing her teach and reading her books brings impartation, clarity, and empowerment to anyone who is ready to live in total victory over satanic powers and shift into the next realm and dimension in their lives.

—Micah Stampley
Minstrel and Psalmist

Practical and spiritual applications abound in this book from Cindy Trimm. If we understand the critical times in which we live (and we do), we must understand that godly power and authority are available and necessary for victory in every aspect of life. Cindy Trimm lays out strategic, logical, and effective maneuvers for warring in the heavenlies. This is an essential book for such a time as this!

—Dr. Teresa Hairston
Founder/Publisher, *Gospel Today Magazine*

The Rules of Engagement is a revolutionary, life-changing view of spiritual warfare. Cindy Trimm's comprehensive manual exposes adversarial tactics and strategies while illuminating seldom-taught truths and principles regarding strongholds and their origins. As a publisher, I have read many books written on spiritual warfare. However, I found this book to be a powerful tool for dethroning the enemy. Its prayers and declarations can be applied by any believer for guaranteed spiritual victory and success in every area of life.

—Theresa Tavernier
Founder/Publisher, Saved Magazine

The
RULES
of ENGAGEMENT

CINDY TRIMM

CHARISMA
HOUSE

Most CHARISMA HOUSE BOOK GROUP products are available at special quantity discounts for bulk purchase for sales promotions, premiums, fund-raising, and educational needs. For details, write Charisma House Book Group, 600 Rinehart Road, Lake Mary, Florida 32746, or telephone (407) 333-0600.

THE RULES OF ENGAGEMENT by Cindy Trimm
Published by Charisma House
Charisma Media/Charisma House Book Group
600 Rinehart Road
Lake Mary, Florida 32746
www.charismahouse.com

Unless otherwise noted, all Scripture quotations are from the King James Version of the Bible.

Scripture quotations marked AMP are from the Amplified Bible. Old Testament copyright © 1965, 1987 by the Zondervan Corporation. The Amplified New Testament copyright © 1954, 1958, 1987 by the Lockman Foundation. Used by permission.

Scripture quotations marked NAS are from the New American Standard Bible. Copyright © 1960, 1962, 1963, 1968, 1971, 1972, 1973, 1975, 1977 by the Lockman Foundation. Used by permission. (www.Lockman.org)

Scripture quotations marked NIV are from the Holy Bible, New International Version. Copyright © 1973, 1978, 1984, International Bible Society. Used by permission.

Scripture quotations marked TLB are from The Living Bible. Copyright © 1971. Used by permission of Tyndale House Publishers, Inc., Wheaton, IL 60189. All rights reserved.

Design Director: Bill Johnson
Cover design by Jerry Pomales

Copyright © 2008 by Cindy Trimm
All rights reserved
Library of Congress Cataloging-in-Publication Data:
Trimm, Cindy.
  The rules of engagement / Cindy Trimm.
    p. cm.
Includes bibliographical references and index.
ISBN 978-1-59979-340-5
1. Spiritual warfare. I. Title.
BV4509.5.T74 2008
235'.4--dc22

                              2008025464

E-book ISBN: 978-1-59979-718-2

This publication is translated in Spanish under the title Las reglas de combate, copyright © 2008 by Cindy Trimm, published by Casa Creación, a Charisma Media company. All rights reserved.

13 14 15 16 17 — 15 14 13 12 11

Printed in the United States of America

This book is dedicated to Prophetess Juanita Bynum.
You gave the world No More Sheets, My Spiritual Inheritance,
Matters of the Heart, Woman on the Frontline,
and the Threshing Floor Revival.
You gave me an opportunity that changed my destiny. Thank you.

CONTENTS

FOREWORD

WAR! THE LORD says in Matthew 24:6–7, "And you will hear of wars and rumors of wars. See that you are not troubled; for all these things must come to pass, but the end is not yet" (NKJV, emphasis added). If we are to keep hearing of wars and rumors of war, we need to understand the rules of engagement for the wars that surround us.

When we hear the word war we have thoughts of destruction, sorrow, grief, loss, conflict, and death. However, the Lord says clearly, "See that you are not troubled." Our inner man will not be unsettled if we know the rules of engagement!

I can still remember the day I got up early and went from our bedroom to the couch. As I lay down and began to meditate and get my mind set on the Lord for the day, an interesting thing happened: a blackboard appeared before me. Visions are very interesting. I can't say that I have had many, but the few God has graced me with have been dramatic.

I began to see words appear on this blackboard. The hand of God seemed to be writing before me, just as He wrote in the days of Daniel. I saw the following words: anti-Semitism, militant Islam, covenant conflict, women arising for My purposes, lawlessness, the transference of wealth, over-throwing thrones of iniquity, and prepare for war. "Prepare for war" seemed to be the illuminating cornerstone of the vision.

I said, "Lord, what are You showing me?" "This is the future war of the church," He said. I got up and began writing what He had shown me, and this is now a classic history book of the last decade and season of war. At the beginning of the new millennium, there was little understanding on war and how to maneuver in and through the season ahead. Then came September 11, 2001. War then became a reality in the world around us! I believe the Lord Himself put us in a supernatural accelerated course and began to develop rules of engagement for this season of confrontation and interaction in the wars around us.

War is like the game of chess. Much like various pieces in a game of chess, each of us plays a key role in God's end-time strategy or future plan for full-ness in the earth realm. Like chess, the only way we can be defeated is to fail to think ahead and anticipate the enemy's moves. When we become Christians, we are born onto a battlefield. Our choice is not whether we want to enter into a conflict; rather, war has already been declared against us. Our only choice is whether we want to be trampled by the enemy or learn to fight and win.

To be efficient in the rules of engagement, one must know the promises of God. Peter said that God has given us His precious and magnificent assurances and that through them we can become partakers of His divine nature (2 Pet. 1:4). God has given us promises that relate to every area of life. He has promised us abundant provision, healing, and many other blessings.

Cindy Trimm has developed a manual that answers questions and creates understanding that prepares us for war! We must know why we are at war! We must know who our enemy is and how he operates against the church! We must know who we are and how God is preparing us for this future war! We must have our strategy for victory. In *The Rules of Engagement*, Cindy Trimm leads you into the most in-depth understanding of WHY and HOW to win the wars around you. Therefore, never fear the rumors of war.

Ask any soldier what matters most when you're on the battlefield and you'll likely get a twofold answer: who are you fighting against, and whose side are you on? It's crucial to know who you are aligned with. Who enlisted you? Who trained you for war? Whose tactics do you adhere to, and whose commands will you follow to death? *The Rules of Engagement* answers these questions.

As Christians, we are warriors who have been called and enlisted by the holy God of this universe. We are warriors of the cross. In the heat of battle, we must remind ourselves of these truths about the God who enlisted us: He is the God above all gods. His Son has paid the price for our ultimate victory. Satan's headship has already been broken by the power of the cross. Jesus has already conquered death, hell, and the grave. We need not fear death but only resist its sting. The Spirit of God still reigns supreme in the earth to comfort us in the midst of distressing times. He is the only restraining force of evil and is there to give us strategies to overcome every ploy the enemy has set against our lives. The earth belongs to God, and He has a plan linked with the fullness of time. We, His children, might get knocked down, but we will never get knocked out. He is love, and perfect love in us will cast out all fear of the future.

With everything going on in the earth, we must never forget that He is God. We know that He is always in command. Yet if that's the case, why is there so much confusion around us? Why are nations forever in conflict and people groups warring against each other? Why does lawlessness continue to escalate throughout the world? If He is God and has already won the victory, what exactly is our role in the midst of the warfare we encounter on a daily basis?

The truth is, we are fully engaged in a covenant conflict, which means that we are warring to see the blessings of a holy, supreme God spread throughout the earthly realm. Psalm 24:1 declares that the "earth is the LORD's, and the fullness thereof." God has a plan of fullness for the earth. His desire is for wholeness. Yet the war between God and evil is unfolding, which will determine how His fullness will be manifested in the earth in our generations and those to come. *The Rules of Engagement*, destined to be a classic for the generations ahead, will assist you to walk on a daily basis as a victorious warrior who understands the boundaries of confrontation and overcoming.

We already know that the headship of Satan has been broken forever. However, how do we enforce and engage the enemy to remain broken and his head submitted to the authority of Christ in us? If we win the war in this generation, the generation that follows will experience blessings. The enemy still believes he has a right to shut the portals of heaven so that we, as God's children, will be confined to a decaying earth realm where death attempts to cast a shadow. Not so! God has made all wisdom available for His children. We can access that wisdom today. We can ascend into heavenly places and gain what is necessary to release in the earth. As blood-bought, redeemed children of a holy God, we can wield the sword of the Spirit in the earth and declare, "On Earth as it is in heaven!" Though the enemy has attempted to prevent God's blessings from manifesting in the earth, we can prepare a way for those blessings to be revealed.

This is a crucial time for believers. We have the opportunity to be as "wise as serpents" (Matt. 10:16) by being like the sons of Issachar. These were men from the renowned tribe in Israel who served as counselors to King David. Scripture records that they were a group "that had understanding of the times" (1 Chron. 12:32). In the same way, we must discern the times, taking full advantage of the otherworldly wisdom God offers us. When we do, we will be prepared for the unfolding wars of our time. We thank you, Cindy Trimm, for a manual to assist us in all the wars ahead! Thank God for *The Rules of Engagement*!

—Dr. Chuck D. Pierce
President, Glory of Zion International Ministries, Inc.

ACKNOWLEDGMENTS

T O MY LORD and Savior, Jesus Christ: Thank You for entrusting me to deliver this literary treasure, and for giving me Bishop Goodwin C. and lady Ruby Smith, my spiritual mentors and pastors for thirty-two years. You nurtured and nourished "success."

I am forever grateful to be blessed with a loving and supportive family who continues to be my strength and inspiration. Praise is continuously on my lips for my staff, partners, and ministry volunteers: Jewel Edwards, Holley Richardson, Tekia Smith, Virginia Matthis, Calvin Anderson, Perisean Hall, Dawn Alli, Peggy Clemens, A. Monica Jackson, Opal Jasper, Robin Green, Jimmie Green, Eugenia Roberts, Dr. Rita Claxton, Annette Ortega, Regina Crider, Wendy Williams, Janice Ruff, Claudette Hinds, Claudette McAlpin, Elke Pettiford, Sharon Harris, Marcus and Yamia Green, Melva Hodge, Debbie Leakey, Doloris Hughes, the leadership and members of Embassy Center of Empowerment, the city of David, KU Bermuda staff, KU alumnae and alumni.

Finally, there can never be a great book without an even greater publisher. Thank you, Stephen Strang, Barbara Dycus, Lucy Kurz, Woodley Auguste, Jevon Bolden, Dinah Wallace, Margarita Henry, Nicole Caldwell, Jerry Pomales, LeAnn Moorhead, Susan Simcox, Laurene Burgwin, Patricia Blount and the entire Strang Communications family! And to all my supporters and ministry partners around the world, thank you for believing in me.

INTRODUCTION

BASIC TRAINING

SALM 144:1–15 RECORDS the prayer of a skilled warrior by the name of David. From his days as a shepherd boy and throughout his reign as king of the nation of Israel, God empowered him in the art, science, and technology of strategic prayer and spiritual warfare.

His skill and expertise were gained as God, in His sovereignty, placed him in the midst of a variety of battles, including encounters with bears and lions, confrontation with Goliath, and the battle he fought with his son Absalom, whose defiant insurrection almost cost David his kingdom. In this psalm, David lets us know that it was Jehovah-Gibbor, the mighty Man of war, who taught him warfare strategies and tactics and provided the divine empowerment for success. He lifts his voice in adulation to honor his General. He declares, "Blessed be the Lord, my Rock and my keen and firm Strength, Who teaches my hands to war and my fingers to fight—My Steadfast Love and my Fortress, my High Tower and my Deliverer, my Shield and He in Whom I trust and take refuge, Who subdues my people under me" (Psalm 144:1–2, AMP).

From David's life experiences, I have learned that the only way you can become a skillful warrior is to be trained and placed in the midst of a battle. It is only when you are placed in the furnace of afflictions, and when all hell seems to break loose around you, that you can truly be trained in the art of strategic prayer and spiritual warfare. Practice does not make perfect. Perfect practice makes perfect. You will never get the level of training you need in order to become an effective prayer warrior by engaging in "war games." You must face the real enemy on the real battlefield. Simply reading the Bible or attending workshops and conferences will never make you an effective warrior. Proverbs implies that knowledge without experience and wisdom is folly. (See Proverbs 14:18; 16:22.)

The intent of this book is to help you to effectively war in the heavens for new spheres of power/jurisdiction so that the kingdom of God is promoted and established in new realms, regions, and terrestrial domains, and to move from a defensive position in the realm of the spirit to an offensive one. (See Daniel 9:1–12:3; Ephesians 6:11–18; Revelation 12:4, 7–9.)

I have discovered that although I had been praying earnestly and scripturally in the past, many of my prayers were either sabotaged or counterattacked by the enemy. As I prayed and asked God why, He showed me that I was praying fervently but not effectively because I was praying amiss. I was praying from an incorrect perspective and position. Satan was able to gain the upper hand in my warfare because I ignorantly prayed "earthbound" prayers. He told me that I needed to fight my battles and wage warfare where it really belongs: in the heavenlies. He also reminded me that I was seated in heavenly places in Christ Jesus, above principalities and powers. (See Ephesians 2:20–22; 3:6.) I then realized that they were not above me, oppressing and controlling my destiny with their diabolical activities. I was above them! Armed and dangerous with this revelation, I was able to enforce my prayers with much authority and confidence in knowing that whatsoever I desired, when I prayed I would receive favorable results. (See Mark 11:23–24.)

As you delve into this carefully prepared manual for spiritual warfare, there are some tools that you will need at all times. No soldier can rely on another's rations, weapons, or experience. It is time for you to get yourself armed. You are well into your training. As a matter of fact, the war is raging on even now.

Below are several instructions that you must hold on to as you engage in spiritual warfare.

1. Make certain you have the right tools.

We will be covering a lot of ground in this book. You may have come across other books that give you all of the Scriptures and prayers written out for you to recite in order to address certain issues and spiritual maladies. Since the intention of this book is to instruct and train, I will not always do that here. Get ready to receive some *on-the-job training*. I want you to get familiar with your own battleground, identify your own strengths and weaknesses, and be well acquainted with your Commander in Chief—Jehovah-Gibbor. Therefore, you will need a personal copy of God's Word, the sword. You will also find that in times of revelation you will need a prayer journal or even a recording device to quickly document the *rhema* word God may give you concerning a certain issue or person. (See Revelation 1:19.) In addition to those items, you may find good use for a notebook, pen, and highlighter. Things are about to get good!

2. Engage in the proper preparation.

First Corinthians 14:4, 14 and Jude 20 instruct us to pray in the Spirit because it will edify us and charge us up in the Holy Spirit (give us power to pray more effectively). This time in the Spirit can also be done by singing as you spend time in worship, praise, and thanksgiving. Recalibrate your spiritual atmosphere by playing worship or anointed instrumental music. This will help you to break through spiritual barriers and barricades and to move beyond the veil into the secret place (Ps. 91). The following prayer often helps me enter into the secret place during my times of worship. Perhaps you may want to pray it as well.

> *My heavenly Father, in the name of Jesus I enter into Your gates with thanksgiving and into Your courts with praise. I bless Your name. You are great and greatly to be praised. I worship You and adore You. (Continue to worship God, and thank Him for health, strength, etc.) I thank You, Father, for clothing me in a robe of righteousness, which covers me because of the shed blood of Jesus Christ. It is in Him I live and move and have my being (Ps. 100:4; Isa. 61:10; Acts 17:28).*

3. Rid yourself of encumbrances.

According to Hebrews 12:1, a few other actions are needed as you prepare for spiritual warfare. You need to make sure you confess your sins (Ps. 24:3–4; Prov. 28:13), examine yourself and determine if you need to repent of something or release (forgive) someone, and cast your cares and burdens upon the Lord (1 Pet. 5:7). Remember, you do not fight spiritual battles in your own strength; you fight them in the strength of the Lord.

4. Maintain the proper perspective, posture, and position.

When you observe a soldier, you immediately notice his stance and his position. His head is up, his eyes are alert and aware of his surroundings, and he is always in position. This is a lifesaver in wartime, if there ever was one. It is imperative that a soldier knows his position and where he should be at all times.

Therefore, as you are fighting for the army of the Lord, you will want to keep the right perspective. According to Revelation 4:1, you need to keep a heavenly, panoramic view, far above principalities and powers (Eph. 1:21–23; Col. 1:18). As you take your posture, you need to stand offensively (Eph. 6:11), stand consistently (v. 13), and stand armed and dangerous (2 Cor. 10:4–5). Your position is in the heavenly places in Christ Jesus (Eph. 2:6). Remember, as He is in the world, so are we (2 Cor. 10:7; Rom. 6:4–5). To maintain this position, your communication must be right on and always connected. Pray "throne-room" prayers (Heb. 4:14–16; 8:1–5; 10:19–23) to keep you aligned with your headquarters. Throne-room prayers are prayers that are prayed from the realm of faith.

Praying from the right position with the right perspective and with confident assurance that your prayers and petitions are being heard will give you the assurance that the answers are on the way (1 John 5:14–15). You are not praying defensively, countering an attack hurled upon you from the realm of the spirit to you who *stand* upon the earth. You are praying from your heavenly position in Christ Jesus, who has been exalted above all principalities and powers and is the head of the church, of which you are a part of the body. You are praying offensively, in heavenly places, having received power over all the power of the enemy (Eph. 1:20–23, 2:6; Phil. 2:5–11; Luke 10:19).

5. Make certain you are properly adorned.

Put on the Lord Jesus Christ, and make no provisions for the flesh—lust, envy, strife, bitterness, fornication, hatred, and so on (Rom. 13:14; Gal. 5:19–20). Ensure you are fully clad with the whole armor of God, according to Ephesians 6:13–17.

6. Effectively use your authority.

The blood of Jesus Christ gives you the right to enter the holiest of places and to petition God for the deliverance that you or someone else may need (Heb. 10:19–23). You can boldly enter, knowing that you are clean and your requests will be honored. Because you are fighting on God's side, you have a right to claim His Son's name and authority. When you say the name of Jesus, everything must submit (Phil. 2:9–11). You also come armed with the authority of the Word—the sword of the Spirit (Eph. 6:16–18).

Remember, God has placed Satan and his cohorts under your feet, so do not just sit and wait for something to happen. Stand, put your foot down, make no covenant, show no mercy, and take the victory in Jesus's name (Deut. 7:1–2; Luke 10:19; Eph. 6:11–18).

7. Effectively use your weapons.

The sword of the Spirit is the Word of God, the blood of Jesus Christ, the anointing and fire of the Holy Spirit. Marching, walking, stomping, dancing, clapping, silence, praying in the Spirit, tithes, offerings, and shouting are all powerful weapons you can access from your spiritual arsenal. We will talk more about these weapons in chapter 8, "Gearing Up for Battle—What Are Your Weapons?"

THE TIME IS NOW

The Bible clearly states that the purpose for which Christ was born was to destroy the works of Satan. We know that Christ completed His mission on the cross. Scripture clearly states that Christ's job description was the exact antithesis of the enemy's. According to John 10:10, Christ came to bring life, but Satan came "to steal, and to kill, and to destroy" (John 10:10). Satan is relentless in his attempts to undermine the plans and purposes of God. He is skillful at even disguising himself in order to remain undetected. As believers, we need not be afraid, but be aware and empowered with the knowledge that we have the ability to identify the works of the enemy. God has given us His power to tread on serpents, scorpions, and over all the power of the enemy so that according to Luke 10:19, "Nothing shall by any means hurt [us]."

The time has come when God has stirred up the hearts of all believers to rise up and take their rightful places as His official representatives in the earthly realm. Our role is to activate and enforce the authority God has given us. As an empowered believer, you should no longer be satisfied with standing on the sidelines or accepting anything from the enemy. There is a real battle going on. There are no demilitarized zones in this battle. Thank God we have been given the assurance that, in this warfare, we are fighting the good fight of faith. The outcome has been decided, and our victory has been downloaded into the equation. It is time to beat the devil at his own game.

I have never seen an age like this, where there is such a desire to see souls saved and the church filled with the glory of God. God is birthing His plans in every nation and among all peoples. The kingdom of heaven is prevailing as the end of the age quickly approaches. We are getting ready for the final showdown: when the saints of God will deliver the final blow to the enemy and deliver the kingdoms of this world to Him. We will not only bind the strongman, but we will also render him hopelessly helpless in preventing the next move of God in our personal lives, churches, ministries, communities, and nations.

The Rules of Engagement is by no means an exhaustive commentary. Instead, it was written with the intention of being used as a handy, user-friendly, easy-to-read reference book. It has been designed to give you victory in all your battles and to divinely empower you to penetrate and plunder the kingdom of darkness while promoting and populating the kingdom of heaven. This book will take your life to new heights in God, new dimensions in knowledge, and new realms of authority as you are divinely empowered to:

1. Assess situations and circumstances accurately based on spiritual laws and principles
2. Recognize and identify the presence and activities of principalities and their subordinate spirits
3. Sever the root causes of satanic influences and demonic activities
4. Gain and maintain spiritual authority over regions and territories
5. Gain and regain control over your life and relationships, ministries, and businesses

As you give this manual your undivided attention, you will be empowered with truth and equipped with powerful weapons of warfare. Anticipate that the Spirit of truth is not only liberating you but also freeing everything and everyone associated with you in Jesus's name.

Utilize these powerful, practical tools and insights designed to give you victory in all your battles, and let the earth resound in concert with the heavenly hosts, saying, "The kingdoms of this world are become the kingdoms of our Lord, and of his Christ; and he shall reign for ever and ever" (Rev. 11:15).

PART I

RULES OF ENGAGEMENT

YOU—REDEFINED

True Dominion Starts With Knowing Who You Are

E. M. BOUNDS once said, "God's great plan for the redemption of mankind is as much bound up to prayer for its prosperity and success as when the decree creating the movement was issued from the Father, bearing on its frontage the imperative, universal and eternal condition, 'Ask of me, and I will give thee the heathen for thy inheritance and the uttermost part of the earth for thy possession.'"[1]

As a believer, you hold the key to advancing the kingdom of heaven and destroying the works of the enemy. According to Matthew 18:18, "Whatsoever ye shall bind on earth shall be bound in heaven: and whatsoever ye shall loose on earth shall be loosed in heaven." This text speaks of the legalities and technicalities of the kingdom, relative to your authority on Earth. You are God's official agent here on Earth. Therefore, whatever you allow, heaven allows, and whatever you disallow, heaven disallows. In part 3, "Binding the Strongman," we will talk more about how to operate within the rules of the kingdom to produce victory in the earth.

But right now, I want you to understand the power behind two principle war weapons: prayer and the Word of God. The combination of the two provide the one-two punch that ensures the enemy is knocked out of your life, family, business, ministry, community, and nation every time. The Bible gives us example after example of how true this is. We are going to look at one example of how prayer changes a whole nation's allegiance and another example of how the Word silences the enemy.

EFFECTUAL PRAYER PRODUCES SUPERNATURAL RESULTS

One of our examples of this is Elijah. First Kings 17:1 records, "And Elijah the Tishbite, *who was* of the inhabitants of Gilead, said unto Ahab, *As the*

LORD God of Israel liveth, before whom I stand, there shall not be dew nor rain these years, but according to my word" (emphasis added). Elijah had all the authority of heaven behind him when he pronounced this judgment over Ahab's kingdom, for they had disgraced God and had given themselves to idol worship. It may appear that Elijah capriciously decided to withhold rain, but no. If you look closely at James 5:17, you will see the secret of his power: "Elijah was a man just like us. *He prayed earnestly...*" (NIV, emphasis added). Earnest prayer from this righteous man produced supernatural results. (See James 5:16.)

Elijah knew the power of prayer, and throughout his dealings with Ahab, he maintained clear communication to the God of heaven. His place was well established in God; therefore, he had a right to speak against things that were not in line with what God commanded. He knew that as he pronounced his judgment over things that displeased God, God would pronounce the same judgment.

What we must learn from Elijah's example is that because God created us in His image and after His likeness, crowning us with His glory and establishing us as His earthly representatives, we have authority in the earth to decree God's judgments (Gen. 1:28; Ps. 115:15–16). Adam and Eve may have fallen into sin, but we have been restored to our high place in God through the sacrifice of Jesus Christ. What was lost has been regained and returned to us by our General and mighty Man of war. It is up to us to enforce that authority (Ps. 8:4–6; 115:16; Luke 10:19; Eph. 2:2). Our authority and dominion can be activated in the same way as Elijah's—through fervent, earnest prayer.

When I look at the state of the world, I have come to the conclusion that the world does not need more churches, more revivals, more choirs, more psalmists, or more minstrels. What the church needs is more men and women of prayer. Prayer is a divine technology that, when implemented, gives God permission to intervene in the affairs of humanity. If there was ever a time when the world could use some divine intervention, it sure is now.

I read a story titled "Spurgeon's Boiler Room." It told of five young college students who were spending a Sunday in London. They went to hear the famed C. H. Spurgeon preach. While waiting for the doors to open, the students were greeted by a man who asked if they would like to see the heating plant of this church. It was mid-July, so they were not interested in seeing a hot place in any building. The story continues:

They didn't want to offend the stranger, so they consented. The young men were taken down a stairway, a door was quietly opened, and their guide whispered, "This is our heating plant." Surprised, the students saw 700 people bowed in prayer, seeking a blessing on the service that was soon to begin in the auditorium above. Softly closing the door, the gentleman then introduced himself. It was none other than Charles Spurgeon.[2]

In every dispensation and generation, God has had a man or woman who partnered with Him for the redemption of humanity. These men and women partnered through prayer. Abraham, Moses, Hannah, David, Solomon, Anna, Paul, St. Francis of Assisi, Martin Luther, Brother Lawrence, John Wesley, David Livingston, Oswald Chambers, E. M. Bounds, D. L. Moody, Watchman Nee, Corrie ten Boom, David Yonggi Cho, and the list goes on. These individuals and many others partnered with God to change the state of the world. Charles G. Finney said, "Effective prayer is prayer that attains what it seeks. It is prayer that moves God, effecting its end."[3] To this end, I believe that in this dispensation, every church should have a "boiler room," with a modern-day "Spurgeon" as its tour guide.

THE WORD SILENCES THE ENEMY

When you use the Word of God in prayer, it silences the enemy. This is what happened to Jesus in the wilderness. The voice of the enemy spoke to Him on three occasions. You have to understand that the conversation was not verbal, but mental. Spiritual warfare is the counsel of the human mind and any other spirit (including the human spirit) other than the Spirit of God as the following text describes:

Then Jesus was led up by the Spirit into the wilderness to be tempted by the devil. And after He had fasted forty days and forty nights, He then became hungry. And the tempter came and said to Him, "If You are the Son of God, command that these stones become bread." But He answered and said, "It is written, 'Man shall not live on bread alone, but on every word that proceeds out of the mouth of God.'" Then the devil took Him into the holy city; and he had Him stand on the pinnacle of the temple, and said to Him, "If You are the Son of God throw Yourself down; for it is written, 'He will give His angels charge concerning You'; and 'On their hands they will bear You up, lest You strike Your foot against a stone.'" Jesus said to him, "On the other hand, it is written, 'You shall not put the Lord your God to the test.'" Again, the devil took Him to a very high mountain, and showed Him all the kingdoms of the world, and their glory; and he said to Him, "All these things will I give You, if You fall down and worship me." Then Jesus said to him, "Begone, Satan! For it is written, 'You shall worship the Lord your God, and serve Him only.'" Then the devil left Him; and behold, angels came and began to minister to Him.

—Matthew 4:1–11, NAS

Notice Jesus fought with the Word of the Lord and brought His thoughts under its authority. You must do the same. The devil was after Jesus's authority and dominion in the earth realm. He is after yours. Do not give it away. You must fight every thought that does not align itself with the Word of God and fight with God's Word. Cast the thoughts down, and bring them under the authority of the Word and under the lordship of Christ.

When the enemy created a mess of this world, according to the first chapter of Genesis, God used words (the spirit of His mouth) to bring the world back into order and alignment according to His original design and plan. Since we are created in the image and after the likeness of God, we too have the same power (Gen. 1:26). It is the power of the spoken word that gives you life or death and releases blessings or curses (Prov. 18:21). You must effectively use anointed words to destroy the works of the enemy in your life, home, ministry, community, and, ultimately, the world. Replace all idle, ineffective words with anointed words. Second Thessalonians 2:8 says that Satan will be consumed with the spirit of God's mouth (words) and destroyed by the brightness of His coming (the anointing). Yokes will be destroyed, burdens will be lifted, your life and the lives of those you love will be revolutionized, your ministry will be energized, and the enemy will be horrified once you combine your two most powerful weapons—the Word and prayer—and begin to pray what I call anointed "word prayers." These are prayers that combine key Scripture verses and the prayers you are led to pray by the revelation of the Holy Spirit.

Above all, remain vigilant in your prayers and mediation on the Word. Because you are armed with these weapons, you can rest assured that although the enemy will attempt to exact himself upon you, you can go into every battle with the knowledge of 2 Corinthians 2:14: "God...always causeth us to triumph in Christ, and maketh manifest the savour of his knowledge by us in every place." Indeed, "No weapon that is formed against thee shall prosper" (Isa. 54:17).

As you begin to receive revelation from this book, I pray that as Adam was ushered into the Garden of Eden, a wealthy place, God will also usher you into your wealthy place. Psalm 66:12 says, "You sent troops to ride across our broken bodies. We went through fire and flood. But in the end, you brought us into wealth and great abundance" (TLB). I decree and declare that God will bring complete victory in the areas the enemy has gained a stronghold in. May your mind become like the Garden of Eden prior to the Fall—a place of peace and serenity, saturated with the presence of God.

If you have suffered any loss, I also decree and declare that the anointing of Job for restoration be released upon you. Things that the enemy stole, destroyed, or undermined are being restored to you twofold. What a wonderful encouragement the following scripture has been to me, and I pray that it will encourage you to prevail in prayer:

> And the LORD turned the captivity of Job, when he prayed for his friends: also the LORD gave Job twice as much as he had before. Then came there unto him all his brethren, and all his sisters, and all they that had been of his acquaintance before, and did eat bread with him in his house: and they bemoaned him, and comforted him over all the evil that the LORD had brought upon him: every man also gave him a piece of money, and every one an earring of gold. So the LORD blessed the latter end of Job more than his beginning: for he had fourteen thousand sheep, and six thousand camels, and a thousand yoke of oxen, and a thousand she asses. He had also seven sons and three daughters.
>
> —Job 42:10–13

In this season, your relationships are being healed, your money is coming, and your "gold" is being released. Your latter end shall be more glorious than your beginning. Your possession shall multiply, and your family constellations shall have a second go at life. You will have an encounter with the God of the second chance. Be encouraged, and remember to pray without ceasing (1 Thess. 5:17).

TWO

YOUR MILITARY HEADQUARTERS AND THE COMMANDER IN CHIEF

True Victory Starts With Knowing Whose You Are

T HE SOLDIER HAS the army. The marine has the Marine Corps, the sailor has the navy, the pilot has the air force, search and rescue has the coast guard, and the believer has the church. We are the defense system in the kingdom. These are, of course, speaking in the most general terms. These five military branches perform many more duties than their names suggest. However, they each must report to the main body of the United States Department of Defense, which then reports to the commander in chief, the president.

As we examine the earthly organization of the United States military, we can begin to see some similarities in the spirit realm. As 1 Corinthians 15:46 says, "The spiritual did not come first, but the natural, and after that the spiritual" (NIV). In the spiritual, we see the church is arranged and divided by the five-fold ministry: apostles, prophets, evangelists, pastors, and teachers (Eph. 4:11). Ideally, each branch of ministry has a head, someone to whom others with the same gifts can be accountable. While all of us reign in heavenly places with God, and we no longer need an intermediary to go to God for us, we can still see that those in authority are given a greater measure of responsibility and must report to our Commander in Chief—Jehovah-Gibbor, the mighty Man of war.

All churches are not so clearly defined, but it is important that we recognize and submit to spiritual leadership and authority within the church. Any effective military operation functions at its peak only when each officer is in line, knows his position, and submits to his senior officer's commands. We need to understand that we are not battling in this war individually. The actions we take, the way we follow an order from God, and how we stay in communication with headquarters can and will affect those around us. We can make excuses about our leaders not following God and choose not to follow them, but what are we doing within our realm of authority to watch their backs? This is what real soldiers do—they look out for each other, sometimes to the death. Knowing your place and following godly orders is crucial to each one of us battling effectively in the spirit. God has placed powerful generals in the earth. It behooves us to submit to them.

THE CHURCH IS HEAVEN'S EARTHLY DEPARTMENT OF DEFENSE

The church is heaven's official agency in the earth for carrying out the "foreign" policies of its heavenly government through prayer and other methodologies and strategies. As such, it functions somewhat like a legislative body. The church has been divinely instituted for the purpose of keeping the earth realm free from the aggressive advancements of the kingdom of darkness. As His governmental official, we represent (re-present) the King and His kingdom. Therefore, when we pray, we are praying that heaven will invade Earth on our behalf.

Prayer keeps you connected to your headquarters. Prayer puts you to work, especially when you obey 1 Thessalonians 5:17: "Pray without ceasing." Prayer puts God to work because He states in Isaiah 45:11, "Ask me of things to come concerning my sons, and concerning the work of my hands command ye me," and in Psalm 2:8, "Ask of me, and I shall give thee the heathen for thine inheritance, and the uttermost parts of the earth for thy possession." Prayer also puts the angelic host to work according to Genesis 18:1–19:29, warring on our behalf, protecting us from the unseen, and ministering to us in our hours of need.

As I said above, God has given the church the fivefold ministry gifts. From the wisdom and insight given to those with those gifts, the policies, principles, and mandates of the kingdom are communicated to the entire spiritual military. As ambassadors and military officers of the kingdom of heaven, we are given the commands to:

1. Influence the world and affect change in the lives of those who are bound by the kingdom of darkness
2. Impact the major systems of the world—social, political, economical, educational, familial, cultural, and so on—

through forceful, effectual action in the spirit, causing a strong response leading to kingdom rule. As Acts 16:16–26 tells the story of how Paul interrupted a town's spiritual, educational, economic system by calling out a soothsaying demon, we too are to go into dark places and cause "exceeding trouble," teaching them the customs of the kingdom of heaven that are contrary to the laws of the kingdom of darkness. Prayer invades darkness.

3. Infiltrate enemy territory, saturating it with the light of God. Our presence should be invasive. Light invades darkness, leaving no places for dark shadows. Acts 8:1–24 tells us how Philip went into the city of Samaria and had the demons running out of the possessed people, crying out with loud voices. They were terrified of the authority that Philip had. He freed the people of debilitating diseases and healed them of their afflictions. He spoke the name of Jesus and of the kingdom of God, and many in this dark city came to the light and were baptized.

4. Implement and establish the behaviors, characteristics, and directives of the kingdom. We are to put into action the policies of God in the earth realm. Binding and loosing is one way of implementing kingdom customs in the earth. The following verses show how the kingdom can be implemented and its effect on the people in the earth:

Then they that gladly received his word were baptized: and the same day there were added *unto them* about three thousand souls. And they continued stedfastly in the apostles' doctrine and fellowship, and in breaking of bread, and in prayers. And fear came upon every soul: and many wonders and signs were done by the apostles. And all that believed were together, and had all things common; and sold their possessions and goods, and parted them to all *men*, as every man had need. And they, continuing daily with one accord in the temple, and breaking bread from house to house, did eat their meat with gladness and singleness of heart, praising

God, and having favour with all the people. And the Lord added to the church daily such as should be saved.

—Acts 2:41–47, emphasis added

For unto us a child is born, unto us a son is given: and the government shall be upon his shoulder: and his name shall be called Wonderful, Counseller, the mighty God, the everlasting Father, the Prince of Peace. Of the increase of *his* government and peace *there shall be* no end, upon the throne of David, and upon his kingdom, to order it, and to establish it with judgment and with justice from henceforth even for ever. The zeal of the LORD of hosts will perform this.

—Isaiah 9:6–7, emphasis added

That the God of our Lord Jesus Christ, the Father of glory, may give unto you the spirit of wisdom and revelation in the knowledge of him: the eyes of your understanding being enlightened; that ye may know what is the hope of his calling, and what the riches of the glory of his inheritance in the saints, and what *is* the exceeding greatness of his power to usward who believe, according to the working of his mighty power, which he wrought in Christ, when he raised him from the dead, and set *him* at his own right hand in the heavenly *places*… which is his body, the fulness of him that filleth all in all.

—Ephesians 1:17–20, 23, emphasis added

THE CHURCH IS THE OFFICIAL EMBASSY OF THE KINGDOM OF HEAVEN

In the natural an embassy is a building containing the offices of an ambassador and staff of diplomatic representatives, a place where ambassadors meet, a diplomatic center where policies and mandates are communicated, a place for debriefing its ambassadors, and a place where ambassadors receive diplomatic immunity.

In looking at the church as our headquarters, we can see how, in many ways, it serves the same purposes for the army of God that an embassy does for its ambassadors. While God calls us soldiers, we are also ambassadors of the kingdom. We are acting as godly representatives in the earth.

Now then we are ambassadors for Christ, as though God did beseech *you* by us: we pray *you* in Christ's stead, be ye reconciled to God.

—2 Corinthians 5:20, emphasis added

For which I am an ambassador in bonds: that therein I may speak boldly, as I ought to speak.

—Ephesians 6:20

That sendeth ambassadors by the sea, even in vessels of bulrushes upon the waters, *saying*, Go, ye swift messengers, to a nation scattered and peeled, to a people terrible from their beginning hitherto; a nation meted out and trodden down, whose land the rivers have spoiled!

—Isaiah 18:2, emphasis added

Because this is true, the church is the official embassy of the government of heaven. We use the church building as a place for the fivefold ministry leaders to work and minister to people within the church as well as to win unbelievers to Christ. We also use it as a central meeting place to fellowship together, to learn of our new assignments and commands, to be debriefed on the next move of God, and to discuss administrative and legislative matters concerning the body of Christ. The apostle Paul foretold of the growing importance of the body of Christ to meet together. In Hebrews 10:25 he says that we should not forsake the "assembling of ourselves together, as the manner of some is; but exhorting one another: and so much the more, as ye see the day approaching." We need the meeting together of the body of Christ so that we can support each other to stand even in the heat of battle.

Like the embassy, the church also stands as a place of refuge, a place of spiritual asylum and sanctuary. We can run to the church when we are battle weary and beaten down. In the Old Testament, the altar in the temple was a place where those who feared for their lives could go and grab on to the horns of the altar. No one could touch them there. (See 1 Kings 1:49–51.)

THE CHURCH IS THE ENEMY OF THE DEVIL

Everything the devil is and does is contrary to God's laws. He is rebellious, and because he continually seeks to bring harm on God's creation, he is an enemy of God. We are God's children and desire to live for Him. We stand for the principles of God to overtake the world and bring it to a victorious end. In that fact alone, the church is Satan's archenemy, and we have been given power to subdue him (Gen. 1:28; Luke 10:19).

We have a connection to God that makes us more powerful than anything the enemy may do to thwart the move of God on the earth. The devil is not the biggest threat or enemy of the church—ignorance is. He tries to keep us in the dark about how powerful we are and how strategic our connection with God is in relation to his schemes. He does everything he can to keep us blind to who we are because he fears us—both individually and collectively. He deceives us into believing that he has more power than he really does.

We must know and understand that the enemy seeks to usurp God's authority and infiltrate this world with a political strategy of fear, deception, and temptations. This is the extent of his weapons. His policy is rooted in iniquitous attitudes and sinful actions. He seeks to prevail, but he cannot and will not. The Bible says in Matthew 16:18 that the gates of hell will not prevail against the church. We are built on the rock, which is Jesus Christ, and because God has built the church, we will be successful in all that we do. The enemy cannot stop us because we have been given power over all his abilities. We are a force to be reckoned with. We have power over all the power of the enemy, but we cannot relinquish our power to him lest he defeat us.

JEHOVAH-GIBBOR—YOUR COMMANDER IN CHIEF

Now that we have an understanding of the structure of our spiritual headquarters, let's spend some time talking about the leader of heaven's department of defense. Our Commander in Chief is the Lord Jesus Christ, and He is an informed leader. He knows the enemy, his arsenal, and the terrain. He is not one of those hands-off leaders who only want to hear good reports. He sees all and knows all.

Our Commander especially knows His troops. He created us. Therefore, as He calls His commands and sets forth His decrees in the earth, He does so knowing how it will influence us. God knows how much of the battle we can bear and always provides a safe way of escape for us. First Corinthians 10:13 says, "There hath no temptation taken you but such as is common to man: but God is faithful, who will not suffer you to be tempted above that ye are able; but will with the temptation also make a way to escape, that ye may be able to bear it." Our leader is merciful and compassionate toward us.

As the almighty, omnipotent Commander, He encourages us to lay our burdens on Him. This is very different than the stereotype we see in some movies where the old sarge is barking orders at the new recruits. But God says that He will bear us up and strengthen us in our weaknesses.

> Come unto me, all ye that labour and are heavy laden, and I will give you rest. Take my yoke upon you, and learn of me; for I am meek and lowly in heart: and ye shall find rest unto your souls. For my yoke is easy, and my burden is light.
>
> —Matthew 11:28–30

> But he said to me, "My grace is sufficient for you, for my power is made perfect in weakness." Therefore I will boast all the more gladly about my weaknesses, so that Christ's power may rest on me. That is why, for Christ's sake, I delight in weaknesses, in insults, in hardships, in persecutions, in difficulties. For when I am weak, then I am strong.
>
> —2 Corinthians 12:9–10, NIV

We also have a leader who knows what we are going through. He became a Man just so He could come up through the ranks, like each one of us have, and redeem us. He is able to identify when we need to press into Him and bear into the trial or when we need a sweet respite provided by His grace and mercy that is new every morning. He is not a hard taskmaster, but because He is familiar with us from the inside out (Ps. 139), He knows exactly what we need in order to grow and be a stronger warrior. Hebrews 4:15–16 says, "For we do not have a high priest who is unable to sympathize with our weaknesses, but we have one who has been tempted in every way, just as we are—yet was without sin. Let us then approach the throne of grace with confidence, so that we may receive mercy and find grace to help us in our time of need" (NIV).

His training exercises are not always easy to accomplish, but they are ever so effective and strategic in achieving the plans that He has for our lives. He gives us the tools, weapons, strategies, and tactics to be overcomers in this spiritual war.

> Blessed be the Lord, my Rock and my keen and firm Strength,
> Who teaches my hands to war and my fingers to fight—My Stead-
> fast Love and my Fortress, my High Tower and my Deliverer, my
> Shield and He in Whom I trust and take refuge, Who subdues my
> people under me.
>
> —Psalm 144:1–2, AMP

To recap: a real war is raging. It is a war between the kingdom of light and the kingdom of darkness. The church has been assigned as a part of heaven's defense system. Every believer is automatically drafted into its military department of defense, and there are no demilitarized zones. Our Commander in Chief has instructed us in Ephesians 6:10–18 to "be strong in the Lord, and in the power of his might. Put on the whole armour of God, that ye may be able to stand against the wiles of the devil. For we wrestle not against flesh and blood, but against principalities, against powers, against the rulers of the darkness of this world, against spiritual wickedness in high places. Wherefore take unto you the whole armour of God, that ye may be able to withstand in the evil day, and having done all, to stand. Stand therefore, having your loins girt about with truth, and having on the breastplate of righteousness; and your feet shod with the preparation of the gospel of peace; above all, taking the shield of faith, wherewith ye shall be able to quench all the fiery darts of the wicked. And take the helmet of salvation, and the sword of the Spirit, which is the word of God: praying always with all prayer and supplication in the Spirit, and watching thereunto with all perseverance and supplication for all saints."

With this armor girded about us, the church is ready for its mission of defending the kingdom of light, protecting it from all foreign intrusion while maintaining an atmosphere that is internally free from revolt and insurrection. It must also actively infiltrate and penetrate (not isolate and alienate itself from) the world's systems with the message of the King and His kingdom, doing the works of Him who sent us, plundering the kingdom of darkness to populate the kingdom of light, and liberating prisoners of war from the tyrannical rule of Satan who has blinded their minds.

In the next chapter, we are going to get our stripes and be activated into war.

THREE

ACTIVATION INTO WAR

Getting Your Stripes

IN THIS CHAPTER, I have compiled a list of injunctions that will serve as an activating force announcing your presence and active-duty status in the spirit. The declarations made in this chapter are placed in the form of a prayer, similar to an officer's swearing-in statement. Each of these are scripturally based. I have referenced the scripture from which each section is constructed.

Use this prayer daily, and pray it aloud. Memorize it. Use the Scripture references in your daily devotions. Study them. They will empower you to fight the good fight of faith. Watch circumstances and situations change for the better. Remember, it is only when you are placed in the middle of a battle or an impossible situation, and when there is no one or nothing that can save or deliver you but God, that a true warrior is born. Instead of giving up, giving in, or falling prey to the strategies of the enemy, consider your times of struggle, testing, and temptation as divine opportunities to be trained in the art of strategic prayer and spiritual warfare. Be assured that these times are authentic training grounds that God has selected to bring you into true dominion. As it was for David, they just might be the very grounds that God uses to train you for the ultimate event: the maximization of your potential and the fulfillment of purpose.

The Bible states in Job 22:27–28 that you should "make thy prayer unto him, and he shall hear thee." The word *make* means "to compose, construct, or design." Each one of the following declarations have been composed, constructed, and designed based on Scripture. Scripture references are given at the end of each declaration, and at the end of the book a glossary is provided for greater insight and understanding. As you pray, pray with the assurance that "the gates of hell shall not prevail" (Matt. 16:18). Remember, these declarations are made to fight against spirits and not people. Show no mercy; take no hostages!

PRAYERS OF ACTIVATION FOR SPIRITUAL WARFARE

As God's official legislator and law-enforcement agent:

I come in the name of the resurrected Jesus, whose I am and whom I serve, "that at the name of Jesus every knee should bow, of things in heaven, and things in earth, and things under the earth; and that every tongue should confess that Jesus Christ is Lord" (Phil. 2:10–11; see also Ps. 82).

I affect and enforce God's original plans and purposes over and against the plans and purposes of Satan (Dan. 6).

I decree and declare that in this battle no intrinsic (internal) or extrinsic (external) weapon, be it emotional, financial, social, physical, psychological, interpersonal, spiritual, or organizational, formed against me shall prosper (1 Sam. 17:47; Isa. 54:17; Jer. 51:20; John 14:30; 2 Cor. 7:5; Eph. 4:27).

I place upon myself the armor of light and of the Lord (Rom. 13:12; Eph. 6:13–17):

- Truth to cover my loins (Ps. 51:6)
- The breastplate of righteousness to cover my heart and chest cavity (Ps. 5:12; 2 Cor. 6:7)
- The gospel of peace to cover my feet (Isa. 52:7)
- The shield of faith to defensively and offensively cover my body (Heb. 10:38; 11:1, 6)
- The helmet of salvation to cover my head (Isa. 59:17; 1 Thess. 5:8)
- The sword of the Spirit, which is the Word of God (Eph. 6:17; Rev. 1:16)
- The Lord Jesus Christ (Rom. 13:14)

- A robe of righteousness (Isa. 61:10)
- The glory of God is my reward (Isa. 58:8).

I decree and declare that the weapons of my warfare are not carnal but mighty through God (1 Sam. 17:45; Rom. 13:12; 2 Cor. 10:3–6; Eph. 6:13–18).

I pull down strongholds and cast down vain imaginations and every high thing that lifts itself against the knowledge of Jesus Christ. My thoughts are now subject to the lordship of Christ (Isa. 14:13–14; Ezek. 28:2; 2 Cor. 10:5).

I speak that God's anointing destroys every yoke in my life and that my soul, spirit, and body now function in order according to divine systems of protocol (1 Cor. 9:27; 14:40).

I decree and declare that I am healed and Spirit filled; sickness and disease are far from me (Isa. 53:5).

I establish divine parameters, boundaries, and borders and legislate and establish the laws of the kingdom of heaven to govern all activities within (1 Chron. 4:10; Ps. 147:14; Isa. 60:18).

I overrule (disallow and veto) every diabolical sanction, subverting activity, injunction, directive, mandate, or order that opposes the will of the Lord concerning my life, ministry, and family (Matt. 18:18).

I nullify diabolical decisions and rulings concerning my ministry, my life, and the lives of family members, friends, and associates (Isa. 38:1–5; 39:6–8; Matt. 16:19).

I take control over the airways, galaxies, systems, spheres, stratospheres, hemispheres, atmospheres, realms, regions, and domains (Jer. 1:10; Matt. 16:19; 18:18; 1 Cor. 6:2–3; Eph. 2:6; Rev. 5:10; 11:12).

I dispossess master spirits and employ Michael, other archangels, and the angelic host to handle any satanic contentions, disputes, strivings, and resistance concerning this injunction (2 Kings 7:5–7; 2 Chron. 32:21; Dan. 3:24–25; 6:22; 10:13; Ps. 91:11; 103:20; Heb. 1:14).

I declare successful divine and angelic undertakings, undergirding, reinforcements, and assistance. According to Your Word in Psalm 103:20, angels now "excel in strength" to marshal and protect my personage, property, and possessions (2 Kings 6:17; Dan. 3:15–30; Acts 12:1–10).

Jehovah-Gibbor, contend with those who contend with me; fight against those who fight against me. Take hold of shield and buckler, and stand up for my help! Draw out also the spear and javelin and close up the way of those who pursue and persecute me. Clothe Yourself in Your garments of war. Muster Your devices; gather Your weaponry and ammunition from Your divine arsenal. Make bright Your arrows, gather Your shields, and let vengeance be Your ultimate goal as You overthrow the chariots, horses, and riders. Let terror strike the hearts of my enemies and cause their hearts to fail.

I decree and declare that by You I run through troops and leap over walls. You are my God: the God who girds me with strength and makes my way perfect. It is You who makes my feet like hinds' feet, giving me stability so that I am able to stand firmly and progress on the dangerous heights of testing and trouble. You set me securely upon my high places. You teach my hands to war and my fingers to fight, granting me supernatural strength and abilities so that my arms break a bow of steel. You are my Rock, my Shield, and my Strong Tower. You have equipped me with the shield of Your salvation, and Your right hand establishes me as a victor in this battle. Beat down the enemy. Give me his neck. Cause me to pursue and overtake them until they are wounded and consumed, falling at my feet, never to rise again. Establish my name in the heavens. Let them who hear of me submit and obey me.

I announce that it is You who have blessed me. It is You who empowers me. It is not by my might nor by my power, but by the Spirit of the Lord. For when the enemy shall come in like a flood, Your Spirit lifts up a standard against him (Exod. 15:3; Deut. 32:41–42; Ps. 7:13; 18:29–50; 35:1–8; 144:5–7; Isa. 42:13–14; 59:16–19; Hag. 2:22).

I forbid and disallow further opposing activities of any satanic personalities with diabolical assignments concerning my life, ministry, and family, and I wage a war with them (Neh. 4:14).

I disapprove and prohibit any demonic interception and interference or resistance (Dan. 10:1–13).

I resist satanic contentions, intentions, provocations, and negotiations concerning my life and my soul, and superimpose prophetic purpose and divine destiny over and against all activities and opposing forces that are contrary to the will of God in Christ Jesus concerning my life (1 Sam. 1:1–8; 1 Kings 22:1–23; 1 Chron. 21:1–2; Job 1:7–12; 3:25; Jude 9).

I bind satanic harassment and rebuke satanic concentrations (2 Sam. 11:1–2). I bring to a halt and prohibit all satanic surveillance (1 Sam. 18; Matt. 26:4; Mark 11:18; Luke 6:11; Acts 16:16–19).

I lift false burdens and remove feelings of heaviness, oppression, and depression. I cast them upon the Lord who sustains. I shall not be moved (Ps. 12:5; 54:2; 55:22; Isa. 10:27; 61:3; Matt. 11:28–30; John 14:1).

I decree and declare that by the anointing, all covenants, contracts, chains, fetters, bondages, proclivities, and captivities that are contrary to, oppose, or hinder the fulfillment of God's original plan and purpose are broken. I am liberated from generational/satanic/demonic alliances, allegiances, soul ties, spirits of inheritance, and curses. I sever them by the sword of the Lord, the blood, and the Spirit. I speak to my DNA and declare that I am free from any and all influences passed down from one generation to another—biologically, socially, emotionally, physiologically, psychologically, spiritually, or by any other channel unknown to me but known to God. I resist every spirit that acts as a gatekeeper or a doorkeeper to my soul, and I renounce any further conscious or unconscious alliance, association, allegiance, or covenant. I open myself to divine deliverance. Father, have Your way now! Perfect those things concerning me (Deut. 5:9; 7:8–9; Eccles. 7:26; Isa. 61:1; Acts 8:9–13; Gal. 5:1; 1 Thess. 5:23–24; 2 Tim. 2:25).

I decree and declare that a prayer shield, the anointing, fire walls, smoke screens, and a *bloodline* form hedges of protection around me and hide me from the scourge of the enemy, familiar spirits, and any and all demonic personalities, making it difficult, if not impossible, for them to effectively track or trace me in the realm of the spirit. There shall be no perforations or penetrations to these hedges of protection (Exod. 12:13; Job 1:7–10; Ps. 91; Zech. 2:5).

I release my name into the atmosphere and declare that prayer warriors, intercessors, and prophetic watchmen are picking me up in the realm of the spirit. I speak that they will not cease or come down from their watchtowers until their assignments have been completed. I decree and declare that they will conduct their intercessory assignments under the direction of the Holy Spirit and Jesus Christ, who is my chief intercessor (Jer. 27:18; Ezek. 3:17; Luke 18:7; John 16:13; Rom. 8:26–27, 34; Heb. 7:25).

I decree and declare that the Spirit of the Lord is upon me—the spirit of wisdom, understanding, divine counsel, supernatural might, knowledge, and of the utmost fear of Jehovah. As I advance, I am divinely empowered and increase in skill and understanding (Isa. 11:2–3; Eph. 1:17–18; Col. 1:9–11; 3:10).

I obliterate and annihilate satanic impressions, illusions, projections, perceptions, suggestions, suspicions, and deceptions set up as a decoy or an ambush to my soul and those assigned to pray with me, for me, on behalf of me, and those who work with me, are assigned to me, and interact with me daily (1 Kings 22:5–40; Acts 13:50; 2 Thess. 2).

I forcefully resist the wiles of the devil and prohibit the hijacking of divine thoughts, inspiration, revelation, insight, wisdom, knowledge, and understanding emanating from the throne room of my heavenly Father, especially those who initiate, stimulate, sustain, and reinforce my kingdom authority in the earth realm and in the heavenlies, and who facilitate God's redemptive purpose (Matt. 13:19; Eph. 6:11).

I put a halt to all distractive, disturbing, and destructive measures. For this reason was the Son of God made manifest, that He would destroy the works of the enemy (John 2:15–17; Acts 16:16–19; 1 John 3:8).

I prevail against satanic inhibitions, prohibitions, and all limitations. I decree and declare that all invisible and invincible walls are destroyed (Josh. 6:1; Col. 1:16).

I execute divine judgment against satanic/demonic activities, and I war in the spirit of Elijah and Jehu (1 Kings 18; 2 Kings 9:1–10:28).

I disapprove, nullify, dismantle, cancel, and forcefully oppose any satanic operations, maneuvers, manipulations, subversions, strategies, tactics, plots, plans, and ploys that are designed to hinder, prevent, frustrate, foil, deny, or delay God's original plans and purposes from their quick, swift, and speedy manifestation, particularly in their correct time and season (Dan. 7:25).

I prohibit the alteration and changing of any time or laws concerning my life and ministry or the life of my family. I move synchronized and syncopated to the choreographic, symphonic, and orchestrated movements of God (Gen. 1:1–5; Dan. 6:1–15; 7:15–27).

I establish that if laws, statutes, codifications, bills, charters, and constitutions are changed, they are changed in my favor so that I may prosper in the place of my assignment and the land in which I am domiciled (Dan. 6:25–28).

I decree and declare that my times and seasons are in the hands of the Lord and they shall not be altered or adjusted by anyone or anything. I function under the anointing of the sons of Issachar, and God gives me the divine ability to accurately discern my times and seasons (1 Chron. 12:32; Ps. 31:15; Eccles. 3:1–8; Daniel 2:21–22).

I decree and declare that the eyes of my spirit function with 20/20 vision for correct understanding and interpretation of divine movements. My ears are in tune with the correct frequency of the Spirit, and I have clear transmission (2 Kings 6:17; Job 42:5; Ps. 119:18; Isa. 29:18; Jer. 1:11–16; 2 Cor. 4:4; 7:2; Eph. 4:18; Rev. 4:1).

I decree that this day I operate according to God's divine timetable/calendar. I decree that God's agenda is my agenda. I am not my own; I have been bought with a price. I therefore submit myself to Him alone. I declare that, like Jesus, "I come: in the volume of the book it is written of me" (Ps. 40:7; see also Ps. 139:16; 1 Cor. 7:23; James 4:7).

Father, overthrow the plans of troublemakers, scorners, scoffers, mockers, persecutors, and character assassins. Expose satanic representatives and grant unto me divine strategies and tactics to identify, resist, and overcome plots and plans established for my demise (Esth. 9:25; Ps. 5:10; 7:14–16; 34:21; 35:1–8; 52:5; 83:13–17; 141:10; Prov. 26:27; 28:10; Dan. 3, 6; Matt. 7:15–23; 2 Cor. 11:14–15):

- Draw out Your spear and stop them in their way.

- Let them be confounded and put to shame.

- Let them fall by their own counsels.

- Let them be turned back and brought to confusion.

- Let them be as chaff driven by the wind.

- Let the angel of the Lord persecute them.

- Let their way be through dark and slippery places, with the angel of the Lord pursuing and afflicting them.

- Let them be put to shame and dishonor who seek and require my life.

- Let them be turned back and confounded who plan my hurt.

- Let destruction come to them suddenly.

- Let them fall to their own destruction.

- Let destruction come upon them unaware.

- Let them stumble and fall into the very destruction they have contrived for me.

- Let them be wounded and destroyed by the very weapons they have devised for me.

- Let them be caught in the same net that they set for me.

- Let them fall in the very pit that they dug for me.

- Let them be hung by the very noose they constructed for me.

- Let them be burned in the very fire they have lit for me.

- Let them be consumed by the very beasts they have prepared for me.

- Strike them down in the very act of their mischief.

- Let their mischief be returned to them twofold.

- Pluck them out of their dwelling place.
- Root them out of the land of the living.
- Let evil slay them and desolation be their lot.
- Make them like a wheel turning in confusion.
- Make them as the stubble before the wind.
- Make them as wood burned by fire.
- Persecute them with Your tempest.
- Cause fear and terror to grip their hearts.
- Let them be confounded and troubled forever.

I employ the hosts of heaven to war against the hosts of darkness (1 Sam. 17). Take command over, bring to a halt, and place a moratorium on further demonic movements and satanic activities emanating from:

- The underworld and its six regions (Isa. 14:9, 15; 38:18; Dan. 7:1–28; Rev. 20:13–14)
- Death (Job 34:22; 1 Cor. 15:55)
- Hell/Sheol/Hades (Isa. 14:19)
- The grave (Isa. 38:10; Ezek. 31:15)
- The pit (Ezek. 32:23)
- The abyss, the lower region of the pit (Isa. 38:17; Ps. 30:3)
- Regions of the sea (Job 41:1–31; Ezek. 26:16)
- Heavens (Eph. 2:6; 6:12; Rev. 12:7)
- Terrestrial, subterrestrial, and celestial domains (Isa. 14:12–14; Jer. 1:10; Luke 11:16–26; Rom. 8:14–23; Phil. 2:10)

I superimpose the prophetic word over all abortive measures, strategies, and tactics of the enemy (1 Tim. 1:18–20).

I overrule and overthrow, according to Isaiah 54:17, ill-spoken words, ill wishes, enchantments, divinations, spells, hexes, curses, witchcraft prayers, and every idle word spoken contrary to God's original plans and purposes.

I reverse the curse associated with these utterances and decree and declare that they shall not stand, they shall not come to pass, they shall not take root, and their violent verbal dealings are returned to them twofold.

I declare that every lying tongue is wrong and that truth prevails. Put a hook in their nostrils, bridle their lips, and hide me from the scourge of their tongues (Job 5:21; Ps. 5:6–10; Isa. 37:29).

I come against falsehoods, slander, speculation, accusation, misrepresentation, and character assassination. Father, cause the heavens to bow down with divine judgment; cast forth lightning to scatter them; shoot out Your arrows to destroy them; send Your hand from above and rid me of them. I will lose no ground or territory through their undermining efforts or initiatives (1 Kings 21:1–16; Ps. 144:5–7).

I prohibit the accuser of the brethren from operating or influencing the soul or mind of anyone who comes into contact with me (Rev. 12:10).

I reverse the effect of any stigmas and declare that divine favor, grace, honor, and well wishes now replace any and all negative feelings, perceptions, and thoughts concerning myself, my family, and the work/ministry that I am called to accomplish.

I decree and declare that nobility and greatness are my portion (Gen. 12:1–3; Ps. 5:12).

Father, frustrate the signs of witches and warlocks who withstand the anointing as You did with Jannes and Jambres in the days of Moses. Confound the omens of the liars, astrologers, psychics, prognosticators, sorcerers, and the like. Make fools of diviners, and make their dark knowledge foolishness (Isa. 44:25; 2 Tim. 3:8).

Rebuke and dismantle satanic alliances, and arrest them by the Spirit. Let every covert and/or clandestine effort and endeavor fail (2 Chron. 20:35; Neh. 4:7–8; Esth. 3–9; Job 5:12–14; Ps. 35:4; 55:9; 70:2; 83:17; 129:5).

- Disappoint the devices that they have crafted so that their hands cannot perform their enterprise.
- Take them in their own crafty and devious ways.
- Let them meet with darkness in the daytime and grope in the noonday as in the night.
- Release divine viruses to invade satanic databases, and command that they be consumed and destroyed.
- Let all future diabolical communications and networking fail. Any attempts shall only yield incoherency and misunderstandings.
- Send a spirit of confusion among them.
- Let their tongues be divided.
- Overrule and overthrow sabotage, subversions, and setbacks.
- Let every attack of retaliation fail.

Confirm the words of Your servant in their midst, and perform the counsel of Your messengers (Isa. 44:26).

Send divine angelic, prophetic assaults and maneuvers against diabolical intelligence (Josh. 5:13–14; Ps. 103:20–22).

Arrest those who operate in the spirit of Jezebel or Belial. Let them not resist the anointing, usurp authority, or gain any ground in the natural or in the realm of the spirit (1 Sam. 10:27; 1 Kings 19:1–5; 21:1–16).

I prohibit satanic manifestations and speak that divine "abortive" measures and "miscarriages" occur in satanic wombs and incubators (2 Cor. 10:5).

Now Father, You have given me a great work to accomplish. I war for the releasing of finances and all resources that belong to me. Everything prepared for me before the foundation of the world, that pertains to my life (ministry, calling) and godliness comes to me now. I shall not/will not be denied. I shall not/will not accept substitutes. I call in resources from the north, south, east, and west. I decree and declare that every resource necessary for me to fulfill God's original plans and purposes comes to me without delay now (2 Pet. 1:3).

I decree and declare that the wealth of the wicked is no longer laying up for me but is released now. Let those who hold on to my wealth longer than they should be afflicted and tormented without relief until they release what rightfully belongs to me. I command Satan to "cough it up," spit it out, loose it, release it, and let it go (Job 20:15–18; Ps. 66:12; Eccles. 2:26).

Jehovah-Jireh, loose the loins of kings! In the name of Jesus, command that the two leaved gates be opened. Go before me and make the crooked places straight. Break in pieces the gates of brass, and cut asunder the bars of iron. Grant unto me, according to Your riches in glory, Your tender mercies and immeasurable favor, the treasures of darkness, and hidden riches of secret places (Isa. 45:1–3). I declare that the Cyrus anointing flows unhindered and uncontaminated in my life (Isa. 60:10–17; Phil. 4:19).

Lift up your heads, O ye gates (keepers of the gates), and be lifted up forever, you age-abiding doors (doorkeepers) that the King of glory, the Lord strong and mighty, the Lord of hosts, may come in (Ps. 24:7–10). I announce my awareness that cannot deny Him access. Therefore, I will not and cannot be denied of what rightfully belongs to me!

I decree and declare the releasing of the forces of the Gentiles, the gold and silver from my prophetic Tarshish, and my prophetic queen of Sheba to come laden with every precious possession/resource/endowment fit for the sons and daughters of the King of kings.

I decree and declare that I shall suck the milk of the Gentiles at the breast of kings (Isa. 60:16). I shall be enlarged as the abundance of the sea is converted unto me (Isa. 60:5). The sons of strangers shall build up my walls, and their kings shall minister unto me (Job 27:16–17; Isa. 60).

I decree and declare that my God has brought me into my wealthy place, and I dwell in my prophetic Goshen. I increase in substance and prosper in the land whereto I abide and am sent as an ambassador of God. As His official representative, all diplomatic and aristocratic rights, privileges, respect, and honor are extended to me. Grace, truth, goodness, and mercy are my bodyguards.

I decree and declare wisdom is my counselor; the Holy Spirit is my consultant; Jesus Christ is my advocate. God, El Elyon, my only judge has declared and I therefore establish that my officers are peace, my exactors righteousness, my walls salvation, and my gates praise (Gen. 47:27; Isa. 60:17–18).

I decree and declare that my set time of favor will not be frustrated (Ps. 102:13).

I release upon my life, ministry, the lives of every family member, associate, and friend the following anointings for wealth and prosperity so that God and God's name alone is glorified:

- Jabez anointing (1 Chron. 4:10)
- Abrahamic anointing (Gen. 12:1–3)
- Melchizedek anointing (Gen. 14:18; Heb. 5:6–10)
- Joseph anointing (Ps. 105:21)
- Jacobian anointing (Gen. 28:1; 30:43)

- Isaac anointing (Gen. 26:1–14)
- Messiah's anointing (Luke 8:1–3)
- Solomaic anointing (1 Chron. 29; 2 Chron. 9)
- Sevenfold Edenic anointing (Gen. 1:28, 30; 2:15)
- Uzziahian anointing (2 Chron. 26:5–15)
- Joshua anointing (Josh. 6:1–3)

I am daily loaded with benefits (Ps. 68:19).

I come against the spirit of deprivation. The Lord prospers the work of my hands. By Him and through Him I accomplish great exploits. Again I reiterate, I shall not be denied (Dan. 11:32)!

I declare success and progress in Jesus's name (2 Cor. 2:14).

I decree and declare that the kingdom of heaven rules and reigns (Rev. 11:15).

I send these words forth as Euroclydon winds in the realm of the spirit to demolish and destroy the enemy's camps. Cause the four winds of the Spirit and of heaven to blow as destroying, conquering winds (Jer. 51:1; Acts 27:14).

I decree and declare that this prayer and all future prayers take on the characteristics of divine projectiles in the realm of the spirit and that they hit the bull's-eye (Ps. 57:4).

I decree that the laws that govern this prayer and all spiritual warfare strategies and tactics are binding by the Word, the blood, and by the Spirit (1 John 5:7–8).

I decree that every spirit released from their diabolical assignment now becomes a part of Jesus's footstool (Ps. 110:1).

I seal this prayer in Jesus's name...amen!

PART II

YOUR ENEMY

FOUR

THE BATTLEFIELD *IS* YOUR MIND

Where All Is Won or Lost

T HE MOST PRECIOUS commodity in the earth realm is the mind. Not only is God vying for your minds, but the enemy is vying for your minds as well. Revelation 18:11–16 states that in the last days, the intellectual property of the soul will be one of the commodities bought and sold in the marketplace and used to drive entire economies:

> And the merchants of the earth shall weep and mourn over her; for no man buyeth their merchandise any more: the merchandise of gold, and silver, and precious stones, and of pearls, and fine linen, and purple, and silk, and scarlet, and all thyine wood, and all manner vessels of ivory, and all manner vessels of most precious wood, and of brass, and iron, and marble, [thyine: or, sweet] and cinnamon, and odours, and ointments, and frankincense, and wine, and oil, and fine flour, and wheat, and beasts, and sheep, and horses, and chariots, and slaves, and souls of men [slaves or bodies]. And the fruits that thy soul lusted after are departed from thee, and all things which were dainty and goodly are departed from thee, and thou shalt find them no more at all. The merchants of these things, which were made rich by her, shall stand afar off for the fear of her torment, weeping and wailing, and saying, Alas, alas, that great city, that was clothed in fine linen, and purple, and scarlet, and decked with gold, and precious stones, and pearls!

The story of the prodigal son in Luke 15:11–32 is a compelling story that shows how the enemy works against us through our thoughts. In this story, we see how the god of this world seduced an uninformed young boy into wasting his substance (time, talent, treasure, gifts, ability, inheritance, anointing, experience, etc.). When the average person thinks of warfare, images of war-stricken places are conjured up. Very seldom does a person think of the mind as being the battlefield. There are a couple realities that this story brings out about spiritual warfare.

1. The battle is not with flesh and blood.

Make note that in verse 12 the son demands the portion of his inheritance that was to be divided between him and his older brother after their father died, but the father gives his son what he asks for. Further down we see that he quickly "wasted his substance with riotous living" (v. 13). If you understand what it means to be a child of wealth and means, you will know that this son would have been reared in an environment where financial steward-ship was paramount. The fact that he demanded his inheritance before time and squandered it foolishly tells us that something or *someone* got a hold of his thoughts, telling him lies about what he deserved and that he shouldn't have to wait to receive what is due him. Good parents generally tell their children to be patient, to not grow up too fast, and to use their time and resources wisely. The son rebelled against everything that his father would have taught him up to that point, and that kind of rebellion is indicative of a demonic spirit at work. Spiritual warfare in its purest form is the council of the human mind by any other spirit other than the Spirit of the Lord. You must discern the spirit that is at work overtly or covertly.

Ephesians 6:12 says, "For we wrestle not against flesh and blood, but against principalities, against powers, against the rulers of the darkness of this world, against spiritual wickedness in high places." It is obvious that this son is neither having a fight with his father nor is anyone pushing him out of the nest before it is time. There is an internal spiritual struggle that influenced the son's actions, and giving in to that struggle caused his demise.

The same is true for us. Our warfare is not with human beings but with the devil and his demons, who propagate doctrines of devils, heresies, Lucife-rian ideologies, satanic philosophies, and diabolical imagery. Our enemy, Satan, attempts to defeat us with strategy and deceit through well-laid plans and deliberate deceptions and manipulation. When he speaks to our minds in an attempt to derail us from following a path that leads us to the fulfill-ment of purpose and destiny, he never speaks to us in the second person ("you"). He uses the first person ("I") to deceive us into believing that the thoughts running through our minds are our thoughts and not suggestions, projections, prompting, or urges emanating from him. He begins his warfare strategy by bombarding our minds with a cleverly devised pattern of little nagging thoughts, suspicions, doubts, fears, wonderings, reasonings, and theories. He moves slowly and cautiously, deliberately and patiently. He will never say, "*You* are sick," "you are poor," "you should leave your church," or "you are never going to make it." He will say, "*I* am sick," "I am leaving this church," or "I am never going to make it," because he really wants us to believe that the thoughts he places in our minds are ours.

I remember returning home one night after ministry. I sat on the edge of my bed, and all of a sudden, "I" felt sad. Thoughts started racing through my mind, and my internal dialogue was incredibly and unusually negative. Since I am a basically positive person, initially I dismissed it as fatigue. However, the thoughts became so overpowering that I began to entertain them as if they were mine. I wanted to leave the ministry and forget about everything and everyone. Then the Holy Spirit rose up in me and instructed me to fight against the thoughts. I took on a posture of prayer and spiritual warfare, commanding the spirit to go.

After binding and loosing and releasing the spirit from its assignment, I heard a *whoosh* sound and felt a presence leave my bedroom through the window. The thoughts and emotions I claimed as mine were really spirits of depression, death (trying to abort my ministry, purpose, and destiny), and frustration. This is how deceptive the weapons of the enemy are. Remember: when spirits come, they come to give diabolical counsel to your mind because this level of warfare is spiritual, not carnal.

2. The mind is the greatest battlefield.

The spiritual struggle presented in the story of this lost son further proves the value of our minds. It is not any outside, physical need that causes the son to ask for his money. He is at war within himself between the good that God has for his life and the bad that the enemy has strategically planned for him. The mind is the greatest battlefield. Within it the fate of a man's eternity is decided, souls are lost or won, and destinies are fulfilled or fizzled out. Here is a simple principle you can apply as you learn about beating the enemy at his own game. If you don't really know what to pray about, observe what the enemy is doing and pray the opposite.

We can assume that the father was confident in the promises of God and knew the truth of 2 Corinthians 1:20: "No matter how many promises God has made, they are 'Yes' in Christ. And so through him the 'Amen' is spoken by us to the glory of God" (NIV). The promise he must have held on to was, "Train up a child in the way he should go: and when he is old, he will not depart from it" (Prov. 22:6). This allowed him to release his son into the world to be taught and rescued by Jehovah-Adonnai. In the end, the son was not overtaken. The Bible says that "he came to himself" (Luke 15:17). He finally came to his senses. His mind was restored. His soul was redeemed. The battlefield of his mind was reclaimed for the kingdom.

STAKING CLAIM OVER THE BATTLEFIELD OF THE MIND

Achieving the kind of victory that was won in the previous story requires discipline. To get this discipline, the first thing is to know what thoughts qualify to legitimately be in your mind. Philippians 4:8 says, "Finally, brethren, whatsoever things are true, whatsoever things are honest, whatsoever things are just, whatsoever things are pure, whatsoever things are lovely, whatsoever things are of good report; if there be any virtue, and if there be any praise, think on these things." If your thoughts are not true, honest, just, pure, lovely, of good report, or praiseworthy, do not allow those thoughts to take root in your mind.

The second thing is to remove the thoughts that should not be in your mind. According to 2 Corinthians 10:4–5, we have the power in Jesus Christ to pull down the strongholds Satan tries to erect in our minds and cast down "imaginations, and every high thing that exalteth itself against the knowledge of God, and bringing into captivity every thought to the obedience of Christ."

Let us break down the divine strategies that God gives us in the above text:

1. You must pull down thoughts that do not qualify.
This action denotes an entire demolition, a clearing away and annihilation of something. It also denotes the conquering of opposing forces and hostile partisans. Francis Frangipane said, "The pulling down of strongholds begins

with repentance. When Jesus sent out His disciples, 'they went out and preached that men should repent. And they were casting out many demons and...healing them' (Mark 6:12–13)."[1]

2. You must eradicate strongholds (*ochuroma*[1])

A stronghold is a pattern and idea that governs individuals, nations, and communities. They are mind-sets, thought patterns, and processes that cause people to act, react, and respond in a particular manner contrary to the ways of God and a godly lifestyle. Strongholds are things that you rationalize and justify. You may say things like, "My whole family is like this," "I can't help it. I was born like this," "This is just the way I am," or "Everybody acts and thinks this way." Your rationalization and justification of certain thoughts, behavior, and attitudes form a stronghold. Strongholds can also be cultural entrenchment.

You have to understand that God wants to give you a better way of living and operating in the earth realm. All successful deliverance must begin by first removing that which defends the enemy. In speaking of spiritual warfare, the apostle Paul enlists the word *stronghold* to define the spiritual fortresses wherein Satan and his legions hide and are protected. These fortresses exist in the thought patterns and ideas that govern individuals and organizations as well as communities and nations. We must not allow the enemy to hide himself and his tactics within these fortresses. Every arsenal of the enemy must be removed and replaced with the mighty arsenal of the Word of God. "For the word of God is living and active and sharper than any two-edged sword, and piercing as far as the division of soul and spirit, of both joints and marrow, and able to judge the thoughts and intentions of the heart" (Heb. 4:12, NAS). Through deliberate ingestions of God's Word, the strongholds of the enemy can be forced out and the things of God can come in and occupy our thought life.

Here are several types of strongholds we must be aware of:

- Demonic/satanic. These will be discussed at length in chapter 6, "Weapons of Mass Destruction" and in chapter 10, "Reconnaissance."

---

1 Strong's #3794.

- Territorial. These represent the hierarchy of dark beings who are strategically assigned by Satan himself to influence and control nations, communities, and even families. Certain demonic forces mass to different regions to fortify particular kinds of evil.[2]

- Ideological. These concern Satan's worldview through philosophies that influence culture and society. These strongholds are portrayed in 2 Corinthians 10:5 "Casting down imaginations, and every high thing that exalteth itself against the knowledge of God, and bringing into captivity every thought to the obedience of Christ."[3]

- Personal. They are things that Satan builds to influence your personal life—personal sin, your thoughts, your feelings, your attitudes, and your behavior patterns.[4]

- Divine. These are strongholds erected by Jehovah-Gibbor to protect the kingdom and its warriors. (See Psalm 18:2–3; Proverbs 18:10.)

- Military. These are strongholds that are put up by the army of God (you and I) to protect itself from enemy fire. (See 1 Samuel 23:14, 19.)

3. You must cast down imaginations.

Part of this phrase comes from the Greek word *kathaireo*, which means "casting down" or "smiting down."2

Imaginations is a derivative of the Greek word for "image" (*ekon*); it involves the two ideas of representation and manifestation. This term denotes a tool used for engraving or to cut into something which produces an image, which is then used to make an impression of that which the instrument engraved.

---

2 Strong's #2507.

4. You must bring thoughts into captivity.

In order to recognize what is wrong in us, we must perceive God's standard of right. We must learn to look objectively at any thoughts or attitudes that fail to conform to the likeness and teaching of Jesus. Those thoughts must be captured and wrong attitudes crucified in order to secure victory. Repent of those thoughts, asking God to forgive you of your unbelief. Then arrest the thoughts and replace them with the confession of your faith, the Word of God.

5. You must renew your mind.

Let your mind be renewed by reading and studying the Word of God. "When you do this you are tearing down a stronghold of defeat that once oppressed you and you are beginning to replace it with the godly stronghold of faith. As you continue being renewed in the spirit of your mind by the Word of God, you will begin walking in tremendous power and peace. You will enter the godly stronghold of faith."[5]

Jesus tells us in John 8:31–32 how we are to stay victorious over the lies of Satan: "Continue in my word, then are ye my disciples indeed; and ye shall know the truth, and the truth shall make you free."

REPENTANCE BRINGS A CHANGE OF MIND

The mind is the greatest battlefield because our minds occupy a large place in our lives, and our thoughts easily influence our actions. It is difficult to estimate how much of the world's philosophy, ethics, knowledge, research, and science flow from the powers of darkness. But of one point we are certain: all arguments and proud obstacles against the knowledge of God are the fortresses of the enemy.

It is true that Satan uses the mind to secure our consent to set up strongholds, and with each enticement the enemy gains more ground in our battlefield. We cannot separate temptation and thought; temptations are offered us in the form of thoughts. Since our thoughts are so exposed to the power of darkness, we need to learn how to guard them. This work begins the day we accept Jesus into our lives and repent for all of the mess that we allow to reign over us. The original definition of *repentance* is "a change of mind." Because our minds had been so united with the devil, it is vital for us to receive from God a change of mind before we can receive a new heart (Acts 11:18).

With this new heart we must understand that we still have the choice to allow evil spirits the opportunity to attack, and unless we voluntarily give him this ground, he has no right to encroach on our freedom. We have it within our power through Christ to oppose every tempting thought, and by our word it shall be stopped.

In this next chapter, you will be given highly classified intelligence into the inner workings of Satan's army and the kingdom of darkness. The Bible says that we are not ignorant of the devil's devices; therefore, we have no right to blame our lack of knowledge for our defeat. As you enter this chapter, you will see that as a soldier of God, there are no excuses for defeat. Our Commander has more than adequately trained and briefed us for victory.

FIVE

KNOWING YOUR ENEMY

Spiritual Intelligence Agency (SIA)

N EW STUDENTS OF the Bible, and even veterans with firm spiritual foundations and studies, often wonder about this figure called Satan. Is Satan a literal being? Is hell a literal place? Is there really a kingdom of darkness? By thoroughly studying the Word of God, you will acquire a greater understanding of Satan and his kingdom, thus eliminating ignorance, which is one of his greatest weapons.

There are two kingdoms mentioned in the Bible. The line on the battlefield has been drawn between the kingdom of darkness and the kingdom of light. Every individual must choose one side or the other. As believers, thank God we have been delivered from the authorities that rule in the kingdom of darkness. God has ordained that even as Christ is the head of the church and the church is His body, we are assured of victory over every demonic force in Jesus's name. (See 2 Corinthians 2:14; Colossians 1:13.)

Although the Bible makes it clear that we have won the victory over Satan and his evil kingdom through Christ, there is still a war waging for our souls. Therefore, we must be aware of who this enemy is and how he operates. Throughout the rest of this chapter, I am going to give you important things to know about the enemy so that you can be empowered in your personal life to stay on the side of victory. Keep your sword—the Bible—open. We are going to move quickly!

1. The kingdom of darkness is a literal, spiritual kingdom.

Think of the kingdom of darkness as you would any other earthly, terrestrial nation or country. However, there is one difference; that difference lies in its essence. The kingdom of darkness, although literal, is not physical but spiritual in nature. (See Jude 6; Revelation 18.)

2. It was instituted by Satan and a host of fallen angels.

The Bible tells how this kingdom of darkness was created. Having seduced approximately one-third of the angelic host, Satan proceeded to organize a foiled insurrection that subsequently led to their expulsion from heaven. What an event! Jesus describes it as a light show in the heavens (Luke 10:18; Rev. 12:3–13).

3. This satanic kingdom has a cosmological system.

The word *cosmology* speaks of the dynamic arrangement of the universe and the world. God created the world in an orderly fashion. Satan has created a perverted imitation of it. By using such people as Cain and other rebellious men as pawns, he has successfully constructed a world that in reality is nothing more than just a great magic show with illusions, smoke, and mirrors to fool the blinded eyes of man. Although illusory in nature, Satan has succeeded in creating a well-organized system of evil (Gen. 4:9–24). In this particular portion of Scripture, we see the terrestrial foundation of the kingdom of darkness taking shape and form through the creation of eight out of the twelve existing systems that comprise our world:

1. Social system (culture, entertainment, language, marriage, or family)
2. Entertainment
3. Environmental
4. Economical
5. Governmental
6. Educational
7. Technological
8. Religious (humanistic, atheistic, and anti-God)

These systems, originally designed by God to provide the optimum environment for mankind to fulfill its purpose and maximize potential, and to reach its destiny, have now become the strongholds of demonic forces. Today we can witness the effects of the presence of the enemy in this world. Governments are corrupt, approximately half of all marriages end in divorce, and families that once were safe havens for children are now plagued with abuse and domestic violence, leaving the educational institution wanting. Satan eroded and corroded the foundation and fiber of societies and institutions, creating the bedrock for sin and iniquity to be perpetuated intergeneration-ally. (See Genesis 6:1–7; Revelation 18:9–10, 23–24.)

4. God has given us authority and power to expose Satan's tactics and overcome his attack.

Satan rules the kingdom of darkness. Remember, he is the prince of the power of the air and not the earth. Man has been given dominion over the earth realm (Gen. 1:28; Ps. 115:15–16). The enemy's activities are illegal because disembodied spirits were not given authority to operate on the earth. This is why Satan had to possess the body of a snake in order to gain legal access. Possession is his current strategy for control in the earth realm. He knew the law of undertaking any initiatives in the earth realm. Flesh and blood is the spiritual protocol for operating here, a protocol that even God subjects Himself to. When God wanted to redeem the world, He came in the form of the flesh through Jesus Christ our Lord, our commanding officer, our General and mighty Man of war who has given us authority over all the power of the enemy. It is up to you and me to enforce that authority (Ps. 8:4–6; 115:16; Luke 10:19; Eph. 2:2).

5. Satan has set himself up to be a god in the earth realm.

He is an imposter and an impersonator (Isa. 14:12–14). Since God aborted his diabolical *coup d'état* (aggressive takeover) in the third heavens, Satan now attempts to become a god over the inhabitants of the earth. You must put up a resistance (James 4:7).

6. Satan and his demonic cohorts have the ability to oppress, possess, and terrorize humanity.

You must identify the spirits, take your authority over the enemy, and bind their activities in Jesus's name. (See Isaiah 14:15–21; Daniel 7:25–27; Mark 3:27; Revelation 12:7–13.) You will learn more about this as you proceed through this book.

7. This kingdom of darkness has a sophisticated economy.

As with any other earthly kingdom, it trades and transacts business. Satan has built an entire evil empire by utilizing the most precious of all commodities—intellectual properties and the very souls of men. When it comes to humanity, many people have replaced their love of God with the love of money. First Timothy 6:10 declares, "For the love of money is the root of all evil: which while some coveted after, they have erred from the faith, and pierced themselves through with many sorrows." Throughout history we can trace many sinful, unholy, and ungodly activities and atrocities to this inordinate affection and idolatrous stronghold in the minds of men. Like the black widow spider that lures her prey to its demise into her web, this satanic economic system will lure any and every soul it can into a web designed for death and destruction. (See Ezekiel 27:2–26; Revelation 18:11–22.)

8. The kingdom of Satan is a kingdom of darkness.

When we speak of the kingdom of darkness we speak of any territory or domain where there is an absence of God, divine revelation, purpose, and destiny. Spiritual blindness is another weapon of mass destruction. In short, this is an effective weapon because, even if truth is presented, the blinded cannot see unless there is divine intervention through salvation, healing, and deliverance. The Living Bible gives us the reason for this level of spiritual blindness in 2 Corinthians 4:4: "Satan, who is the god of this evil world, has made him blind, unable to see the glorious light of the Gospel that is shining upon him or to understand the amazing message we preach about the glory of Christ, who is God." (See also Genesis 1:2–4; Deuteronomy 28:29; Job 12:25; Isaiah 59:10.)

9. The kingdom of darkness is accessible to both spirit beings and human beings who either visit or make their abode there.

Fallen angels dwell there. This kingdom of darkness is not far removed from us at all. As human beings, we can abandon the laws of God—the laws that would bring us the peace that surpasses all understanding—and live in the kingdom of darkness as well. In Revelation 18:1–4, the Bible speaks of Babylon. Babylon is to the kingdom of darkness as Washington DC is to the United States, or London is to England. Think of it as you would the capital of your country.

10. Like our own worship of the Lord our God, the kingdom of darkness also has a mode of worship.

Just as your worship brings you into the presence of God, satanic worship will bring you into the presence of Satan. Remember, worship is not just an activity in a church or synagogue; it also is the lifestyle you choose to live on a daily basis. The question that I pose to you today is, Does your life bring glory to God or to Satan? (See Daniel 3:1–15; Revelation 17:1–6.)

11. The kingdom of darkness can be experienced by both the physical senses and the spiritual senses.

The experience of the kingdom of darkness can be physical, and it can also be spiritual. I am sure you know someone who has fallen into drug abuse, alcoholism, or despair. These are physical ills, but they also have the power to render the person spiritually bankrupt under its influence. Scripture warns us to stay away from the kingdom of darkness and its activities, values, principles, and standards (Col. 2:20–21; 1 John 2:15–17).

THE KINGDOM OF DARKNESS: AN ELABORATELY ORGANIZED KINGDOM

The kingdom of darkness is well equipped and very ready to fight a pitched battle using any and all means at its disposal. Remember, you are engaged in a battle with a very organized system of protocol and chain of command. The following is a description of the kingdom of darkness. This may be the first time you are learning about the elaborately organized kingdom and nation of darkness. But like all good generals, it is to your benefit to be well aware of the inner workings of the enemy.

1. Principalities

The word *principality* comes from the Greek word *archomai*, which, literally translated, means "first in rank and order." Principalities derive their power directly from Satan and are the highest-ranking entities in Satan's army. They influence the affairs of humanity at a national level, impacting laws and policies. They are so purpose specific that they often embody world leaders. Take Hitler, for instance. A careful examination of his life will undoubtedly point toward definite, demonic influence. (See Ezekiel 28:11–19; Acts 8:6–25; Ephesians 3:10.)

2. Powers

Next in the chain of command we find powers. The Greek word for power, *exousia*, speaks of delegated authority. These are demonic spirits that derive their jurisdictional and delegated authority from principalities. They affect and infect structures, systems, and the five pillars of our society: marriage, family, government, education, and church. (See Ezekiel 28:1–10; Colossians 2:15.)

3. Rulers of the darkness of this world

Kosmokrator and *skotos*3 are the Greek words used for this category of spirits. These spirits are very high-ranking officers that have specialized jurisdiction over the twelve cosmological systems of the universe and rule in the kingdom of darkness. They are responsible for blinding the minds of people to truth and for facilitating sin, wickedness, and iniquity within the nations of this world. They are also responsible for keeping people in a state of darkness. (When I speak of darkness, I am not merely speaking of the absence of light, but of the absence of God. God is light and divine inspiration.) They affect the thoughts, feelings, and perceptions of humanity through mass media, music, movies, fashion, sports, philosophies, and religious ideologies. (See Colossians 1:13; Revelation 16:10; Jude 6, 13.)

4. Spiritual wickedness in high places

The Greek phrase *pneumatikos poneria epouranios* speaks of types of spirits found in high and lofty places that are responsible for anything that is perverted, depraved, debased, warped, or corrupt. This spirit is spoken of as working from high, lofty, and heavenly places that speak of not only celestial zones and dimensions but also the mind, which is a type of a heavenly place. It influences, seduces, and falsely inspires actions, perceptions, motivations, fantasies, imaginations, and appetites through the overt or covert attack and influence of the mind, affecting terrestrial and celestial domains. (See Jeremiah 1:10; Luke 11:16–26; Romans 8:14–23.) According to Daniel 10:10–13 these spirits, operating in the second heaven, frustrate and prohibit the manifestation and answers to believers' prayers. Perceptions, mindsets, paradigms, ideologies, and belief systems are twisted and perverted to accommodate the personality of these evil spirits. (See Isaiah 14:12–14; 2 Corinthians 10:4–5; Ephesians 2:6; 3:10.)

---

3 Strong's #4655

5. Devils and demons

Literally translated from the Greek word *daimonion*, *demon* means "distributor of fortunes."4 A demon or devil is a supernatural spirit that possesses the nature of Satan and has the ability to give and distribute fortunes (mammon of the unrighteous), possess man, and control mind-sets and activities. Devils can be worshiped, make people sick, communicate, and involve themselves in a host of other diabolical activities. (See Matthew 6:24; 8:16, 28; Revelation 16:13–14.)

6. Spirits of the underworld

These spirits work with high witchcraft operations (Isa. 14:9; Ezek. 32:17–32; Job 41). As mentioned before, the underworld has six regions, and none of which are places you would ever want to go:

- Death (1 Cor. 15:55; Job 34:22)
- Hell/Sheol/Hades (Isa. 14:19)
- The grave (Isa. 38:10; Ezek. 31:15)
- The pit (Ezek. 32:23)
- The abyss—the lower region of the pit (Isa. 38:17; Ps. 30:3)
- Regions of the sea (Job 41:1–31; Ezek. 26:16)

7. Spirit birds

Remember when Noah sent out the dove who returned with an olive branch, or when God used a bird to bring food to Elijah the prophet? Satan also has spirit birds at his disposal, only they are unclean and hateful (Rev. 18:2).

8. Spirit horses and horsemen

Before there were tanks, airplanes, and Scud missiles, men used horses and horsemen when they went to war. As in the natural, so it is in the spiritual. The spiritual battlefield is filled with spirit horses and horsemen (Rev. 9:15–19; Hag. 2:21–22).

9. Familiar spirits

We can encounter familiar spirits who work for Satan. They are like reconnaissance teams. Their job is to spy and take reports back to headquarters

---

4 Strong's #1140

(Lev. 20:6). Familiar spirits are demonic agents whose main assignments are to become well acquainted with a person or groups of people. In the Old Testament we find that familiar spirits are mentioned in several places, including: Leviticus 19:31; 20:6, 27; Deuteronomy 18:9–14; 2 Kings 21:6; 23:24; 1 Chronicles 10:13–14; 2 Chronicles 33:6; Isaiah 8:19. In the New Testament, we clearly see familiar spirits at work. A few examples can be found in Matthew 9:32; 12:43–45; 15:22; 17:15–18; Mark 5:1–20; 9:17–26; Acts 16:16–18; 19:15–16.

These demonic spirits propagate the will of their master, Satan. They are responsible for satanic surveillance, diabolical reconnaissance, and vigilante activities. They are spirits with assignments emanating from a highly developed and complex satanic operation designed to kill, steal, and destroy. In order for you to understand their functions, roles, and portfolio, modern computer terminologies will explain some of their activities. They gather information through observation, and create a comprehensive dossier on the person to whom they are assigned. This information would then be passed on to another recording spirit to be downloaded into satanic databases for future reference. If Paul was born during this century, perhaps "the handwriting" he refers to in Colossians 2:14 would read "Database."

Familiar spirits usually operate independently of the human spirit. However, they have also been known to possess human beings who become agents. In 1 Samuel 28:7 Saul sought a woman who operated by familiar spirits. He told his servants to "Seek me a woman that hath a familiar spirit, that I may go to her, and inquire of her. And his servants said to him, Behold, there is a woman that hath a familiar spirit at Endor."

In this text a familiar spirit has formed an unholy alliance with the witch of Endor, who crosses over to the "dark" world and sees demonic activities. A familiar spirit, who is aware that Saul's anointing has been lifted and who is aware of the desolate state of his spiritual life, communicates with the familiar spirit who had been assigned to the prophet Samuel. The two decide that their plan to put another stake in Saul's prophetic coffin would be to impersonate Samuel, which would be a simple diabolical endeavor because the spirit assigned to him would know everything about him, right down to his deportment, decorum, persona, and unique physiological characteristics.

A familiar spirit of one person can communicate with the familiar spirit of another person. That is why, in the instance of abuse, the abused can be in another city or state and feel the presence of the abuser, who can pick up his activities and whereabouts. This is because they form strong lines of communication between themselves. When there is a covenant made, it is not only made between the persons, but also the between the familiar spirits assigned to them. They form attachments in the realm of the spirit, which are often difficult to break. You should never establish any kind of association with anyone or any institution without first getting a green light from the Father.

Familiar spirits know the person to whom they are assigned so well that they can even imitate them. This ability produces the deceptive element in a séance. People are often convinced that the diviner is talking and communing with their dead relatives or loved ones. These are not dead relatives but very evil spirits, attempting to hold them captive in the darkness of their underworld activities. The Bible warns us against establishing any kind of communication with familiar spirits. Leviticus 19:31 clearly tells us not to regard "them that have familiar spirits, neither seek after wizards, to be defiled by them: I am the LORD your God." I believe Saul was aware of this commandment. To go as undetected as one who ignores a commandment of God, Saul attempted to hide his real identity by camouflaging himself. As you read the account of his rendezvous experience with the witch of Endor, you will notice that the familiar spirit knew who he was in spite of his masquerade. First Samuel 28:3–25 gives us further insight to the activities of familiar spirits. As you read this account, please observe the following:

- Samuel is dead.
- The witch sees "gods" ascending out of the earth (regions of the underworld). These are actual familiar (demonic) spirits disguising themselves as Samuel.
- The response of Saul was fear. Second Timothy 1:7 states that God does not give you the spirit of fear.

Familiar spirits form confederations, tracking activities of men and women of God, divine visitations, and kingdom initiatives through religious spirits as well. Acts 16:16–21 records another instance where we read of a young woman who was able to work with familiar spirits. The intent was to discredit Paul's ministry by deceiving the people, causing them to believe that he was associated with her.

Familiar spirits know your "hot spots." They know which buttons to push. They know your weaknesses and strengths, likes and dislikes, passions and pet peeves, what gets you going, what upsets you, what distracts you, your desires, your ambitions—everything!

Familiar spirits have three different assignments:

1. Geographical assignments (Mark 5:1–10)
2. Cultural assignments (Num. 33:50–55)
3. Individual assignments (1 Sam. 28:3–9; 1 Chron. 10:13)

To accomplish their goals and purpose, they can use:

1. Animals (i.e., black cats, frogs)
2. Talisman (any object or piece of clothing that witches and warlocks and other workers of the craft use to transfer spells and hexes)
3. People whose lives are characterized by demonic/satanic alliances

Familiar spirits act as informants to a larger network of demons who function as a kind of satanic intelligence. (See Daniel 11:30.) Their portfolios include their roles as informants and council to Satan and other highly specialized principalities, powers, or rulers of the darkness of this world. I can imagine them reporting to satanic councils, bringing to the table information that would be utilized in the designing of attacks and strongholds, and creating weapons of mass destruction designed to kill and destroy individuals, families, ministries, communities, and nations.

Familiar spirits observe very strict protocols. Although they are not employed to attack, in addition to the aforementioned tasks, their job descriptions would also include the examining of spiritual hedges of protection built around believers in an attempt to identify and locate perforations. Job 1:7–11 and 3:25 record examples of this activity. Fear created a perforation in Job's hedge, thus allowing Satan to send in his agents to steal, kill, and destroy.

In fulfilling their roles as counsel to Satan, high-ranking principalities, and powers, they offer suggestions to them as to how best to keep an individual in bondage. In this instance, gatekeepers and doorkeepers would be employed to allow or prohibit access to an individual, family, community, nation, organization, or ministry. Every city, country, family, person, and any living entity has gates and doors, hence Psalm 24:7–10: "Lift up your head, O ye gates; and be ye lift up, ye everlasting doors; and the King of glory shall come in. Who is this King of glory? The LORD strong and mighty, the LORD mighty in battle. Lift up your heads, O ye gates; even lift them up, ye everlasting doors; and the King of glory shall come in. Who is this King of glory? The LORD of hosts, he is the King of glory. Selah."

Concerning you as a human being, you have three gates and nineteen doors to your soul and body that provide portals through which spirits enter. They are as follows:

Portals Through Which Spirits Can Enter the Soul or Body	
Gates	**Doors**
Lust of the flesh	Olfactory (2)
Lust of the eyes	Visual (2)
Pride of life	Auditory (2)
	Kinesthetic (1)
	Gustatory (2)
	Reproductive/sexual (4)
	Elimination (2)
	Motion and movement (2)
	Action and accomplishments (2)

Make God the Father, God the Son, and God the Holy Spirit your new gate and doorkeeper.

10. Unclean spirits

Satan even commands unclean spirits—yes, the same spirits Jesus cast out. As the Word suggests, this spirit is responsible for lewd, promiscuous, and immoral activities. (See Mark 1:27.)

11. Evil spirits

Satan commands vicious and malicious spirits that are responsible for promoting terrible, dehumanized conditions. They work in concert with other spirits to cause misfortunes, mishaps, and accidents and to incite criminal activities. (See Luke 7:21.)

12. Seducing spirits

Satan commands seducing spirits, which are responsible for attracting and drawing you into a wrong or foolish course of action. Many fall victim to this kind of spirit. (See 1 Timothy 4:1.)

13. Archangels

Satan was a created being, along with all other angelic beings. He was also one of the highest-ranking angels, along with Michael and Gabriel. According to Ezekiel 28:11–17 and other passages of Scripture, Satan had a kingdom on Earth. He fell and led a host of angels into rebellion against God. He was thrown out of heaven, and has become a ruler of this world's systems: the prince of the power of the air. He is cunning, wicked, and insidious. He opposes all that is of God and everything that is good. (See Isaiah 14:12–14.)

SATAN'S NAMES

Most of us know that Satan has more than one name. When Jesus went about delivering people and casting out demons, He called the demons out by name (Mark 5:9–15; Luke 8:30). By Jesus's victorious example, it would be better for us on our battlefield to be prepared by knowing these names:

1. Lucifer (Isa. 14:12–14)
2. Devil and Satan (Rev. 12:9)
3. Beelzebub (Matt. 10:25; 12:24)
4. Adversary (1 Pet. 5:8–9)
5. Belial (2 Cor. 6:15)
6. Dragon (Rev. 12:3–12; 13:1–4; 20:1–3)
7. Serpent (2 Cor. 11:3; Rev. 12:9)
8. The god of this world (2 Cor. 4:4)
9. The prince of this world (John 12:31)
10. Prince of the power of the air (Eph. 2:1–3)
11. Accuser of the brethren (Rev. 12:10)
12. The enemy (Matt. 13:39)
13. The tempter (Matt. 4:3)
14. The wicked one (Matt. 13:19, 38)

THE NATURE OF SATANIC SPIRITS

People often make the error of believing Satan is a caricatured being with red horns and a pitchfork. Satan is much more than that, and he is powerful. Here are some characteristics of Satan and his demons:

1. They are not human (Eph 6:12).
2. They are evil (Judg. 9:23).
3. They are intelligent and wise (1 Kings 22:22–24).
4. They are powerful (Mark 5:1–18).
5. They are beings with personalities (Acts 19:15–16).
6. They talk and communicate (Mark 5:6–7).
7. They feel (Matt. 8:29).
8. They have knowledge (Acts 19:15).
9. They congregate and fellowship (1 Cor. 10:20–21).
10. They "preach" doctrines (1 Tim. 4:1).
11. They have desires (Matt. 8:28–31).
12. They have a will (Matt. 12:43–45).
13. They can work miracles (Rev. 16:13–14).
14. They possess supernatural strength (Mark 5:1–18).
15. They fear God (James 2:19).
16. They travel (Mark 5:7–12).
17. They impersonate people (1 Sam. 28:3–9).
18. They know their fate (Matt. 8:29).
19. They recognize those who have power over them (Acts 19:13–15).
20. They are responsible for every evil known to man (Eph. 6:11).

THE SCOPE OF THEIR ACTIVITIES AND PROOF OF THEIR PRESENCE

The scope of demonic activities is both broad and diverse. Among them are:

1. Deafness and dumbness (Matt. 9:32–33)
2. Blindness (Matt. 12:22)
3. Grief (1 Sam. 1:7–8)
4. Vexation (Matt. 15:22)

5. Provocation (1 Chron. 21:1)
6. Murder (Ps. 106:36–38)
7. Suicide (Matt. 17:15)
8. Idolatry (1 Kings 22:53)
9. Convulsions (Mark 9:20)
10. Lusts (John 8:44)
11. Confusion and strife (James 3:15–16)
12. False worship (Deut. 32:17)
13. Error, heresy, and false doctrine (1 Tim. 4:1–2)
14. Sickness and disease (Matt. 4:23–24)
15. Torments (Matt. 15:22)
16. Deception (1 John 4:1–6)
17. Lying (1 Kings 22:21–24)
18. Wickedness (Luke 11:26)
19. Fear (2 Tim. 1:7)
20. Worldliness (1 John 2:15–17)
21. Bondage (Rom. 8:15)
22. Discord (Prov. 6:16–19)
23. Violence (Mark 9:22)
24. Betrayal (John 13:2)
25. Oppression (Acts 10:38)
26. Persecution (Rev. 2:10)
27. Jealousy (1 Sam. 19:1–11)
28. False prophecy (1 Sam. 18:8–10)
29. Stealing (John 10:10)
30. Fighting/wrestling (Eph. 6:10–18)

Now that you are more knowledgeable about the structure and organization of the kingdom of darkness, let's move on to see what kinds of weapons the enemy uses so that we know how to effectively plan our defense and offense.

SIX

WEAPONS OF MASS DESTRUCTION

Hiroshima of the Spirit

T HE ENEMY FORMS and forges a great variety of weapons. Some are more apparent than others, such as abuse and afflictions. Others are not as evident, such as the spirit of indifference and frustration.

In several places, the Bible portrays Satan as a crouching lion waiting for the most opportune moment to pounce upon his unsuspecting prey. First Peter 5:8 exhorts us to "be sober, be vigilant; because your adversary the devil, as a roaring lion, walketh about, seeking whom he may devour." The word *may* is the key word in this passage. It says to me that Satan cannot devour everyone. He cannot devour you if you are aware of his tactics and strategies, because the weapons you fight with are far greater than his according to 2 Corinthians 10:4–5. From this scripture alone we can conclude that the weapons the enemy uses against us are primarily carnal in nature: ones that involve the mind, will, and emotions.

In order to defend against Satan and his deceptive attacks, we must first understand what we are defending against. Imagine, for example, that you are a general with tens of thousands of soldiers and weapons at your command. The battlefield is pitch black—and as events would have it, you don't at this moment have night-vision goggles and equipment. You know out there somewhere is another general with his battalions, but you don't know how many soldiers he has on the battlefield. You don't know if your soldiers will be facing tanks, cannons, planes, or missiles. You don't know whether the terrain is mountainous or wet and swampy. Can you plan a battle effectively? Absolutely not! Everything would be guesswork. Both you and your soldiers would be at a disadvantage and in greater danger of being killed. Our general, the Lord Jesus Christ, is not an uninformed general. He knows the enemy, his arsenal, and the terrain. The battlefield is the mind, and the weapons...well, you are about to discover.

THE ENEMY'S WEAPONS AGAINST THE CHILDREN OF GOD

What follows at the end of this chapter is a list of intrinsic (internal), extrinsic (external), and esoteric (obscure/hidden) weapons the enemy could possibly employ in his attack against you. For ease of reference, weapons have been alphabetized. Scripture references are given to provide further biblical insight and revelation of how the enemy utilizes these weapons. Read each section carefully and prayerfully.

ABANDONMENT

Abandonment is when a person withdraws their presence and support from another person or organization; reneges on their duty, responsibility, and obligation; and betrays covenant or commitment. The enemy seduces people, particularly those who play a key role in the life of another person or organization's development and progress, to renege on commitments and contracts and to walk away from relationships and responsibilities. This act of abdication has the power to cause great emotional pain, financial hardship, spiritual misalignment, organizational chaos, and confusion in the abandoned. Abandonment can be physical, psychological, and emotional and can occur with one's job or career, a political or military post, and within family relationships. Paul experienced ministerial abandonment, but God provided for him three individuals—Timothy, Mark, and Luke—to encourage and refresh him during his season of testing. (See 2 Timothy 4:9–18.)

Issues arising from abandonment, such as the inability to trust, manipulation, shame, fear of rejection, loneliness, suspicion, addictions, codependency, and a host of other maladaptive sets of behavior interfere with the victim's ability to foster future healthy and loving relationships.

ABORTION

There are two perspectives I want to give concerning abortion. First, I offer the traditional. According to the *American Heritage Dictionary*, abortion is an induced termination of pregnancy and expulsion of an embryo or fetus. Once the woman or young girl consents and actually undergoes an abortion, she becomes both victim and perpetrator. The abortion does not merely make a person "unpregnant," but it also molds both the woman and those who support and perform abortion into murderers. It opens the door for a spirit of death to destroy other areas of their lives, creating cycles of death that allow the enemy to access their lives to steal, kill, and destroy not only the quality of their lives but also business ventures, relationships, and ministries. It also sends the spirit of death down to future generations. Long-term ramifications are mind-boggling.

The second has to do with spiritual abortion. The spirit of abortion not only affects the physical womb, but it also affects all twenty-six wombs of the spirit. These weapons are meticulously crafted to destroy an individual, businesses, ministries, organizations, or any other entity's chance of maximizing potential or the fulfillment of purpose. Other abortive activities that the enemy is involved in are murder, accidents, premature deaths, sabotage, and less obvious activities such as laziness, gossip, fear, underbelief, and slander. Each one of these abortive activities affects one or more areas of a person's life and has the power to terminate things such as ministries, business opportunities, relationships, purpose, and potential.

Spiritual abortion kills the many different blessings that heaven is pregnant with for you, your dreams and visions, plans and purpose, desires and aspirations. The delivered adult Hebrew slaves never made it into the Promised Land. Their entire future prosperity and life was aborted because of fear and unbelief. There is such a high level of misunderstanding when it comes to abortion that the enemy has created a stronghold in many societies through misunderstanding and miseducation of the masses.

ABUSE

Abuse is defined as the mistreatment of something or someone, and it can manifest itself in various forms: physical (punching; hitting; slapping; pinching; shaking; less-than-adequate care and support; and improper administration of drugs, treatments, or medication), psychological (repeatedly making someone feel unhappy, anxious, afraid, humiliated, or devalued), sexual (acts that involve physical or nonphysical harassment, precludes consent, or the power imbalance is too great for their consent to be considered valid), financial or material (the misuse of a vulnerable person's money, property, possessions, or insurance, or blocking access to these material goods; denying the rights of a competent adult to complain, to vote, or to seek independent legal advice; and stealing a vulnerable person's money, property, possessions, or insurance; or extortion through threats and misappropriation), institutional (the practice of an abusive regime or culture that destroys the dignity and respect to which every person is entitled and occurs when the individual's wishes and needs are sacrificed for the smooth running of an institution, organization, or home), social (intentional or unintentional exclusion from a valued activity, denial of access to community events/groups, or denied access to friends and family), discriminatory (oppressive and discriminatory attitudes toward a person's disability, including physical or learning disability, ill mental health, or sensory impairment; race; age; gender; religion; cultural background; or sexual orientation).

ACCIDENT

When I talk about accidents, I am not only referring to those that are seemingly caused by human error but also unexplainable events caused by forces outside of human instigation. I believe that satanic forces can instigate catastrophic events. These occurrences are abortive undertakings designed to frustrate or foil the will of God in the earth realm. In Acts 27:9–44 one of Jesus's disciples narrated an event that is an example of a satanically orchestrated accident waiting to happen. This passage shows a well-planned attempt by the enemy to sabotage the mission of Jesus in the country of the Gergesenes, where therein awaited a demon-possessed individual divinely scheduled for deliverance that day. Had the enemy successfully completed this undertaking, lives would have been lost and the demoniac would have remained under the control and influence of Satan.

ACCUSATION

Accusation is the act of attributing blame and wrongdoings. This is one of the enemy's weapons of choice when it comes to disturbing personal peace, undermining purpose, and destroying faith in God, particularly if the accusations are fabricated. The accuser of the brethren will not only personally accuse you, but also, like a master chess player, he uses other people as pawns to bring you to the point of hearing him declare "checkmate" and defeating you completely. Whenever you see individuals accusing one another, or you begin to accuse and point fingers, ask yourself this question: Is the accuser of the brethren at the helm of this? Accusations can go from one extreme to the other: the blatant, such as indictments and impeachments; and the sublime, such as insinuations and innuendos. (See Daniel 6:1–7; Revelation 12:10.)

ADDICTIONS

There are both popular and professional definitions for the word *addiction*. When a layperson attempts to define what an addiction is, usually they will describe a person who is addicted to something that creates an unhealthy habit or a social disease. According to the *American Heritage Dictionary*, an addiction is a compulsive physical or psychological need for habit-forming substances, activities, or experiences. (See Luke 21:34; Romans 6:16.) An addiction is also characterized by a behavior performed in response to an obsession. Addictions can spin off into what is psychologically termed as obsessive-compulsive disorders (OCD). For ease of reference, I have listed addictions under two headings:

1. Substance: alcohol, heroin, tobacco, solvents, cocaine, crack, cannabis, caffeine, steroids, tranquilizers, hallucinogens, amphetamines, ecstasy, painkillers, barbiturates
2. Social: overexercising, sex, sexual perversions, pornography, eating disorders (anorexia, bulimia, overeating), techno-addictions (computer games, cyber sex), work, gambling, oniomania (compulsive shopping)

ADULTERY

Adultery is a voluntary sexual relationship between a married person and a person other than their spouse. It is a form of betrayal that involves the breaking of a covenant and is an elaborately crafted weapon of mass destruction. This satanic tool is used to corrode the institutions of marriage and family and ultimately causes the very fabric of a just and moral society or nation to fray at its seams. The adulterer or adulteress betrays their marriage vow and lies in order to cover up their sin. The deceptive nature of adultery is that the individuals involved believe no one else is hurt by their activities. The feelings of betrayal, hurt, sadness, anger, and grief are caused not just because one of the partners engages in a sexual relationship with another, but also because the exclusivity and secrecy of the relationship causes feelings of betrayal and intense emotional pain. To know that your partner is sharing an intimate spiritual or emotional connection with someone else can be extremely disconcerting.

ADVERSITY

Adversities are calamitous circumstances and conditions that cause anguish, affliction, distress, physical discomfort, and psychological damage. These life-altering and sometimes life-threatening events can be national, financial, physical, organizational, ministerial, spiritual, or psychological in nature. (See Proverbs 24:10; Colossians 1:24.)

AFFLICTIONS

An affliction is a pathological (deviation from normalcy) condition of mind, body, soul, or spirit that produces suffering, sicknesses, disease, or conditions difficult to treat, cure, or overcome by human interventions. The ultimate cure, of course, is divine intervention. The list of afflictions include: trials and tribulations, sorrows of the soul (depression, rejection, inferiority complex, loneliness), physical ailments, emotional hardship, misfortunes, satanically induced vexation, satanic/demonic provocation, incurable disease and sickness, adversity, abandonment, calamities and catastrophes, distress, and medical emergencies.

ANGER

The Hebrew word for anger is *anaph*, which, when literally translated, means, "rapid breathing from passion."[1] An angry person is often spoken of as someone who boils with anger, or who is hotheaded. This is because extreme anger affects every part of our being. The Holy Spirit's presence in our lives should be the gatekeeper to our soul. The enemy wants to make you or people associated with you emotional volcanoes, erratically erupting and disrupting peace. Don't let your (or anyone else's) hot temper and emotions get the best of you, creating irrational, ungodly responses and behavior, fear, trepidation, and hostile environments for others to live in. The enemy would love to have you live a life driven by anger rather than being led by the Spirit of God. He wants to make you an emotional puppet on a diabolical string and open prey to the enemy. According to Proverbs 25:28, "He that hath no rule over his own spirit is like a city that is broken down, and without walls." (See also Genesis 49:6–7.)

ANXIETY

Anxiety is the apprehensive, uneasy, and distressed state of mind concerning real or imagined future possibilities, probabilities, or eventualities. This condition causes a kind of mental prison that, when not counteracted by faith in God, will invite fear, hopelessness, depression, worry, and dread to become fellow inmates who will place your present and future on lockdown. To render this weapon ineffective, the apostle Paul encourages us to use our anxieties as prayer points and prophetic praise reports (Phil. 4:6).

APATHY

When the spirit of apathy is present, it causes a person to become indifferent and desensitized to circumstances or conditions, ultimately producing a literal numbing of the soul and an emotional calcification of the heart. Having spent many years in bondage, the children of Israel were attacked with this weapon. The psalmist recorded their blues in Psalm 137:1–4: "By the rivers of Babylon we sat and wept when we remembered Zion. There on the poplars we hung our harps, for there our captors asked us for songs, our tormentors demanded songs of joy; they said, 'Sing us one of the songs of Zion!' How can we sing the songs of the LORD while in a foreign land?" (NIV).

APPROVAL-SEEKING ACTIVITIES

People who engage in approval-seeking activities are people who will do anything to get affirmation and acceptance from others. Approval-seeking individuals lack personal power, self-worth, dignity, and a sense of significance. Approval-seeking activities are driven by fear. The instigating spirit will cause you to fear negative responses and feedback and to become so approval dependent that you barter away all your time, energy, and personal preferences just for affirmation and approval. Sometimes these activities will come across as noble and altruistic. If you carefully examine the motivations behind most activities, you will notice they are usually instigated by the need to be seen, affirmed, or accepted. Activities can range from saying yes when you really want or should say no (becoming a yes-man), or a total denial of self. But in saying no, deep down inside if you really explore what is going on, you are engaging in activities that invalidate your significance and importance as an individual free to make decisions independent of another's opinion.

Approval-seeking shenanigans will cause you to become a feel-good junky addicted to the affirmation of others and focusing solely on their affirmations. You let others have their way with you, say whatever they want to you, treat you any way they want, walk all over you, and treat you like a doormat in exchange for a hit of praise. Of course, you love when they call you good, godly, saintly, and angelic. Your personal preference and opinion, critical thinking, purpose, vision, and desires are inconsequential when juxtaposed to another. For you, approval seeking becomes the quintessential definition of degradation, self-betrayal, and self-abuse, destroying authenticity and integrity of self.

ARGUMENTS

Arguments are carnal, self-centered, or demonically instigated verbal conflict, disagreement, or irrational presupposition presented to support an erroneous thought, opinion, or position. This weapon is used to seduce people away from the truth, to avoid responsibility, or as an alibi to cover the truth. Many relationships, ministries, and marriages end up sabotaged, undermined, or destroyed because of this particular weapon. At all costs, a child of God should avoid this kind of controversy because according to Titus 3:9, it is useless and unprofitable. (See also 2 Timothy 2:23.)

ATTACHMENTS

As the word suggests, an attachment is that which Satan uses to maintain alliances and connection to something that is not good for you or has the power to undermine and destroy purpose, potential, and destiny because it facilitates carnality and unrighteousness. Attachments can exist on many levels and can take on many different forms, such as food, people, conditions, environments, or behaviors. They can exist prior to salvation and long after a person receives the Lord as his or her Savior. A good example of this is contained in the account of Simon the sorcerer in Acts 8:18–24. Even after his conversion, residue from his activities in the occult was still evident. Although he had been converted, he still needed deliverance.

ATTENTION-SEEKING ACTIVITIES

In life you will run across people who will do anything to gain center stage and to be at the center of everyone's attention. These individuals usually are starved for attention, plagued with the spirit of jealousy, or just plain insecure. Stemming from their upbringing, this state usually is the result of having not received appropriate attention in their unique love language.

AVOIDANCE

Avoidance activities are socially, emotionally, or psychologically generated disorders whereby a person shuns responsibilities or circumvents account-ability through justification, excuses, or alibis. Usually a person who is skilled in this area will be seduced into living a hermit-type life, avoiding confron-tational situations, uncomfortable conditions, or anything that moves them out of their abnormal comfort zone.

BACKLASH

Backlash is the spiritual repercussion an individual experiences after making spiritual inroads in prayer and gaining new territories through spiritual warfare activities. This is satanic *quid pro quo*; as the saying goes: "You kill my cat, I'll kill your dog." Do not be intimidated. Be like David—don't give up or give in. Don't throw in the towel or raise a white flag of defeat. If the enemy causes any losses or setbacks, pursue, prevail, and recover all! (See 1 Samuel 30:1–8.)

BACKSLIDING

The word *backsliding* is an old English term used to describe the regressive action of an individual who, having made progress toward a more ethically, morally, and spiritually enriched life, reverts back to a less-than-admirable life of immorality, spiritual depravity, and spiritual and emotional immatu-rity. When the spirit of backsliding hits you, it has the potential to cause you to move out of a higher level of operating in the spirit to a lower, inferior state of existence. (See Jeremiah 3:6–14; 2 Thessalonians 2:1–3.)

Bad Reputations

In Philemon 1:10–11, Paul makes an appeal on behalf of a brother who apparently had a bad reputation. A reputation is the value, assessment, or a kind of social rating placed upon a person based on the perception of their character, image, and activities. The Bible clearly states, "Man looketh on the outward appearance" (1 Sam. 16:7). We can have good reputations or bad reputations. Another person's assessment of us can be accurate or inaccurate. Perception is reality to the person perceiving. The enemy uses this fact to twist and distort our perceptions.

Bands

In the Bible days, a band was a thin strip of flexible material used for encircling and binding one object to another, or to hold a number of objects together. Using this analogy, bands can therefore be referred to as satanic restraining devices that prohibit progress, growth, and development by causing a person to be bound to situations, circumstances, conditions, people, habits, thought and behavior patterns, activities, and substances. Bands can be physical, psychological, or emotional. (See Leviticus 26:13; Isaiah 52:2; 58:6.)

Besetting Sin

According to Hebrews 12:1, a besetting sin would be any hindrance that Satan uses to thwart the progress of a believer so that he cannot finish a particular course of action.

Betrayal

Betrayal is a powerful weapon that robs a person of his or her trust in something or someone through the violation of covenant, contracts, or verbal agreements. This weapon causes intense grief of the soul. There are two pieces of advice I want to give you if you have been betrayed. First, never allow yourself to take on the role of a victim. And second, do not give your personal power away. Remember, you have a God who will never betray you.

He has made a covenant with you that He will never break. (See Psalm 55:4–6, 12–14.)

BITTERNESS

Bitterness, the fruit of unforgiveness, causes deep-seated resentment, hatred, and ill will. This acrimonious emotion is the result of anguish, disappointment, or severe grief. It is believed by many psychotherapeutic practitioners and spiritual leaders that bitterness is the root cause of arthritis and a host of other emotional, spiritual, psychological, and physiological maladies. Bitterness is a weapon that, once effectively utilized against you, will affect every facet of your life. It erodes relationships, taints perception, contaminates anointing, and hinders true liberty in the spirit. The spirit of bitterness, acting as a doorkeeper, will make its victim hostile, antagonistic, acrimonious, and open to other demonic activities. (See Jeremiah 4:18; Hebrews 12:15.)

BLIND SPOTS

Has anyone ever pointed out a proclivity, action, habit, or attitude that you supposedly demonstrated and that you swore was incorrect? Do you know anyone who, no matter how many people accuse them of saying or doing something, they simply cannot see what people are referring to? Have you ever been told something about yourself by more than one person that you flatly denied because you couldn't see what they were talking about? This is what we call a blind spot. They are things in our lives that we do unknowingly that offend, hurt, or insult others. Remember, even if these things are obvious to others and a person points them out to you, you will not be able to see what they are talking about. (See Psalm 51:6; 2 Corinthians 3:14; 4:4.)

BONDAGES

Bondage is a condition where a person is placed in a state of subjugation to an "owner" or a "master" who psychologically, emotionally, or physically restrains them by force, power, or influence. Bondage has many faces, wears many masks, and creates emotional, physical, financial, and spiritual prisoners out of its victims. People can be in bondage to such things as drugs, alcohol, and sex. (See Exodus 13:3.)

CARES OF THE WORLD

Cares of the world can be anything causing a believer to pursue worldly things, business ventures, and the acquisition of possessions at the expense of their pursuit of God, His Word, and His kingdom. (See Matthew 13:22.)

CARNALITY

Carnality is the appetite of the flesh and soul. (See 1 Corinthians 3:3–4.) It is the preoccupation with one's appetite and satiation of urges, drives, and desires.

CELESTIAL BARRICADES

Have you ever prayed and felt that your prayers were just hitting the ceiling? Have you ever attempted to pursue a God-given idea, mandate, or mission, only to feel as if every attempt was hindered by some unseen force? You might have encountered what I call a "celestial barricade." Celestial barricades are satanic maneuvers, barriers, blocks, encumbrances, and hindrances that obstruct, hinder, and prohibit movement in the spirit realm and frustrate the progress of a vision, dream, mandate, mission, prayer, or the plan of God for your life. (See Daniel 10:12–13.)

CHAINS/FETTERS/SHACKLES

Chains, fetters, and shackles are anything that confine movement, hinder progress, and cause captivity, oppression, and bondage. (See Judges 16:5–6, 18–21; Psalm 68:6.)

COMPLACENCY

Adam and Eve were prosperous until complacency set in. Israel had become socially and politically prosperous under the leadership of Joshua until the spirit of complacency set in. Complacency kills passion, strangles drive and motivation, and lulls a person's senses to sleep until they are unaware of their deficiencies, their need for God, and the need to do something about their condition. This spirit is so powerful that it will cause you to lose your sense of urgency, vigilance, and awareness, and to walk through life unconscious. (See 1 Corinthians 15:34; Ephesians 5:14.)

COMPROMISING

·The enemy uses this weapon to cause you to make concessions to things that are spiritually detrimental. In the case of a believer, it is the lowering of a biblical standard and the abatement of a conviction. (See Romans 14:16; James 1:8.)

CONDEMNATION

The spirit of condemnation causes mental and emotional torment by satanically imposing an overwhelming sense of guilt, long-term remorse, and shame in spite of a confessed sin and a repented heart. Remember—God convicts; Satan condemns. (See Romans 8:1.)

CONFEDERATES

A confederate is one who supports another in a criminal act as an accomplice or an ally. (See Psalm 83:5; Isaiah 7:2.)

CONTAMINATED ANOINTING

A contaminated anointing is caused when someone who is ministering, ministers without full and total submission to the Holy Spirit. The pure anointing becomes contaminated because it flows from the soulish realm rather than a regenerated and consecrated spirit. (See Jude 10–13.)

COVERT OPERATIONS

Covert operations are high-powered, camouflaged, satanic strategies used to hinder and frustrate the work of the Lord, to distract ministers, to destroy their influence and ministry, and to utterly destroy the lives of saints in general. (See Acts 16:14–20.)

COVETOUSNESS

Covetousness causes an individual to lust for what rightfully belongs to others. This spirit acts as a doorkeeper to jealousy, hatred, envy, strife, murder, slander, adultery, and a host of other evil works of the flesh. (See Romans 13:9.)

CULTURE

Cultures form when two or more individuals band together in response to perceived needs and then combine their abilities and resources to meet those needs. Once formed, cultures are responsible for socially transmitting behavior patterns, arts, beliefs, institutions, and all other products of human work and thought. Culture shapes your awareness of everything around you and how you react to things. Many times the enemy attempts to seduce believers into placing more emphasis on their earthly culture rather than the culture of the kingdom of God, which takes precedence over all national, organizational, and parochial cultures. (See Acts 8:5–13.)

DEATH

Death is the most deadly weapon Satan has in his arsenal (pun intended). It demands the attention of humanity and the curiosity of science. It commands the attention of all media and culture. It promotes the sale of newspapers, books, and life insurance and provides plots for Hollywood. Death even has a way of causing people to carefully weigh their actions from the perspective of eternity. Death incorporates those occurrences that are untimely and unexpected, such as suicides, homicides, accidents, loss of reputation, loss of hope, or divorce. The pain and agony experienced by those mourning their losses are often so intense and unbearable that they become vulnerable to its seduction and swept away into eternity by its dark and spindly hands. Untimely death aborts destinies, executes purpose, and assassinates potential. (See Jeremiah 9:21.)

DECEPTION

This weapon causes fraudulence, duplicity, underhandedness, cheating, and the willful betrayal of confidence and trust. This surreptitious behavior requires you to be vigilant, alert, and discerning of the spirits working and lurking around you. Take nothing and no one for granted. Although the enemy uses all forms of deception, the highest form of deception is self-deception. Deuteronomy 11:16 warns us to "take heed to yourselves, that your heart be not deceived, and ye turn aside, and serve other gods, and worship them." (See also Joshua 9:1–12; 1 Corinthians 6:9; 2 Timothy 3:13.)

DEGENERATIVE DISEASES

From the moment we are conceived, the processes of life are carried out by our biological executor called DNA. Our DNA holds the genetic code for our life, health, and for the unique physical features of our bodies. DNA has the divine blueprint for our body, programming our cells to maintain optimum health from birth to death. The body is a magnificent biological system that provides an earth-suit for our spirits and, once filled with the Holy Spirit, provides a vessel through which God conducts His affairs in the earth realm. Degenerative diseases are the means by which Satan interferes with the life God wants for us all. (See Job 33:21; Psalm 22:14–17; John 5:1–6.)

DELUSION

This weapon causes man to hold on to false perceptions, images, concepts, beliefs, and opinions generated by demons, embracing them as if they were truth and reality. (See 2 Thessalonians 2:11.) The delusion may manifest itself as any of the following types: persecutory (the individual believes he or she is being threatened or mistreated by others), grandiose (the individual believes that they are extraordinarily important people or are possessed of extraordinary power, knowledge, or ability), jealous (the individual focuses on the suspected unfaithfulness of a spouse or sexual partner), "erotimatic" (an individual convinces themselves that some person of eminence, usually someone they do not have close contact with or have never met but with whom they frequently have corresponded, is in love with them), somatic (a false belief focused on a delusional physical abnormality or disorder, like false pregnancies), and *folie à deux* (an extremely rare type of shared delusion, resulting from a close relationship with someone else who already has a delusions disorder).

DEPRESSION

Depression has become a prevalent mental disease in our world today. This weapon causes psychotic or neurotic conditions, and emotional and physiological disorders. (See Psalm 69:20; 119:28; Matthew 26:38.) It is characterized by an inability to concentrate, insomnia, constant feelings of extreme sadness, lack of motivation, irritability, withdrawal tendencies, weight loss or gain, loneliness, fatigue, and thoughts of suicide, especially when the spirit of hopelessness sets in. As the word implies, it creates an overall feeling of heaviness. This spirit attacked Elijah, David, and Jesus. While Jesus overcame His depression through prayer and David through the reading of God's Word, Elijah overcame his depression though divine intervention. God instructed him to get up and get going.

DEPRIVATION

Deprivation is the condition of being extremely poor, destitute. (See 2 Kings 6:25.) It divests a person of his or her God-given dignity and a good quality of life. Deprivation falls under the following categories: social (being restrained from enjoying interaction with certain people based on social or economic differences), sleep (extended periods of wakefulness or a decrease in sleep over an extended period), privacy (the divestment of the right to be free of unsanctioned intrusion), parental (physical and emotional detachment of parents from children), financial (withdrawal of financial support; loss of income; unemployment; underemployment resulting in a lack of money for food, housing, clothing, and transportation), early childhood (insufficient or lack of food, housing, clothing, safety, nurturance, love, guidance, care, concern, or direction), and emotional (privation of affection, attention, direction, empathy, nurturance, strength, and understanding)

DISCOURAGEMENT

Many believers suffer from feelings of hopelessness in their Christian walk and ministry. These emotions are characteristic of the spirit of discouragement that occurs when a particular expectation is unmet. "Why art thou cast down, O my soul? and why art thou disquieted in me? hope thou in God: for I shall yet praise him for the help of his countenance" (Ps. 42:5).

DISILLUSIONMENT

Disillusionment is a powerful weapon of divination that causes a feeling of deep, sorrowful unhappiness and woe. This psychological weapon was forged and successfully used against Elijah, one of the most powerful prophets in the Bible. After experiencing a great victory over the infernal enemies of Israel, Satan retaliated with a death threat issued through the mouth of Jezebel.

This affected Elijah so deeply that he was prepared to give up everything, including his life. (See 1 Kings 19:1–4.)

DISOBEDIENCE

Disobedience is the disposition that defies and resists authority, and the refusal or failure to obey a mandate, directive, or command. It is rebellion against known authority. According to 1 Samuel 15:23, God considers disobedience a form of witchcraft. The thought of disobedience being associated with witchcraft is chilling to me, especially as it relates to believers who sincerely love the Lord and want to serve Him. First Peter 2:13–15 encourages you to "submit yourselves to every ordinance of man for the Lord's sake: whether it be to the king, as supreme; or unto governors, as unto them that are sent by him for the punishment of evildoers, and for the praise of them that do well. For so is the will of God, that with well doing ye may put to silence the ignorance of foolish men." (See 1 Samuel 15:1–3, 13–24.)

DIVINATION

Divination, a word used interchangeably with witchcraft, is characterized by occult activities, deception, control, and fear. (See Exodus 22:18; Deuteronomy 18:10; Jeremiah 27:9.) Individuals utilize satanic and diabolical agents, tactics, and strategies for the purposes of foretelling events and controlling people, animals, environments, things, and situations. Their tactics involve: ill-spoken words, ill wishes, enchantments, spells, hexes, curses, witchcraft prayers, idle words spoken contrary to God's original plans and purposes, talisman, astrology, palmistry, crystal gazing, fortune-telling, false prophecy, soothsaying, and doctrines of devils. (For a more comprehensive look at the spirit of divination, please refer to chapter 9.)

DIVORCE

According to 1 Corinthians 13, love is perfect. Unfortunately, we live in a less-than-perfect world with less-than-perfect people who have grand weddings but not so grand experiences within the institution of marriage. Communication suffers, a partner cheats, relationships crumble, lovers leave, or midlife happens. Divorce for some seemingly becomes the only solution for their disappointment.

Doctrines of Devils

A doctrine is a rule, principle of law, or a statement of official government policy, especially in foreign affairs and military strategies. Doctrines of devils therefore, are those rules, governmental policies, and principles of laws that do not adhere to or reflect biblical principles. Satan is skillful at preaching *another gospel*. The unsuspecting and innocent become easy prey because many seek to be *enlightened* rather than seek God. The New Age movement is an example of this deception. (See Matthew 6:22–23; 1 Timothy 4:1.)

Doctrines of Man

As with doctrines of devils, these are principles or laws men hold and are promulgated through political policies, laws, legislative edicts, educational curricula, religious tenets, and teachings. (See Matthew 15:9.)

Doubt

Doubt is characterized by feelings of uncertainty and misgivings. This was one of the weapons used against Adam and Eve in the Garden of Eden. One of the things you should never allow the enemy to cause you to doubt is the Word of God. Jesus promises us in Matthew 24:35 that "heaven and earth shall pass away, but my [His] words shall not pass away." Doubt is not necessarily a sin. But it has the power to make you sin. Doubt simply says, "I need more information." However, when doubt leads to unbelief, this is where sin enters the picture. It is never a crime to require more information, but make certain you are gaining that information from the correct source. Be careful that Satan does not seduce you into questioning the validity of the Word of God or God Himself. (See Genesis 3:1–7; Mark 11:23.)

Enmeshments

Enmeshment is a popularly used term in family therapy literature when speaking about codependence. It was made popular by the work of Salvador Minuchin.[2] Enmeshment refers to an extreme form of proximity and intensity in family interactions that inevitably corrode and weaken boundaries that define individual autonomy until a kind of fusion occurs. This fusion creates a dysfunctional family culture that emotionally handicaps family members to a point of them not having a clear sense of self, rendering members too weak to function in an individualistic, differentiated way. Generally speaking, this condition leads a person to become psychologically influenced, controlled by, mutually reliant upon, or needing another person to fulfill their own needs or to complete them as a person. According to Melody Beattie in her book *Codependent No More*, enmeshment "causes people to become emotionally and psychologically consumed in a dysfunctional relationship in which they allow someone else's thoughts, opinions, emotions, and behavior to control them."[3] (See 1 Kings 11:1–5.)

ENTANGLEMENTS

When I think of the word *entangle*, I think of someone caught in a web that stagnates growth, progress, or development and keeps a person stuck in circumstances they really want to be delivered from. Entanglements can be social, relational, familial, organizational, spiritual, psychological, or financial in nature. Once God delivers you from anything, be careful because the devil will seek to cause you to fall into the same or similar entanglements again. (See Exodus 14:3; 2 Peter 2:20.)

ETHNICITIES

Ethnicity relates to a particular group of people who share a common and distinctive race or linguistic, religious, or cultural heritage. Satan uses this weapon effectively to keep believers separated. (See John 4:7–9, 19–20.)

EVENTUALITIES

An eventuality is a possibility of something occurring, or the consequence of an action. Eventualities operate by a law called the law of cause and effect. (See Hosea 8:7.) Satan often blinds your mind and deceives you into believing, denying, or ignoring that this principle will be suspended based on your desire or ignorance (Gal. 6:7). A particular outcome may not come to pass immediately after an act that defies biblical principles, but eventually every seed sown will have its harvest. For instance, after a long period of alcoholism, a person gives their heart to the Lord only to discover, months later, that they have sclerosis of the liver. Because the individual feels that God should have healed them since they gave up the error of their ways (alcoholism), demonic spirits may seduce them into believing that God does not care and eventually they backslide. Another example is the power of the spoken word. Idle, capriciously spoken words will eventually manifest into reality. (See Proverbs 18:21.) You have probably heard of a self-fulfilling prophecy. For example: "I never have money at the end of the month," then—you guessed it—when the end of the month comes, you do not have money. Or: "This always happens to me," "If it ain't one thing, it's another," "I'm sick and tired of this." Eventually, you will be both sick and tired.

FALSE BURDENS

To be burdened for people and situations is expected of all saints, especially when it comes to the redemptive purpose of God being manifested. However, Satan wants to put false burdens upon you that cause undue stress, pressure, and discomfort. These burdens are easily distinguishable from the authentic ones in that they are heavy, often unbearable, and do not come from God. Jesus said in Matthew 11:29–30, "Take my yoke upon you, and learn of me; for I am meek and lowly in heart: and ye shall find rest unto your souls. For my yoke is easy, and my burden is light."

FALSE ENTITLEMENT

False entitlement is a spirit that causes people to feel they deserve, have a right to, or have claim to something that is really not theirs. It could be a position, money, attention, a title, clothing, or just about anything. In the Bible, Satan used this weapon through Ahab against Naboth. Ahab wanted property that belong to Naboth and plotted and planned his demise. This spirit is relentless. It will not stop until its lust and covetousness are satiated. (See 1 Kings 21:1–16.)

FALSE EXPECTATIONS

This one weapon, in particular, has been used to destroy many good relationships, ministries, and organizations. Expectations are good to have, particularly those that are reasonable and those that you have for yourself. But when they encroach upon another person's freedom of choice or they are unknown to others, they can become a destructive element. Jesus lost many of His followers because they had false expectations of Him. David overcame this weapon by placing his expectations upon the Lord. (See Psalm 62:5.)

FALSE IMPRESSIONS

The mind is a very powerful thing. The enemy, knowing its capabilities, superimposes erroneous perceptions of reality upon it. This is the weapon that was used against both Paul and Jesus by causing people to falsely perceive them. (See Luke 11:14–19.)

FAMILY ECCENTRICITIES AND IDIOSYNCRASIES

Sometimes Satan will attempt to short-circuit complete deliverance by telling us that there are certain peculiarities in our lives that give us a distinction from other individuals, such as particular actions, perceptions, and behaviors that are characteristic of our family. It could be shyness or a tendency to lie or fight. It is postulated that since certain hereditary characteristics are passed down through our DNA, spirits of inheritance (demonic spirits) can attach themselves to the DNA and be passed down generationally. An example of this is Abraham and his descendants, Isaac and Jacob. They all had the proclivity to lie under pressure. (See Exodus 20:5; 34:7.)

FEAR

Fear is a powerful weapon the enemy uses against the saints. This was one of the weapons used to penetrate Job's hedge of protection (Job 3:25). It is actually used to perforate and penetrate our faith. Fear has a diversity of expressions, but 1 John 4:18 says, "There is no fear in love; but perfect love casteth out fear: because fear hath torment. He that feareth is not made perfect in love."

FIERY DARTS

During biblical days, fiery darts were pointed missiles lit with fire and thrown at a target. Using this as a metaphor, Paul speaks of this weapon in Ephesians 6:16. Today, these spiritual fiery darts can be enflamed by anger, jealousy, bitterness, and rage, and faith is required to counteract their effect and to protect us.

Firebrands

Firebrands were used as a type of weapon. The tail of an animal, such as a fox, would be set on fire, the animal then set loose usually in a field or through a village setting, alighting anything in its path. A firebrand can be likened to intense opposition and "heated" warfare.

> He that passeth by, and meddleth with strife belonging not to him, is like one that taketh a dog by the ears. As a mad man who casteth firebrands, arrows, and death, so is the man that deceiveth his neighbour, and saith, Am not I in sport?
> —Proverbs 26:17–19

Friendly Fire

It is a fact that not all casualties of war are caused by the enemy, but sometimes by those closest to us. This is not to imply that they have malicious intent, that they are motivated to destroy us, or intentionally harm us. But they can be used by the enemy to accidentally hurt or destroy us in spite of their sincere love for us. One of the reasons why this weapon is so powerful is that the actual weapons used are their love and positive regard, rather than their hatred or ill will toward us. Two examples of friendly fire are found in Matthew 16:20–23 and Acts 16:16–23. The first is Peter and Jesus.

Sometimes people are misled into believing that Satan requires insidiously motivated individuals to accomplish his tasks. This is not always the case because his strategy would be too obvious. To accomplish anything in a person's life, particularly if that person is matured in the things of the Lord and sensitive in the Spirit, Satan will have to take a more clandestine approach in his attack against them.

My strong counsel to you today would be to take nothing and no one for granted. The ones we love, and the ones that love us, could very well be used to provoke us into the forfeiture of divine opportunities, ministries, and ultimately the fulfillment of purpose, maximization of potential, and reaching our destiny.

One of the reasons why I believe this particular strategy is so powerful is that we are usually more relaxed around people with whom we are close, so we let our hair down, so to speak. There are four categories of people the enemy will use: family (e.g., Moses, Aaron, and Miriam), friends (Peter and Jesus), business partners and ministerial colleagues (Paul and Barnabas), and confidants, counselors, and mentors (David and Ahithophel).

Frustration

Frustrations result from the failure to reach some valued objective or achieve the fulfillment of purpose. (See Ezra 4:1–5.)

Generational Curses

A generational curse operates by a spiritual law called the "ancestry law." You have probably heard the adage, "The apple does not fall too far from the tree." What this means is that certain characteristics, tendencies, and peculiarities unique to certain families are passed down genetically. So many Christians misunderstand the term *curse*. According to Scripture, a generational curse is the natural outcome of an act of defiant disobedience passed down from one generation to another. (See Exodus 20:5; Numbers 14:18; Deuteronomy 11:26–28.) Ezekiel 18:2 says, "The fathers have eaten sour grapes, and the children's teeth are set on edge." This weapon of the enemy plays itself out in family and community peculiarities, eccentricities, social/ethnic traits, tendencies, oddities, pathological conditions of mind and body, individualities (DNA), passions, motives, intentions, agendas, habits, ideologies, perceptions, temperaments, personalities, illness, and degenerative/congenital diseases.

Gossip

If Satan's characteristic is that of a snake, then gossip can be likened to the venom of a snake. This weapon is made powerful because it uses rumor, hearsay, sensationalized talking, and commentary to undermine and destroy a person's image, influence, reputation, relationships, name, and even future. In my opinion, this weapon has been the cause of more destruction than all wars combined! James writes in James 3:5–6, "Even so the tongue is a little member, and boasteth great things. Behold, how great a matter a little fire kindleth! And the tongue is a fire, a world of iniquity: so is the tongue among our members, that it defileth the whole body, and setteth on fire the course of nature; and it is set on fire of hell." Jesus warns us about the misuse of the tongue and the eternal judgment that awaits individuals who refuse to bring their tongue under the subjection of the lordship of Christ. He states in Matthew 12:36–37, "But I say unto you, that every idle word that men shall speak, they shall give account thereof in the day of judgment. For by thy words thou shalt be justified, and by thy words thou shalt be condemned." (See Ecclesiastes 10:11; 1 Timothy 5:13.)

GUILT

Guilt is caused when a particular principle is violated or a law broken. We also tend to feel guilty when we have not lived up to expectations and standards that we have set for ourselves. If we believe that we "should" have behaved differently or we "ought" to have done better, we likely will feel guilty. Although genuine guilt is a healthy emotion, Satan can pervert it by turning it from a remorseful awareness of having done something wrong to self-reproach. When this happens, we know that Satan has perverted a healthy emotion into a deadly weapon. When guilt assails you, rather than wallowing in your guilt to the point of defeat, pray a prayer similar to Psalm 51:1–12. Overcoming guilt and shame does not mean not caring about your actions. It involves taking responsibility for what you did and coming to terms with it.

HABITS

Habits are unconscious patterns of behavior that are acquired by frequent repetition of a thought, action, or reaction, and that establish a disposition of the mind, character, or mannerism. When a behavior is practiced, day after day, you will naturally train yourself to form habits. As you regularly perform this habit, you become skilled at your behavior. It becomes easy and comfortable for you to take this action over and over again. Ultimately, you begin performing this action automatically. This action has now become your routine behavior. Habitual behaviors can be beneficial and liberating to you because of your ability to perform these tasks without having to consciously think about your every action. Habits can also be destructive. They can limit our effectiveness, stunt our personal growth, cut years from our lives, create antagonistic dynamics in relationships, alienate loved ones, and basically corrode a good quality of life. Bad habits can be likened to playing Russian roulette: disaster is always imminent. (See 2 Peter 2:19.)

HARASSMENT

Harassment is an exasperating and disturbing annoyance or irritation that threatens or undermines personal peace and tranquility. By utilizing this weapon, Satan can oppress and victimize the believer. (See Nehemiah 4:1–3.) Harassment can come in the form of verbal abuse, sexual misconduct, unrealistic demands, stalking, or continuous telephone calls. Types of harassment include: sexual (unwanted, unwelcomed sexual comments or actions, including touching, sexual insults, staring, unwanted "compliments" that make the target uncomfortable, and sexual rumors or innuendo), racial (racist comments and slurs based on skin color, language, or national origin), verbal (name calling, derogatory statements, bullying, insulting, or intimidation), religious (intolerance of someone's religious beliefs), ableist (insulting someone based on a real or assumed physical or mental disability), classist (making fun of, belittling, or demeaning someone based on socioeconomic status), and scapegoating (holding one person or group responsible for a family's, organization's, or community's problems; isolating or rejecting a person or group of people).

HERESIES

Heresies are biblical truths and doctrines contaminated by controversial or unorthodox opinions, false interpretations, and doctrines of man. (See 1 Corinthians 11:19; 2 Peter 2:1.)

HOMOSEXUALITY

Homosexuality, in its broadest sense, is a term created by nineteenth century theorists to describe the lustful predilection, sexual orientation, and emotional interest in members of the same sex. Whether a person is convinced they were born that way, that it is a learned behavior, or that it is a preference, Romans 1:5–28 convinces me that it is a satanically originated, deviant behavior used to undermine the biblical definition of family and marriage and to promote mere stimulation without the ability to procreate.

IDOLATRY

Idolatry is a deep devotion and immoderate affection of an object or a person that displaces the type of love and honor God expects from His creation. (See Psalm 97:7.)

IGNORANCE

Ignorance is the want for knowledge in general, or in relation to a particular subject; the state of being uneducated or uninformed. It is not just the lack of knowledge that destroys, it is the lack of the need for knowledge such as the knowledge of God. See Hosea 4:6.

IMMATURITY

Encarta offers us the following definition for the word *immaturity*: "childish: lacking the wisdom or emotional development normally associated with adults (disapproving)," such as pouting, whining, pleading, nagging, throwing tantrums, dependence, and irresponsibility.

INCEST

Incest is defined as sexual relations between persons closely related enough that marriage would be considered illegal or forbidden. This weapon, used from the days of Lot, has been used for opening doors in many people's lives to perversion, psychotic or neurotic conditions, heinous criminal activities, and intergenerational dysfunctions. (See Genesis 19:30–37.)

INDIFFERENCE

Indifference causes hope, purpose, and vision to be replaced by apathy. According to Nobel Prize–winning author Elie Wiesel, "The opposite of love is not hate, it's indifference. The opposite of art is not ugliness, it is indifference. The opposite of faith is not heresy, it is indifference. And the opposite of life is not death, it is [the failure to value life brought on by one thing only]—indifference."[4] (See Psalm 137:1–4.)

INHIBITIONS

Intrinsic, extrinsic, conscious, or unconscious things that prevent, restrain, block, or suppress. (See Luke 18:35–39.)

INIQUITY

Iniquity is to sin as the root of a tree is to the fruit. Iniquity comes from the Hebrew word *avon* and literally means "to make crooked, perverse, twisted, corrupt, and immoral." In many religious circles, it is recognized as the bedrock of generational curses. (See Numbers 14:18–19; Jeremiah 36:3.)

INSECURITY

Insecurities create a condition that is physically or psychologically unstable, emotionally uncertain, and is marked by a lacking in confidence in one's ability, purpose, and potential. Insecurities often show up, for example, when we are in the midst of someone we perceive to be better, more capable, talented, educated, or attractive than we perceive ourselves to be. (See Exodus 3:9–12.)

INSULTS

An insult can be defined as the abasement, belittlement, degradation, and verbalization of a low opinion of something or someone. The power of an insult should not be underestimated because it has the innate ability of having a long-term effect long after it has been experienced, such as fear, anxiety, depression, low self-esteem, poor self-image, and erosion of confidence. (See Proverbs 18:14.) They can take on the form of swearing, stereotyping, prejudice, racial slurs, off-color jokes, generalizations, accusations, negative personal assessments, blasphemy, inappropriate behavior, or unintentional or intentional breach of protocol. There are four types of insults: pragmatic (methodically delivered so as to offend, humiliate, provoke, scapegoat, or hurt deeply), cathartic (hostile venting of emotions), overt (opinions, feelings, perceptions, or verbal confrontations intended and perceived by both parties), and covert/passive-aggressive (insults that "sink in" later).

INTERFERENCE

This is a satanic act or instance of hindering, impeding, or obstructing God's work and the fulfillment of destiny and purpose. (See Ezra 4:1–6.)

INVINCIBLE OBSTRUCTIONS

Since perception is everything Satan will attempt to affect our perception of what is and what is not possible. He will create a mountain out of a molehill, even though he knows that with God, nothing is impossible. In one instance, the enemy convinced an entire nation that it was not possible to overcome or defeat their obstruction. However, through the power of Jehovah-Gibbor, David overcame Goliath, the "invincible" obstruction of the nation of Israel. (See 1 Samuel 17:22–27, 40–51.)

INVISIBLE BARRIERS

Invisible barriers can be emotional, psychological, spiritual, financial, racial, social, national, regional, global, parochial, or political in nature. The story of Simon the sorcerer demonstrates two categories under which these weapons function. (See Acts 8:5–25.)

1. Extrinsic: Satan skillfully uses a variety of external forces to obstruct, delay, and frustrate the plans and purpose of God. Examples of these forces are cultural limitations, traditions, political legislation, religious practices, social rituals, witch-craft, economic oppression, and miseducation.
2. Intrinsic: Satan also uses a variety of internal forces, emotions, and attitudes. Examples include fear, doubt, habits, iniquities, prejudices, perceptions, attitudes, ignorance, pride, self-deception, and codependence.

IRRITATIONS

The old English word for irritation is *vex*. Irritations are things that get under your skin and can be likened to an annoying fly buzzing around you. Psychological and physical in nature, an irritation is characterized by any stimulus that produces a state of annoyance that distracts one from focus and conscious thinking. It can also give rise to frustration, anger, offense, resentment, and bad feelings. Irritations are very subjective and are predicated on an individual's tolerance level and ability to focus and concentrate. Examples of this are: people talking behind you at a movie, a waitress mixing up your order, tardiness, nagging, skin irritations, etc. (See Numbers 25:17–18.)

JEALOUSY/ENVY

Jealousy is an emotion provoked by any perceived threat to a relationship. Most people use the word *jealousy* interchangeably with *envy*. However, there is a difference. Jealousy stems from insecurity, a sense of ownership, or obsession. A jealous person usually does not want anyone else to share what or who they "possess." Conversely, envy causes a person to covet the possession of another. Jealousy may involve varying degrees of emotions such as sadness, anger, anxiety, and rage. However, many psychologists have defined jealousy as the sense of "distress" or "discomfort" experienced over a partner's real or imagined involvement with another. Even though jealousy occurs in all types of dyadic relationships, extreme cases are commonly associated with romantic relationships. It has been reported that in these extreme cases, jealousy has been known to drive people to commit heinous crimes. (See Proverbs 6:34; Song of Solomon 8:6.)

JUDGMENTALISM

Judgmentalism is the inclination toward making moral judgments based on personal context and preference. People have a tendency to judge others in an attempt to force them into conformity, basically because they feel some kind of fear of their own skeletons in the closet or because what they see in others may be hidden deep within themselves. (See James 4:11–12.)

LACK OF SPIRITUAL ENDOWMENTS

Lack of faith, fruit of the Spirit, wisdom, focus, purpose, hope, or submission falls under this category. (See Daniel 5:27.)

LACK OF SUBMISSION TO AUTHORITY

Lack of submission to authority is caused by the spirits of pride and rebellion. People who do not submit to authority are self-willed, stubborn, and uninformed about the dangers associated with this kind of recalcitrant behavior. Miriam and Aaron, although close kin to Moses, were driven by this spirit and failed to fully submit to their brother Moses's leadership. This spirit led them to rebel against Moses's authority, assuming that because of the similarity in calling, office, and anointing, submission was unnecessary. (See Numbers 12:1–2.)

LAZINESS

The enemy is aware that this powerful weapon often goes undetected because it does not appear demonic at first blush. Slothfulness and inactivity leads to poverty, a lack of fulfillment of purpose, and impotence. The old-timers used to say that idleness is the "devil's workshop." (See Proverbs 26:13–15.)

LIES

Lies are false declarations, distorted facts, and fabricated statements used to deceive or give an incorrect perception. The Greek word for lie is *pseudologos*, where *pseudo* means "false" and *logos* means "word or declaration." (See 1 Timothy 4:1–2.)

LUSTS

Lust can be defined as a strong desire of the flesh and the desires, appetites, and cravings of the soul. To the believer, lust is the cancer of the soul. It produces leanness of the soul so that after it has completed its assignment, according to the apostle James, it brings sin and then death. (See Galatians 5:16, 19–21; James 1:14–15; 2 Peter 2:18; 1 John 2:16.)

MANIPULATION

Manipulation is the employment of shrewd or devious activities and tactics in an attempt to take advantage of another. It is not only used to dominate or control, but also to subtly, underhandedly, or deceptively hide true intentions. Even though manipulation involves a variety of maneuvers, tactics, and ploys, a person who is skilled in this behavior will avoid any overt display of aggression while simultaneously intimidating, bamboozling, and cajoling or coercing others into giving them what they want. Covert activities are most often the vehicle used for interpersonal manipulation. Insecure people or people with power are prime targets for satanic manipulations. In the first instance, Satan wants insecure people to feel more powerless, and in the second instance, Satan wants to usurp power from the powerful. Types of manipulation include:

- Verbal: innuendo, fear, name-calling, flattery, rationalization, avoidance, nagging, crying, screaming
- Relational: whining, coercion, ultimatums, bullying, victimization
- Social: propaganda, media and printed materials, half-truths, white lies, false advertisement, covert oppression/control

MATERIALISM

Materialism is the theory or doctrine that physical well-being and worldly possessions constitute the greatest good and highest value in life. The following terms and phrases best describe and define *materialism*: wealth seeking; prefers extravagance and opulence; self-centered; self-seeking; superficial; believes the bigger the paycheck, the more important the person; competitive; selfish; preoccupied with money; sense of entitlement; pride; comparison; competitive; image is everything; seeks status and power relative to peers/colleagues; will marry for money; cost equates with value; looks down their nose at others; prejudiced opinions; disdains financial insecurity; avoids losing status and control; looking good is more important than comfort; believes in success through appearances; status-seeking; buys status symbols; second place is not good enough; manipulative; has a need for applause; center of attention; not generous; loves to win awards; does things primarily for own benefit; gets angry when they don't get what they want; used to getting their way; prefers instant gratification. (See Mark 8:36.)

MISEDUCATION

Education, the development of understanding, must be distinguished from training, the development of skill. Education in its purest sense is designed to empower individuals to fulfill purpose and maximize potential. Therefore, miseducation is its antithesis. Modern education has been legislatively subverted into training, with taxpayer's precious dollars being squandered to produce skilled individuals whose educational experience has stripped them of eleven essential elements of success and prosperity. These elements produce healthy, emotionally stable, economically empowered, contributing members of any society. They are creative thinkers, self-aware, principle driven, motivated, spiritually aware, self-disciplined, and critical thinkers. They have good life skills, interpersonal skills, crisis management skills, resource management skills, problem-solving skills (vs. victimization), and critical consciousness skills.

Miseducation is responsible for the construction of an artificial consciousness held together by media propaganda at the expense of an authentic critical consciousness, which gives an individual the ability to perceive truth from error; to resist systemic, social, political, psychological, religious, or economic oppression; and to take action against tyrannical, autocratic, iron-fisted elements within a society controlled by the prince of the power of the air, who, according to 2 Corinthians 4:4, blinds the minds of people.

In my research, I came across the following disturbing quote that proves the enemy's deliberate efforts to miseducate entire populations:

> In our dream, we have limitless resources and the people yield themselves with perfect docility to our molding hand. The present educational conventions fade from our minds, and unhampered by tradition, we work our own good will upon a grateful and responsive folk. We shall not try to make these people or any of their children into philosophers or men of learning or science. We are not to raise up from among them authors, orators, poets, or men of letters. We shall not search for embryos of great artists, painters, or musicians. Nor will we cherish even the humbler ambition to raise up from among them

lawyers, doctors, preachers, politicians, statesmen, of which we now have ample supply. [5]

—Frederick Gates, 1913
Director Of Charity
Rockefeller Foundation

To state more clearly, the secular educational system is designed to separate the masses into two classes: the elite minority who become the ruling class, and the brainwashed, nonthinking working class. When the Bible was removed from schools as one of the main text, so was the ability for individuals to translate words, language, and information into comprehension, revelation, and manifestation. God's design for education is unifying and empowering, making it possible for all to benefit and succeed. But now, without the Bible as the main text, we have made ourselves vulnerable to the deception that true success, freedom, and prosperity is not a reality for everyone or must be obtained through unethical means. According to Ephesians 4:14, they are "tossed to and fro, and carried about with every wind of doctrine, by the sleight of men, and cunning craftiness, whereby they lie in wait to deceive."

If this statement is true, then miseducation is an elaborately crafted, satanically imposed, anti-intellectual plan supported by governments (perhaps in some cases ignorantly and in others consensually) to train a skilled-based (not intellectually stimulated) people to work to create wealth for others to enjoy. Since the wealth of the sinner is laid up for the just, we need to be reeducated in order to materialize the next great wealth transfer. Miseducation cripples our ability not only to think critically and solve problems, but it also inhibits us from making the Word of God active in our lives. Real education brings together education and revelation. This is key because without revelation there can be no manifestation and we are not able to see God's promises materialize.

Perhaps the best way to grasp this diabolical weapon is to examine the story of Helen Keller.

As a blind and deaf child, Helen lived much like an animal, rushing from one sensation to another. She was trained to be animalistic, a person surviving a disability, rather than educated to be a person living with a disability, until Anne Mansfield Sullivan was introduced into her world.

Within a short period of becoming Helen's teacher, Sullivan was able to impart the concept of language to her, leaving only one educational mountain left to conquer, which held the secret to unlocking Helen's potential hidden beneath her disability: comprehension and the awakening to meaning. The turning point was when Helen saw the correlation between the water that slipped through her fingers and the word water she had been repeating.

This simple but life-altering event made it possible for Helen to begin understanding instead of simply repeating what Anne was teaching her. Helen had been trained to repeat the word water, but it wasn't until she combined the experience of feeling water and trying to communicate the word water simultaneously that Helen gained the wonderful gift of meaning and comprehension of language. These two elements, once kept from the education process, will keep a group of people unconsciously oppressed and believing that their oppressed state is normal. Up to that point, Helen had been like a well-trained animal, memorizing words, speaking them, and receiving praise from Anne. But now, suddenly, it came to her! The word water actually referred to, pointed to, meant the exuberant liquid that ran through her fingers.

So the true and greatest casualty of spiritual warfare is not the human body, but the human mind. This is perhaps the greatest travesty of this weapon of mass destruction: the demise of the human soul.

Misfortunes

Misfortunes are circumstances that bring calamity, hardship, and difficult and challenging times. This weapon has a variety of faces, namely untimely deaths, loss of income, accidents, and economic hardship. (See 2 Kings 4:1.)

Mistrust

Mistrust is a feeling of uncertainty about a situation or misgivings about a person or organization. (See 1 Samuel 18:1–9.)

MOVING OUT OF THE TIMING OF THE LORD

This is a powerful weapon used against individuals called into ministry. Through a strong satanic provocation, both David and Saul moved out of the timing of the Lord much to the detriment of their destinies. We read in 1 Samuel how the internal pressures of insecurity were used as an intrinsic weapon to cause Saul to disregard the Lord's call to wait. In the case of David, although it was his kingly responsibility to conduct a census of the people, it was not in the timing of the Lord. Hence, not only were there severe personal consequences, but also an entire nation was affected. As we wait on God for our ministry, we must also remember that since our times and seasons are in the hand of the Lord, there is no need to be anxious, rushed, or hurried in the maturation process through impatience or satanic provocation. (See 1 Chronicles 21:1; Romans 12:7.)

NEGATIVITY

Circumstances, situations, and people may sometimes appear as if they have no positive characteristic or value. Sometimes our judgments are based on past experience or irrational thoughts. Negativity alters the perception of an individual and causes them to remove the colorful dynamics of life and the world and paints them gray and grim. Negativity does not only alter a person's present life, but it also alters their future. According to Numbers 14, one day of negativity has the power to take a person into a year's worth of bondage. Sustained negativity changes a person's mood, affects their relationships, and suppresses their immune system. (See Numbers 14:26–34.)

NETS

Nets are things Satan places in your life that lead to situations from which escape is difficult. The Internet has now become one of his modern-day weapons of choice, through which individuals have been introduced and held captive to perverted cyberspace activities. (See Ecclesiastes 7:26.)

OBSESSION

An obsession is a compulsive fixation upon an idea, emotion, or person. Obsessions are open doors to some of the most heinous crimes and twisted activities. (See 2 Samuel 13:1–2, 11–12, 14.)

OFFENSES

Offenses are used by Satan to cause you to transgress based on your displeasure, anger, or resentment of someone's action displayed or words spoken to or against you. When an offense is allowed to remain and fester, the enemy not only uses it to destroy you or the individual, but also this weapon actually undermines spiritual authority. Seek to love the Word of God, especially Scripture that speaks about forgiveness and love. The following two passages from the Bible will inoculate you to the effects of this weapon: Psalm 119:165 and Luke 17:1–10.

OPPRESSION

According to Proverbs 28:3, this weapon is like a "sweeping rain which leaveth no food." It totally ravishes the soul and leaves it wanting as it steals your dignity and quality of life. Thank God that He "anointed Jesus of Nazareth with the Holy Ghost and with power: who went about doing good, and healing all that were oppressed of the devil; for God was with him" (Acts 10:38, see also Ezekiel 22:29).

OVERT OPERATIONS

There are times when Satan's attack upon you requires a less-than-obvious tactic. Equally, there are other times when his attack is "in your face" and obvious. This is what I call an overt attack. It is bold and brazen, and Satan definitely wants to get the glory. (See 1 Samuel 30:1–8.)

PEER PRESSURE

Peer pressure is the external pressure exerted upon an individual by colleagues, friends, and associates that psychologically affects them, causing them to fundamentally conform to a specific code of conduct, mind-set, and basic way of living. Peer pressure makes you live by the standards of man rather than those established by God. Since the word *peer* is defined as, "a person who has equal standing with another or others, as in rank, class, or age," the phrase *peer pressure* preempts the notion that this phenomenon is specific to teenagers. That is to say that no matter how young or old you are, everyone is susceptible to it. (See 1 Samuel 15:19–21.)

PERVERSIONS

Perversions are any kind of action that God considers deviant, corrupt, or vile. Proverbs 17:20 states, "He that hath a froward heart findeth no good: and he that hath a perverse tongue falleth into mischief." (See Genesis 19:1–11.)

POSSESSION

Possession is the state of being ruled, controlled, and dominated by an evil spirit. (See Matthew 8:16, 28; 12:22; Mark 1:32.)

POVERTY

Poverty is a state of economic deficiency characterized by the lack of capacity to obtain the basic necessities of life or material comforts. The unfortunate thing about individuals who experience poverty is that they often blame their state on the Lord rather than on the real culprit—Satan. Poverty causes a lack of access. (See Ruth 1:21; Psalm 12:5.)

PREJUDICE

Prejudice is a preconceived preference or idea that leads to the development of adverse judgment, opinion, or belief prior to and without knowledge or examination of the facts. It is also an irrational suspicion or hatred of a particular group, race, or religion. The enemy uses this weapon to separate and divide. As it relates to the church, this weapon is employed in an attempt to undermine the preaching of the gospel and the unity of the Spirit among believers of different ethnicities, nationalities, and denominational preferences. (See Acts 10:9–15.)

PRIDE

Pride is to the kingdom of darkness what humility is to the kingdom of light. In fact, pride is the foundation upon which the kingdom of darkness is built. Pride is essentially a declaration of independence from God because it produces an inordinate opinion of self and personal superiority. The spirit of pride caused Satan to believe that he could be God. (See Proverbs 11:2; 16:18; 29:23.)

PROJECTIONS

This weapon is formed in the mind of individuals causing them to attribute their attitudes, feelings, or suppositions to another. In our text, Laban accuses Jacob of the very thing he did during Jacob's career within his corporation. He projected his guilt onto another. (See Genesis 31:36–42.)

PROVOCATION

A provocation is a perturbing stimulus that intentionally incites or rouses you to actions and activities that are usually diametrically opposed to the will of God. (See 1 Chronicles 21:1–3, 7–8.)

RAPE

Rape is the violation of the physiological, psychological, and emotional self by another. It is one of the many weapons the spirit of perversion uses to destroy an individual's quality of life.

Although rape is viewed as a violent sexual crime perpetrated by males against females, statistics show that a small number of cases have been reported where the victim has been male. Nevertheless, rape is not about sex. It is more than just an act of sexual violence. It is an act of the exertion of power and control over another person. Rape is life threatening and life altering; it severely traumatizes the victim. For many victims, rape is a defining moment that divides their life into two parts: life before the rape and life after. In some measure, the same is true for those who are closest to the victim including their children and male relationships such as husbands, fathers, brothers, and male companions. For all, one single incidence of rape reshapes and remolds perceptions of self, how they interact with others, and how they and their loved ones conduct the affairs of their lives in the future.

Rape is a disturbingly frequent crime. It is also one of the least-reported crimes in part because many victims fear how they might be treated if they divulge what has happened. (See Judges 19:22–28.)

REBELLION

Rebellion is to the kingdom of darkness as righteousness, peace, and joy in the Holy Spirit is to the kingdom of light. It is the very foundation upon which Satan built his kingdom of sin and iniquity. Rebellion is a demonic disposition that leads to defiance of authority, insurrection, and violence. (See 1 Samuel 15:23.)

REGRET

The weapon of regret is a satanic abortive weapon because it keeps you connected to your past rather than living for the future. Remember, yesterday is in the tomb, and tomorrow is yet in the womb. Regret led Judas to hang himself. His other option would have been confession, repentance, and restoration—three acts that had the potential of salvaging his ministry and giving him a future. Regrets led people to live with "I wish," "what if," and "if only." (See Matthew 27:1–5.)

REJECTION

When God created mankind, He created both male and female in His image. I believe that one of the things that makes man like God is the inherent desire to be recognized, valued, accepted, and appreciated. Rejection undermines that natural, God-given characteristic that predisposes each one of us with the desire to be loved, cherished, and appreciated not for what we do, have, or attain, but for just being an individual who has been fearfully and wonderfully made. Rejection is one of the ways the enemy undermines self-worth, self-esteem, self-image, purpose, and potential. Rejection comes in two basic forms: covert and overt. Covert can be characterized by someone saying they love and support you but never showing it. Overt is more obvious. It comprises verbal, physical, or social ostracizing, isolation, discrimination, and segregation.

Rejection from others often leads to the rejection of self, which produces feelings of worthlessness and inferiority, depression, emotional isolation, introspection, perfectionism, irresponsibility, guilt, and self-hatred. People who have lived under constant rejection eventually have a difficult time expressing feelings, asserting himself/herself, or taking control of his/her life. Rejected people reject as a result of an acquired defense mechanism. (See Mark 8:31; 12:10.) For a greater study, please see chapter 9.

RELIGIOSITY

Religiosity is a system of beliefs, principles, creeds, dogmas, and faith to which an individual adheres. (See Galatians 1:13–14; James 1:26–27.)

RESENTMENT

Resentment is an irrational mind-set created by the enemy that causes a person to feel indignation or ill will toward another as a result of a real or imagined grievance. (See Genesis 4:1–8.)

RETALIATION

Retaliation is a weapon used to get back at someone, especially if you are making spiritual inroads in prayer and spiritual warfare. The more you war against the enemy, the more he will desire to get back at you. The Latin phrase for this is *quid pro quo*. You will advance on one hand, then the enemy will attempt to cause you to lose ground on the other. The ultimate intent is for you to lose control of your emotions, lose hope, and to break your focus. He may retaliate by hitting your finances, family, marriage, friendships, business, or any other area he feels will weaken you in your battle. (See Esther 5:9–14.)

SABOTAGE

Sabotage is used to cause malicious destruction to an individual or the cessation of a work, a cause, a relationship, or a ministry. (See Nehemiah 6:1–6.)

Satanic Concentration

Satanic concentration is the total focus of satanic powers upon a specific object or person. Satan often focuses on one person in a family, a church, a territory, or a group of people to the exclusion of others. Usually this person has a divine purpose that threatens Satan. The following are examples of individuals who came under this attack. Read the references for further exposure and enlightenment: Joseph (Gen. 37–39), the nation of Israel (Exod. 1–12), Esther and Mordecai (Esth. 1–8), Nehemiah (Neh. 4; 6:1–16), and Jesus (the Gospels).

Scandal

In 1 Corinthians 5:1–5 the enemy attempted to not only destroy an individual through scandal, but also to undermine the influence of the local assembly within its community as well. In Matthew 16:21–26, Jesus rebuked Peter because he perceived that Satan had set him up for a scandalous undertaking in His life. In this text, the word *offence* comes from the Greek word *skandalon* and is probably a derivative of another Greek word *kampt*, which is a trap stick (bent sapling) or a snare (figurative cause of displeasure or sin), which gives occasion for someone to trip, stumble, or fall. *Kampt* is the actual feeling of being offended or the thing that causes the offense. *Scandal* is the English translation for this word. *The American Heritage Dictionary* defines this word as "a publicized incident that brings about disgrace or offends the moral sensibilities of society; a person, thing, or circumstance that causes or ought to cause disgrace or outrage."

A scandal can cause irreversible damage to reputation or character, especially if there is a public disclosure of immoral or grossly improper behavior. Scandals cause shame, embarrassment, and disgrace. They can be caused by talk or expressions of injurious, malicious statements that are damaging to one's character. According to Proverbs 22:1, "A good name is rather to be chosen than great riches, and loving favour rather than silver and gold."

Seduction

This weapon is used just as bait is used for fish. It is designed to entice, attract, or draw a person into a wrong or foolish course of action. Seductions can be verbal or nonverbal. (See 2 Kings 21:9; Ezekiel 13:10; 1 Timothy 4:1.)

SHAME

The spirit of shame produces an internal feeling that we are grossly and unbearably flawed as a person. It seduces us into believing that we are inadequate, bad, and no good. These feelings impede the maximization of potential and the fulfillment of purpose. In some people, it can result in low self-esteem and a poor concept of self. Shame can involve family secrets, personal failures, and poor self-image. It can stem from issues like alcoholism, abuse, abortion, bankruptcy, unemployment, or divorce. This weapon is designed to erode the authenticity of who you really are: a person created in the image and likeness of God. Shame brings with it a sense of worthlessness, meaninglessness, depression, compulsive disorders, a deep sense of inferiority, inadequacy, alienation, helplessness, victimization, and isolation. (See 2 Samuel 13:1–2, 14–20.)

SIN

The Hebrew word for sin is *chattath*, from the root *chatta*, and in Greek it is *hamartia*. Both of these words mean "to miss the mark." They are words that intimate something is off target. As it relates to God's Law, they mean that one has failed to meet the standard or missed the targeted mark set by God for us. God's mark or standard is His Law. Therefore sin is the transgression of any of the laws of God. First John 3:4 offers the biblical definition of sin: "Whosoever committeth sin transgresseth also the law: for sin is the transgression of the law." Sin is the transgression of any of the laws of God.

SNARES

In days of old, snares were trapping devices. They primarily consisted of a noose and were used for capturing animals. In your life a snare is a satanic weapon that you should view as a source of danger or something that causes difficulty in escaping circumstances that are designed to cause your demise. Snares may come as a relationship or habit-forming activities. (See 1 Samuel 18:21–25.)

SPIRITS OF AFFINITY

This spirit designs weapons that take a person into idolatry, causing them to lose favor with God. Exodus 20:2–3 states, "I am the LORD thy God, which have brought thee out of the land of Egypt, out of the house of bondage. Thou shalt have no other gods before me." This weapon was used in the life of many biblical characters such as King Solomon, Jehoshaphat, and the children of Israel. (See 1 Kings 3:1; 2 Chronicles 18:1; Ezra 9:14.)

SPIRITUAL MISCARRIAGE

Spiritual miscarriage is spontaneous, diabolically initiated spiritual loss of divine purpose and destiny. This weapon was used effectively against Lot's wife. (See Genesis 19:15–26.)

STIGMATIZATION

This satanic weapon attempts to characterize or brand you as disgraceful or ignominious. It attaches "labels" upon a person, many of which are difficult to "shake off." (See Matthew 12:24.)

STRONGHOLDS

A stronghold is a mental paradigm, ideology, heresy, information, doctrine, dogma, doctrines of men and devils, or any other mind-set Satan uses to control the destiny of an individual. He also uses strongholds to keep entire groups of people (communities, nations, kingdoms) in bondage. This powerful weapon blinds the minds and binds the will. He will use culture, fashion, music, political propaganda, religious and cultic activities, or anything else as a type of fortress, hiding and camouflaging himself so as to go undetected by the masses. (See Romans 1:21; 2 Corinthians 10:4; Ephesians 4:18.)

STUMBLING BLOCKS

Stumbling blocks are those things that obstruct movement and cause spiritual instability. In the original Hebrew text, the word *mikashowl* had the connotation of an individual whose ankles could not support their weight, thus they would constantly stumble and fall. (See Ezekiel 14:3–4; 1 Peter 2:8; 1 John 2:10; Revelation 2:14.)

Suicidal Thoughts

Elijah is one of our greatest examples of the effectiveness of this weapon in the life of a believer. Even Jesus was attacked by this spirit. Just prior to His crucifixion, He was attacked in the Garden of Gethsemane. (See 1 Kings 19:1–4; Matthew 26:38.)

Thorn in the Flesh

A thorn in the flesh is an area of weakness that Satan is allowed to consistently focus on so that, as a result of the existence of the thorn, the individual, like Paul, fosters a total dependence on God and not self. (See 2 Corinthians 12:7.)

Traditions of Men

Traditions are elements of a culture passed down from generation to generation, especially by oral communication and modeling. (See Matthew 15:2–3, 6; Mark 7:3.)

Transference of Spirits

Transference of spirits is the transmigration of a spirit from one person to another. This can happen by laying on hands, association, sexual encounters, incantation, contracts, covenants, oaths, or talisman. (See 1 Corinthians 15:33.)

Unbelief

Unbelief is another powerful weapon. It differs from doubt in that doubt says, "I need more information." Unbelief, on the other hand, says, "No matter how much information you give me, I still don't believe." The first generation of Hebrews who were delivered from the hand of Pharaoh died because of their unbelief. This weapon restrains the power of God. (See Matthew 13:58; Hebrews 4:1–2, 11.)

UNCLEANNESS

This weapon consists of moral, psychological, physical, or environmental defilement. (See Mark 1:23, 26–27.)

UNDERACHIEVEMENT

This powerful intrinsic weapon is used by a demotivating spirit, driving a paradigm that will cause you to:

- Avoid success-related activities
- Doubt your ability
- Assume success is related to luck, education, money, "who you know," or to other factors out of your control. Thus, even when successful, it isn't as rewarding to the unmotivated person because they don't feel responsible or it doesn't increase his/her pride and confidence
- Quit when having difficulty because you believe failure is caused by a lack of ability which you "obviously don't have"
- Choose tasks that are not challenging, passion- or purpose-driven
- Work with little drive or enthusiasm because outcome isn't thought to be related to effort

UNFORGIVENESS

Unforgiveness is the refusal to release someone from an offense or wrong-doing. Unforgiveness grieves the Holy Spirit and is sometimes one of the most difficult sins to confess and to get over because we so often think we must feel it emotionally when we forgive someone. The very act of forgiveness is an act of our will and not our emotions. If unforgiveness is left to fester, it has the potential to give rise to bitterness. Characteristics of unforgiveness include anger, hurt, resentfulness, replaying an event or words spoken, or vengeance. As long as an act of wrongdoing or the assailant remains in your thoughts, you have not forgiven. Sometimes you have to forgive yourself too. Don't grieve the Spirit by holding on to things too long. Cast your cares on the Lord. Forgiving means leaving everything in God's hands, recalling that ultimately, vengeance is His. (See Mark 11:25–26.)

UNHOLY ALLIANCES

Unholy alliances are ungodly, close associations established through demonic influences so as to reinforce satanic plans and purposes in your life. (See Daniel 11:1–6.)

UNSANCTIFIED SOULS

Although many believers are truly and sincerely saved, their souls remain unconverted. (See Luke 22:31–32.) The following are areas in our lives that can become unsanctified: agendas, ambitions, appetites, desires, ideologies, intentions, motives, passions, perceptions, and philosophies.

VAIN IMAGINATION

Narcissism and arrogance of the mind often lead believers into more dependence on self, education, good looks, intelligence, or the likes, than dependence on God. This is a trick of the enemy because without God we are nothing. (See Genesis 8:21; Deuteronomy 29:19; 31:21.)

VENGEANCE/VINDICTIVENESS

Getting back at and getting even with someone are two acts of revenge. Getting revenge should never be on the tongue of a believer. There are universal, spiritual laws that work for us if we are wronged. Besides, God reminds us in Romans 12:19 that vengeance belongs to Him, and that He will repay any wrongdoing. So remember that the next time you are tempted by the enemy to get someone back.

VEXATIONS

The enemy will attempt to overwhelm, harass, and exasperate you—don't let him. This is not your battle; the battle belongs to the Lord. Go into prayer and spiritual warfare against this spirit. Insist that it cease and desist in the name of the Lord. (See Ecclesiastes 4:6; Acts 12:1.)

VIOLENCE

In this text violence is likened to wine, which inebriates and causes a person to lose reason. Violence is hideous because it does not take into consideration laws, personhood, personal possessions, property, or the right to live. (See Psalm 11:5; 73:6; Proverbs 4:17.)

WARS/CONFLICTS

War is the state of open, armed, and prolonged conflict between nations, organizations, and people. The enemy loves to keep things stirring and in motion in order to derail, distract, and destroy. Satan employs demonic spirits to create discord and disharmony in your relationships, especially with those who have a divine assignment. In an attempt to camouflage your real foe, he will attempt to blind you spiritually and emotionally by causing you to focus on the person or situation he uses rather than on the spirit that is behind the conflict. Remember, no matter who or what he uses, he is the culprit behind every conflict and battle. (See 2 Corinthians 7:5; James 4:1.)

WEIGHTS

Weights are satanic burdens. They can come in a variety of shapes and forms, such as emotional weights, which can be yours or someone else's; financial weights; or psychological weights. They are worries, cares, or concerns intended to keep you earthbound. (See Proverbs 11:1.)

WORKS OF THE FLESH

The works of the flesh are carnally motivated activities and self-seeking endeavors that keep an individual from living a kingdom-oriented lifestyle. (See Galatians 5:19–21.)

WORLDLINESS

According to 1 John 2:16, worldliness is characterized by the lust of the flesh, the lust of the eyes, and the pride of life. John's statement contrasts itself with things that are in God as opposed to being in the world. When a person looks for enjoyment, success, and the fulfillment of purpose outside of the will of God, this is worldliness. It is like building your house on sand as opposed to on a firm foundation. When emotional, economic, relational, or spiritual storms come, a worldly person has nothing of substance on which to weather the storms. Worldliness to a Christian amounts to foolishness because even though you may gain carnal things, your gain will be at the expense of your soul. (See Mark 8:36.)

Worry

Worry is an apprehensive or distressed state of mind. Jesus gives us much insight into the futility of worry, especially in light of our alternative—faith and believing in our heavenly Father as Jehovah-Jireh, the provider and the giver and sustainer of life. Worry cannot change anything but your physical and mental well-being. Worry is a contributing factor of high blood pressure, insomnia, anxiety, and a whole host of other conditions. Remember, don't pray if you are going to worry, and don't worry if you are going to pray. (See Matthew 6:27–34.)

Yokes

In biblical days a yoke was a crossbar with two U-shaped pieces that encircle the necks of a pair of oxen or other draft animals working together. One animal would be the leader; the other the follower. If the follower attempted to go in another direction, the lead animal would redirect it by jerking its neck. The jerk would cause discomfort and even pain. This activity was undertaken not only to increase productivity, but also to tame and train less-domesticated animals. Likewise with Satan, he will attempt to yoke you to a spirit whose assignment is to lead you into a direction away from God and the fulfillment of purpose. Yokes are Satan's way of derailing you and altering your destiny. Being yoked to the enemy removes your freedom of choice.

SEVEN

COUNTERATTACKING THE WEAPONS OF THE ENEMY

Ready, Aim, Fire!

AS PROMISED, I am now going to release to you the spiritual counter-attacks to the enemy's weapons of mass destruction from chapter 6. You are ready to take this on. Instead of warm-ups or practice runs, you are going to gain your training in the field. We will move alphabetically down the list, gaining ground as we proceed through each one.

Abandonment counterattack

Ask God to give you your prophetic Timothy, Mark, or Luke on whom you can depend in your time of need. Quote Psalm 27:10: "When my father [covering, anyone responsible to facilitate organizational or relational destiny] and my mother [anyone responsible for financial, emotional, and moral support] forsake me, then the LORD will take me up."

Abortion counterattack

Ask the Lord to forgive you and to free you from all present and future ramifications associated with an abortion or abortive activities. Renounce all satanic contracts and covenants with the spirit of death. Break soul ties and strongholds associated with abortive activities. Bind the spirit of death, and break death cycles from your life, home, business, marriage, children, and loved ones. Confess that your body is the temple of the Holy Spirit, cleansed and sanctified by the blood of Jesus Christ. Close all spiritual portals to your soul from the enemy. Establish Jehovah as the gatekeeper and doorkeeper to your soul. Build prayer hedges around your life, business, ministry, and relationships, and around the lives of your loved ones.

Abuse counterattack

Decree and declare daily Exodus 19:5. I am God's treasured possession. He will cause everything to work together for me because He loves me with an everlasting love. I release myself from being ensnared by unforgiveness and receive divine empowerment to walk away from the abuse and take control over my destiny. I decree and declare that with God all things are possible, and today, according to Philippians 3:13, I forget those things that are behind and reach forth unto those things that are before. Heal me of all hurt and pain: "Thou art my hiding place; thou shalt preserve me from trouble; thou shalt compass me about with songs of deliverance" (Ps. 32:7).

Accident counterattack

Quote Psalm 91:9–12: "Because thou hast [I have] made the LORD, which is my refuge, even the most High, thy [my] habitation; there shall no evil befall thee [me], neither shall any plague come nigh thy [my] dwelling. For he shall give his angels charge over thee [me], to keep thee [me] in all thy [my] ways. They shall bear thee [me] up in their hands, lest thou [I] dash thy [my] foot against a stone." Bind the spirits of inheritance, and decree and declare that you are free from all accidents in Jesus's name. Come against every abortive activity and act of sabotage in Jesus's name.

Accusation counterattack

Ask God to vindicate you in the name of Jesus. Decree and declare that no weapon formed against you will prosper and that every lying tongue is silenced. Come against falsehoods, slander, speculation, accusation, misrepresentation, and character assassination. Ask God to cause the heavens to bow down with divine judgment, to cast forth lightning to scatter His accuser, and to send His hand from above and rid you of them (Ps. 144:5–7). Ask God to prohibit the accuser of the brethren from operating or influencing the soul or mind of anyone who comes into contact with me (Rev. 12:10). Decree and declare that your name is associated with integrity, holiness, righteousness, and uprightness, and that the Lord will vindicate you in due season. Maintain a posture dictated by James 4:7: "Submit yourselves therefore to God. Resist the devil, and he will flee from you."

Addictions counterattack

Decree and declare that according to 1 Corinthians 6:19, your body is the temple of the Holy Spirit. Break the stronghold of addiction. Ask God to remove the appetite for the thing or person. Establish God as the gatekeeper and doorkeeper of your soul. Ask God to bring healing and reconciliation to every person negatively affected by your addiction. Renounce future activities with anything or anyone associated with addictive activities. Ask God to eclipse the addiction with purpose. War in the spirit, and decree and declare that all diabolical strongholds are destroyed and spirits of inheritances are severed and prohibited from influencing any future activities.

Adultery counterattack

The first step toward resolution and healing is naming it for what it is, acknowledging that it happened rather than pretending it did not in the hope that it and the feelings associated with it would just go away. The act of adultery needs to be admitted rather than rationalized or defended. Next, the feelings need to be expressed, not explained, by both parties. There may be fear, anger, hurt, sadness, and grief, or even rage. Petition the Lord to help you to forgive and to empower you to move on in love. Break and renounce sexual soul ties. Ask for forgiveness. Ask God to restore commitment to covenant. Build a hedge of protection around your mind and body. Fast and pray for the desire for the other individual to be broken. Ask God to purify the mind by the blood, the Word, and the Spirit.

Adversity counterattack

Quote Isaiah 59:19, and ask God to give you a strong support system to encourage and gird you up during times of adversity according to Proverbs 17:17.

Afflictions counterattack

Quote Psalm 34:19, and ask God for divine intervention. Declare and decree that you are protected by Jehovah-Gibbor, Jehovah-Nissi, and Jehovah-Rapha. Continue to build prayer shields, fire walls, and prayer hedges around yourself and your loved ones, ministry, and business. Pray the prayers from chapter 3.

Anger counterattack

Decree and declare: "I will not be driven by anger but by the Holy Spirit." Ask God to release the fruit of the Spirit and let it saturate your soul. Bind every spirit that attempts to control your emotions. Claim John 8:36 for yourself and for anyone bound by the spirit of anger: "If the Son therefore shall make you free, ye shall be free indeed."

Anxiety counterattack

Pray according Psalm 20:7.

Apathy counterattack

Pray according to Psalm 42:11, and bind the spirit of apathy and decree and declare that the anointing destroys every yoke and lifts every burden. Receive the joy of the Lord as your strength.

Approval-seeking activities counterattack

Ask God to restore your authentic self. Ask God to remove from your mental and psychological portfolio all attention-seeking activities and to place your feet on a path that leads you to a purpose-driven, principle-orientated life. Bind all feelings of powerlessness and ask God to restore your personal parameters of power, self-worth, and dignity. Loose the spirit that perpetuates irrational thought processes, and make it a part of the footstool of Jesus according to Hebrews 1:13. Decree and declare that your affirmation comes from Psalm 139:14: "I will praise thee; for I am fearfully and wonderfully made: marvellous are thy works; and that my soul knoweth right well."

Arguments counterattack

Pray Titus 3:9.

Attachments counterattack

Break all demonic and satanic attachments. Sever them by the blood and by the Spirit. Decree and declare that you are free from all alliance covenants and contracts that have not originated from the heart and mind of God.

Attention-seeking activities counterattack

Pray according to Jeremiah 31:3.

Avoidance counterattack

Decree and declare, "God hath not given us the spirit of fear; but of power, and of love, and of a sound mind" (2 Tim. 1:7), and "By thee I have run through a troop; and by my God have I leaped over a wall" (Ps. 18:29). Break the spirit of fear and irresponsibility.

Backlash counterattack

Seek God for a divine strategy to counter the attack of the enemy. Gird up the loins of the mind with resolve that you cannot be overcome and defeated because, according to 1 John 4:4, "Greater is he that is in you, than he that is in the world."

Backsliding counterattack

Decree and declare that according to Hebrews 6:18–19, "[I] have a strong consolation...lay hold upon the hope set before us [me]: which hope we [I] have as an anchor of the [my] soul, both sure and steadfast," in Jesus's name. Ask God to make your feet like hinds' feet and to grant you spiritual stability.

Bad reputations counterattack

Pray this prayer or a prayer similar to this: *Father, I cry out unto the God of Abraham, Isaac, and Jacob, the God who is able to change both my name and nature. According to Proverbs 22:1 and Ecclesiastes 7:1, a good name is better than precious ointments, and it is better to be chosen than to have great riches. Therefore I decree and declare that my name is associated with holiness, righteousness, integrity, favor, and excellence. Give me a good name. Amen.*

Bands counterattack

Pray: *Father, please free me from the bands of wickedness.* Utilize the power of the weapons of prayer and fasting (Matt. 17:21).

Besetting sin counterattack

Pray according to Psalm 51.

Betrayal counterattack

Pray this prayer: *Father, as You heal me of my heart of disappointment, bitterness, sadness, anger, rage, and pain, I thank You for all of Your promises. Help me to believe again and to trust again. Amen.* (See 1 Corinthians 1:20.) Remember that your hope is in God.

Bitterness counterattack

Choose to let go and forgive. Ask God to remove the root of bitterness from you and to allow His grace to permeate your mind, soul, and emotions.

Blind spots counterattack

Ask God to reveal to you the truth about yourself and to deliver you from any attitude, behavior, or action that hinders healthy interactions with others. Ask God to remove all spiritual blindness and veils so that you truly can live a life of personal integrity and authenticity of self in Jesus's name.

Bondages counterattack

Pray according to Isaiah 61:1–3.

Cares of the world counterattack

Read Colossians 2:20–21: "Wherefore if ye be dead with Christ from the rudiments of the world, why, as though living in the world, are ye subject to ordinances, (Touch not; taste not; handle not)?" Then read Matthew 6:33: "But seek ye first the kingdom of God, and his righteousness; and all these things shall be added unto you."

Carnality counterattack

"This I say then, Walk in the Spirit, and ye shall not fulfil the lust of the flesh" (Gal. 5:16).

Celestial barricades counterattack

Use a combination of prayer and fasting. Reinforce your prayer efforts by engaging in the prayer of agreement. Ask God to send divine angelic assistance to remove all hindrances and barriers in Jesus's name.

Chains/fetters/shackles counterattack

"Let the high praises of God be in their mouth, and a twoedged sword in their hand; to execute vengeance upon the heathen, and punishments upon the people; to bind their kings with chains, and their nobles with fetters of iron; to execute upon them the judgment written: this honour have all his saints. Praise ye the LORD" (Ps. 149:6–9).

Complacency counterattack

Ask God to grant you an alertness of mind, zeal, and an urgency of spirit. Pray the following: "See then that ye walk circumspectly, not as fools, but as wise, redeeming the time, because the days are evil. Wherefore be ye not unwise, but understanding what the will of the Lord is" (Eph. 5:15–17).

Compromise counterattack

Bind the compromising spirit. Superimpose the spirits of conviction, excellence, and resolve.

Condemnation counterattack

"For God sent not his Son into the world to condemn the world; but that the world through him might be saved" (John 3:17). "If the Son therefore shall make you free, ye shall be free indeed" (John 8:36).

Confederates counterattack

Decree and declare that God will confuse the communications of every satanically orchestrated confederation and disperse their gatherings. Pray the prayers in chapter 3.

Contaminated anointing counterattack

Decree and declare a fresh supply of the uncontaminated anointing. Ask God to sanctify your soul and spirit according to Titus 3:5 by the washing of regeneration and renewing of the Holy Ghost.

Covert operations counterattack

Ask God to expose, destroy, and dismantle every diabolical covert operation. Let the destroying winds of the Spirit blow in judgment against every work of darkness in Jesus's name. Declare and decree Isaiah 54:17: "No weapon that is formed against thee shall prosper; and every tongue that shall rise against thee in judgment thou shalt condemn. This is the heritage of the servants of the LORD, and their righteousness is of me, saith the Lord."

Covetousness counterattack

Pray the following verses: "The meek shall eat and be satisfied: they shall praise the LORD that seek him: your heart shall live for ever" (Ps. 22:26); "Not that I speak in respect of want: for I have learned, in whatsoever state I am, therewith to be content" (Phil. 4:11).

Culture counterattack

"And be not conformed to this world: but be ye transformed by the renewing of your mind, that ye may prove what is that good, and acceptable, and perfect, will of God" (Rom. 12:2). Superimpose the culture of the kingdom of heaven over all-opposing cultures. Decree and declare Luke 11:2: "Thy kingdom come. Thy will be done, as in heaven, so in earth."

Death counterattack

Declare Romans 8:2: "For the law of the Spirit of life in Christ Jesus hath made me free from the law of sin and death"; Psalm 118:17: "I shall not die, but live, and declare the works of the LORD"; and 1 Corinthians 15:55: "O death, where is thy sting? O grave, where is thy victory?"

Deception counterattack

"Howbeit when he, the Spirit of truth, is come, he will guide you into all truth: for he shall not speak of himself; but whatsoever he shall hear, that shall he speak: and he will shew you things to come" (John 16:13). "We are of God: he that knoweth God heareth us; he that is not of God heareth not us. Hereby know we the spirit of truth, and the spirit of error" (1 John 4:6).

Degenerative diseases counterattack

Decree and declare that by the precious blood of Jesus, all sickness, ailments, degenerative conditions, and disease are healed. Make these declarations: I am liberated from alliances, allegiances, curses, and spirits of inheritance. I sever them by the sword of the Lord. He is Jehovah-Ropha, the Lord who heals me. I speak to my DNA and declare that I am free from any and all influences passed down from one generation to another, biologically, socially, emotionally, physiologically, psychologically, nutritionally, spiritually, or by any other channel unknown to me but known to God. Decree and declare total divine alignment genetically, systemically, psychologically, biochemically, physiologically, mentally, and neurologically. Ensure you are feeding your body nutritious fresh fruit and vegetables, drinking sufficient water, exercising, and laughing at least seven times a day. I arbitrarily selected the number seven because it is God's perfect number. "A merry heart doeth good like a medicine: but a broken spirit drieth the bones" (Prov. 17:22).

Delusion counterattack

"And ye shall know the truth, and the truth shall make you free" (John 8:32). Bind every spirit that twists and perverts your mind and thoughts. Ask God to place truth in your heart and to deliver you from all delusions.

Depression counterattack

"To appoint unto them that mourn in Zion, to give unto them beauty for ashes, the oil of joy for mourning, the garment of praise for the spirit of heaviness; that they might be called trees of righteousness, the planting of the LORD, that he might be glorified" (Isa. 61:3). Ask God to remove the spirit of heaviness. Get up, open your curtains, help someone less fortunate than you (visit the hospital, read to someone in the nursing home), start journaling, sing, dance, read the Word of God, play soothing music, go outside, worship, fellowship. Rebuke the spirit of depression. Decree and declare—the joy of the Lord is my strength.

Deprivation counterattack

Bind the spirit of deprivation, and decree and declare that through divine intervention rivers of success, progress, and prosperity begin to flow. Decree and declare that the anointing of Cyrus is released, and it flows according to Isaiah 45:1–3, "Thus saith the LORD to his anointed, to Cyrus, whose right hand I have holden, to subdue nations before him; and I will loose the loins of kings, to open before him the two leaved gates; and the gates shall not be shut; I will go before thee, and make the crooked places straight: I will break in pieces the gates of brass, and cut in sunder the bars of iron: and I will give thee the treasures of darkness, and hidden riches of secret places, that thou mayest know that I, the LORD, which call thee by thy name, am the God of Israel."

Discouragement counterattack

Pray these Bible passages: "My soul, wait thou only upon God; for my expectation is from him" (Ps. 62:5). "The hope of the righteous shall be gladness: but the expectation of the wicked shall perish" (Prov. 10:28).

Disillusionment counterattack

Gird up your mind. Pray without ceasing. Bind the spirit of disillusionment. Ask God to give you a vision of a future characterized by success and to bring your life back into divine alignment. "Put on the whole armour of God, that ye may be able to stand against the wiles of the devil" (Eph. 6:11).

Disobedience counterattack

Pray these verses: "Submit yourselves to every ordinance of man for the Lord's sake: whether it be to the king, as supreme" (1 Pet. 2:13). "Likewise, ye younger, submit yourselves unto the elder. Yea, all of you be subject one to another, and be clothed with humility: for God resisteth the proud, and giveth grace to the humble" (1 Pet. 5:5). "In that I command thee this day to love the LORD thy God, to walk in his ways, and to keep his commandments and his statutes and his judgments, that thou mayest live and multiply: and the LORD thy God shall bless thee in the land whither thou goest to possess it" (Deut. 30:16).

Divination counterattack

Bind the spirit of divination. Decree the lordship of Christ. Pray the "Prayers for Activation Into Warfare" in chapter 3.

Divorce counterattack

Forgive, release, and let go of anger, depression, and bitterness. Ask God to remove feelings of resentment, betrayal, embarrassment, and loneliness. Get on with your life. Rebuild your worth and significance based on purpose and visions for a bright and better future. Take one day at a time. Take responsibility for your own life and feelings.

Doctrines of devils counterattack

Bind the spirit of seduction. Decree and declare that truth prevails. Build prayer shields and hedges around your mind.

Doctrines of man counterattack

Bind the spirit of error. Decree and declare that truth prevails.

Doubt counterattack

Pray that your mind is steadfast, immoveable, and always abounding in the work and Word of the Lord. Decree, according to 2 Thessalonians 2:2, that you are not shaken in your mind, and refuse to be troubled by the attack of several spirits, words, or any circumstance.

Enmeshments counterattack

Break soul ties, psychological and emotional attachments, and strongholds. Renounce codependency, and declare that all present and future relationships are healthy, mutually beneficial, and interdependent.

Entanglements counterattack

Destroy entanglements. Decree and declare that Jehovah gives you the strength and courage to break free of every entanglement. "Stand fast therefore in the liberty wherewith Christ hath made us free, and be not entangled again with the yoke of bondage" (Gal. 5:1).

Ethnicities counterattack

"With all lowliness and meekness, with longsuffering, forbearing one another in love; endeavouring to keep the unity of the Spirit in the bond of peace. There is one body, and one Spirit, even as ye are called in one hope of your calling; one Lord, one faith, one baptism, one God and Father of all, who is above all, and through all, and in you all" (Eph. 4:2–6). "There is neither Jew nor Greek, there is neither bond nor free, there is neither male nor female: for ye are all one in Christ Jesus" (Gal. 3:28).

Eventualities counterattack

Decree and declare that God and God alone holds the key to your future: "'For I know the plans I have for you,' declares the LORD, 'plans to prosper you and not to harm you, plans to give you hope and a future'" (Jer. 29:11, NIV).

False burdens counterattack

Pray this verse from Isaiah: "And it shall come to pass in that day, that his burden shall be taken away from off thy shoulder, and his yoke from off thy neck, and the yoke shall be destroyed because of the anointing" (Isa. 10:27). (See also Isaiah 9:4.)

False entitlement counterattack

Bind the spirit of Belial. Decree and declare that you will not lose anything God has given to you in Jesus's name. Ask God to release angels to marshal and protect the boundaries and borders of all physical, spiritual, and intellectual properties and all your possessions. Build a hedge of protection around yourself and everything and everyone associated with you in Jesus's name.

False expectations counterattack

Pray according to Psalm 20:7: "Some trust in chariots and some in horses, but we trust in the name of the LORD our God" (NIV). You are a God of covenant, and every promise in You is yes and amen. Therefore, I place my hope and faith in You and You alone. Thank You for bringing people into my life whose words and promise I can depend on.

False impressions counterattack

Pray the following prayer: *In the name of Jesus, I obliterate, annihilate, and prohibit satanic impressions, illusions, projections, perceptions, suggestions, suspicions, and deceptions set up as a decoy or an ambush to my soul and those assigned to pray with me, for me, and on behalf of me, those who work with me, are assigned to me, and interact with me daily. Amen.* (See 1 Kings 22:5–40; Acts 13:50; 2 Thessalonians 2:1–10.)

Family eccentricities and idiosyncrasies counterattack

Pray: *I decree and declare that, by the anointing, covenants, contracts, chains, fetters, bondages, proclivities, and captivities that are contrary to, oppose, or hinder the fulfillment of God's original plan and purpose, are broken. I am liberated from soul ties and generational, satanic, and demonic alliances, allegiances, and curses or spirits of inheritance. I sever them by the blood and by the Spirit. I speak to my DNA and declare that I am free from any and all influences passed down from one generation to another, biologically, socially, emotionally, physiologically, psychologically, spiritually, or by any other channel unknown to me but known to God. I resist every spirit that acts as a doorkeeper to my soul and renounce any further conscious or unconscious alliance, association, allegiance, or covenant. I open myself to divine deliverance. Father, have Your way now! Perfect those things concerning me. Amen.* (See Deuteronomy 5:9; 7:8–9; Ecclesiastes 7:26; Isaiah 61:1; Acts 8:9–13; Galatians 5:1; 1 Thessalonians 5:23–24; 2 Timothy 2:25.)

Fear counterattack

Pray Psalm 27:1–6.

Fiery darts counterattack

Pray: *Father, I lift up the shield of faith today and quench the fiery darts of the wicked one.*

Firebrands counterattack

Pray according to this passage of Scripture: "And say unto him, Take heed, and be quiet; fear not, neither be fainthearted for the two tails of these smoking firebrands, for the fierce anger of Rezin with Syria, and of the son of Remaliah" (Isa. 7:4).

Friendly fire counterattack

Ask God to enable you to accurately discern the spirits of man. Bind all illegal activities concerning your life. Decree and declare that a prayer shield, the anointing, and the bloodline form a hedge of protection that hides you from familiar spirits and all other demonic personalities, making it difficult if not impossible for them to effectively track or trace you in the realm of the Spirit. There shall be no perforations or penetrations. (See Exodus 12:13; Job 1:7–10; Psalm 91.)

Frustration counterattack

Release the spirit of Nehemiah upon you. Declare and decree success and progress in Jesus's name.

Generational curses counterattack

Break generational curses in Jesus's name. Live a life of obedience. "Therefore if any man be in Christ, he is a new creature: old things are passed away; behold, all things are become new" (2 Cor. 5:17).

Gossip counterattack

Pray according to Psalm 3 and Psalm 19:14.

Guilt counterattack

Determine to take personal responsibility for recognizing your shortcomings. Ask God for forgiveness, forgive yourself, and make reparations where necessary.

Habits counterattack

Practice self-discipline. Enlist the support of family and friends by sharing with them. This one act of public accountability will make it more difficult to back out or compromise. Enlist a partner when possible. Ecclesiastes 4:9 states, "Two are better than one; because they have a good reward for their labour." Focus on the end reward and have fun. It is so much easier to form a new habit if it is perceived as enjoyable. Be prepared to reward yourself if you achieve your goal.

Harassment counterattack

Pray the "Prayers for Activation Into Warfare" in chapter 3. Reverse, over-rule, and veto every act and ill-spoken and negative word. Bind the enemy, and declare Isaiah 54:17, "No weapon that is formed against thee shall prosper; and every tongue that shall rise against thee in judgment thou shalt condemn. This is the heritage of the servants of the LORD, and their righteousness is of me, saith the LORD."

Heresies counterattack

Declare and decree that truth prevails. Bind the spirit of deception, false-hoods, and lying.

Homosexuality counterattack

"With men it is impossible, but not with God: for with God all things are possible" (Mark 10:27). "I beseech you therefore, brethren, by the mercies of God, that ye present your bodies a living sacrifice, holy, acceptable unto God, which is your reasonable service. And be not conformed to this world: but be ye transformed by the renewing of your mind, that ye may prove what is that good, and acceptable, and perfect, will of God" (Rom. 12:1–2).

Idolatry counterattack

Pray Exodus 20:3, "Thou shalt have no other gods before me."

Ignorance counterattack

Ask God to give you knowledge, understanding, prudence, and wisdom. Remember Proverbs 9:10: "The fear of the LORD is the beginning of wisdom: and the knowledge of the holy is understanding."

Immaturity counterattack

"But speaking the truth in love, may grow up into him in all things, which is the head, even Christ" (Eph. 4:15). "As newborn babes, desire the sincere milk of the word, that ye may grow thereby" (1 Pet. 2:2). "But grow in grace, and in the knowledge of our Lord and Saviour Jesus Christ. To him be glory both now and for ever. Amen" (2 Pet. 3:18).

Incest counterattack

See chapter 9 to bind the spirit of perversion. Decree and declare that the family line is cleansed from all perversions in Jesus's name. Decree and declare that by the anointing, covenants, contracts, chains, fetters, bondages, proclivities, and captivities that are contrary to, oppose, or hinder the fulfillment of God's original plan and purpose are broken. I am liberated from soul ties, generational, satanic, and demonic alliances, allegiances, curses, and spirits of inheritance. I sever them by the blood and by the spirit. I declare that I am free from any and all influences passed down from one generation to another—biologically, socially, sexually, emotionally, physiologically, psychologically, spiritually, or by any other channel unknown to me but known to God. The blood of Jesus Christ sets me free from all soulish and carnal predilections and predispositions of the flesh, and cleanses my body, soul, and spirit of all psychic and generational contaminates. I resist every spirit that acts as a doorkeeper to my soul and renounce any further conscious or unconscious alliance, association, allegiance, or covenant. I open myself to divine deliverance. Father, have your way now! Perfect those things concerning me. (See Deuteronomy 5:9, 7:8–9; Ecclesiastes 7:26; Isaiah 61:1; Acts 8:9–13; Galatians 5:1; 2 Timothy 2:25; 1 Thessalonians 5:23–24.)

Indifference counterattack

Ask God to restore the joy of your salvation and to give you a zeal for life and living.

Inhibitions counterattack

Pray: *I prevail against satanic inhibitions, prohibitions, and all limitations. I decree and declare that all invisible and invincible walls are destroyed.* (See Colossians 1:16.)

Iniquity counterattack

Pray Psalm 32:5: "I acknowledged my sin unto thee, and mine iniquity have I not hid. I said, I will confess my transgressions unto the LORD; and thou forgavest the iniquity of my sin. Selah."

Insecurity counterattack

"For it is God which worketh in you both to will and to do of his good pleasure" (Phil. 2:13). Rely on the enabling power of the Holy Spirit, for the Spirit in you is far stronger than anything in the world. (See 1 John 4:4.)

Insults counterattack

Pray: *I obliterate and annihilate satanic impressions, insults, prejudice, harassments, projections, perceptions, suggestions, suspicions, and deceptions set up as a decoy or an ambush to my soul and those assigned to pray with me, for me, on behalf of me, those who work with me, are assigned to me, and interact with me daily.* (See 1 Kings 22:5–40; Acts 13:50; 2 Thessalonians 2:1–10.) Build prayer hedges and fire walls around your mind, will, and emotions. I overrule and overthrow according to Isaiah 54:17, ill-spoken words, ill wishes, enchantments, curses, and every idle word spoken contrary to God's original plans and purpose. I reverse the effects associated with these insults and decree that they shall not stand; they shall not come to pass; *they shall not take root.* Their violent verbal dealings are returned to them twofold. Amen."

Interference counterattack

Ask God for supernatural intervention. Pray the "Prayers of Activation Into Warfare" in chapter 3.

Invincible obstructions counterattack

Pray 2 Samuel 22:30: "For by thee I have run through a troop: by my God have I leaped over a wall." And pray Matthew 17:20: "If ye have faith as a grain of mustard seed, ye shall say unto this mountain, Remove hence to yonder place; and it shall remove; and nothing shall be impossible unto you."

Invisible barriers counterattack

"Every valley shall be filled, and every mountain and hill shall be brought low; and the crooked shall be made straight, and the rough ways shall be made smooth" (Luke 3:5). Employ the anointing of Zerubbabel and prophesy grace to every mountain (Zech. 4:6–7).

Irritations counterattack

Ask God to remove the irritations or to provide divine inoculations.

Jealousy counterattack

Ask God to deliver you or the person closely associated with you from the spirit of jealousy.

Judgmentalism counterattack

"Judge not, and ye shall not be judged: condemn not, and ye shall not be condemned: forgive, and ye shall be forgiven" (Luke 6:37).

Lack of spiritual endowments counterattack

Ask God to give you your spiritual inheritance and true riches in Christ Jesus. Bind the spirit of lack, and speak abundance. "The young lions do lack, and suffer hunger: but they that seek the LORD shall not want any good thing" (Ps. 34:10). "If any of you lack wisdom, let him ask of God, that giveth to all men liberally, and upbraideth not; and it shall be given him" (James 1:5).

Lack of submission to authority counterattack

"Submit yourselves therefore to God. Resist the devil, and he will flee from you" (James 4:7). "Submit yourselves to every ordinance of man for the Lord's sake: whether it be to the king, as supreme" (1 Pet. 2:13). "Likewise, ye younger, submit yourselves unto the elder. Yea, all of you be subject one to another, and be clothed with humility: for God resisteth the proud, and giveth grace to the humble" (1 Pet. 5:5).

Laziness counterattack

"The hand of the diligent shall bear rule: but the slothful shall be under tribute" (Prov. 12:24). "Love not sleep, lest thou come to poverty; open thine eyes, and thou shalt be satisfied with bread" (Prov. 20:13).

Lies counterattack

"And ye shall know the truth, and the truth shall make you free" (John 8:32). Bind the spirit's lies, falsehood, and error, and loose them from their assignment. Decree and declare that truth prevails.

Lusts counterattack

Pray Galatians 5:16.

Manipulation counterattack

Pray according to Ephesians 6:10–18.

Materialism counterattack

Pray this passage: "But seek ye first the kingdom of God, and his righteousness; and all these things shall be added unto you" (Matt. 6:33).

Miseducation counterattack

Pray according to 2 Peter 3:18.

Misfortunes counterattack

Use the "Prayers of Activation Into Warfare" in chapter 3 for further prayer study on this topic.

Mistrust counterattack

Ask God to reveal the intent and content of a person's heart. Discern the spirit of those operating around you and interacting with you. Ask God to make you more trusting.

Moving out of the timing of the Lord counterattack

Ask God to allow you to move in the anointing of the sons of Isaachar so that you will discern the proper time and season for all things. Decree and declare that you are synchronized and syncopated to the timing of the Lord, moving in His will and with the prophetic "cloud."

Negativity counterattack

Pray according to Philippians 4:8.

Nets counterattack

In the name of Jesus, I take the sword of the spirit and sever all nets and decree and declare that whom the Son sets free is free indeed! I decree and declare that every unholy alliance and association is severed in Jesus's name.

Obsession counterattack

Fast and pray according to Isaiah 58:5–11.

Offenses counterattack

Pray this prayer: *Father, I release (name the person) from all offenses I have held in my heart. Forgive me for my resentment, hatred, anger, and displeasure. Deliver me from this self-imposed bondage. Close every portal that gives the spirit of unforgiveness access to my soul. I worship You as I decree and declare that where the Spirit of the Lord is, there is liberty.*

Oppression counterattack

Pray according to Ezekiel 46:18.

Overt operations counterattack

Pray according to Ephesians 6:10–18.

Peer pressure counterattack

Pray according to Romans 12:2.

Perversions counterattack

"Be not wise in thine own eyes: fear the LORD, and depart from evil" (Prov. 3:7). Break the hold of every evil, unclean power over your life in Jesus's name. Declare that the blood of Jesus Christ cleanses you from all sin. Ask God to remove the appetite for this sin. Break ungodly soul ties, renounce diabolical contracts, and destroy unholy alliances. Shun the very appearance of evil. Ask the Holy Spirit to expose and destroy every stronghold and cleanse you from sexual perversions. Fill your heart and mind with the Word of the Lord, and decree that godly thoughts, visions, and dreams replace immoral, degrading thoughts, dreams, nightmares, and fantasies. Decree and declare your freedom in Jesus's name. "Blessed are the pure in heart: for they shall see God" (Matt. 5:8).

Possession counterattack

"And it shall come to pass in that day, that his burden shall be taken away from off thy shoulder, and his yoke from off thy neck, and the yoke shall be destroyed because of the anointing" (Isa. 10:27).

Poverty counterattack

Bind the spirit of poverty. Ask God to give you an open heaven and divine inspiration, and to open streams of income. Make certain you are paying your tithes and planting seeds. A seed does not necessarily have to be money. You can sow seeds of hospitality, kind deeds, and acts of service and time.

Prejudice counterattack

Pray Galatians 3:28: "There is neither Jew nor Greek, there is neither bond nor free, there is neither male nor female: for ye are all one in Christ Jesus."

Pride counterattack

Pray these passages: "But he giveth more grace. Wherefore he saith, God resisteth the proud, but giveth grace unto the humble" (James 4:6); "Humble yourselves in the sight of the Lord, and he shall lift you up" (v. 10).

Projections counterattack

Pray: *I obliterate and annihilate satanic impressions, illusions, projections, perceptions, suggestions, suspicions, and deceptions set up as a decoy or an ambush to my soul and those assigned to pray with me, for me, on behalf of me, those who work with me, are assigned to me, and interact with me daily in Jesus's name. Amen.* (See 1 Kings 22:5–40; Acts 13:50; 2 Thessalonians 2:1–10.)

Provocation counterattack

Pray that God will grant you the ability to discern the spirit of provocation whenever it is operable. Forcefully resist it in Jesus's name. Decree and declare that you are led by the Spirit of the Lord.

Rape counterattack

Break the silence, speak up, and speak out. Seek Christian counseling. Involve loved ones and family members in the counseling sessions. Seek a powerful, safe, accepting, and supportive climate for you to release painful feelings without fear of criticism, judgment, rejection, or humiliation. Utilize prayer strategy from chapter 3. It may seem as if you will never heal, but in your weakness and sadness, God's strength is made perfect. Build prayer shields, fire walls, and prayer hedges around your life, mind, soul, and spirit. Progress through the grieving process (psychologists offer the first five stages, but I have added the last two): denial, resentment, bargaining, depression, acceptance, regaining personal power, and living life on purpose). Through Jesus Christ there is life after death. Allow the unconditional love of the Father to heal you.

Rebellion counterattack

Pray without ceasing. Bind the spirit of rebellion. Decree and declare that peace, compliance, and obedience are superimposed over the spirit of rebellion.

Regret counterattack

Ask God to empower you to overcome the pain, guilt, shame, and humiliation of the past. Live life on purpose. Live life in the now. Accept forgiveness. Forget the past, and look forward to what lies ahead (Phil. 3:13).

Rejection counterattack

Ask God to show you your true worth in Him. Do not seek affirmation from others at the expense of the affirmation that God gives you. See yourself as God sees you. "To the praise of the glory of his grace, wherein he hath made us accepted in the beloved" (Eph. 1:6).

Religiosity counterattack

Pray Matthew 6:10: "Thy kingdom come. Thy will be done in earth, as it is in heaven."

Resentment counterattack

Ask God to remove the pain and grievance and to supply you with an abundance of forgiveness.

Retaliation counterattack

Decree and declare that no act of retaliation will prosper. Continue to reinforce your prayer shield and hedges of protection. Establish the Godhead as your gatekeeper and doorkeeper.

Sabotage counterattack

Bind and loose the spirit of Sanballat and Tobiah. Ask God to strengthen your hands as you work as unto the Lord. Ask God to supernaturally sustain you. Build prayer shields and hedges around your relationships, personhood, ministry, and business. Obliterate and annihilate satanic impressions, illusions, projections, perceptions, suggestions, suspicions, and deceptions set up as a decoy or an ambush to your soul and those assigned to pray with you, for you, on behalf of you, those who work with you, are assigned to you, and interact with you daily. (See 1 Kings 22:5–40; Acts 13:50; 2 Thessalonians

2:1–10.) Pray: *Father, overthrow the plans of troublemakers, scorners, scoffers, mockers, persecutors, and character assassins. Expose satanic representatives, and grant unto me divine strategies and tactics to identify, resist, and overcome plots and plans established for my demise. Amen.* (See Esther 9:25; Psalm 5:10; 7:14–16; 34:21; 35:1–8; 52:5; 83:13–17; 141:10; Proverbs 26:27; 28:10; Daniel 3; 6; Matthew 7:15–23; 2 Corinthians 11:14–15.)

Satanic concentration counterattack

Pray that a prayer shield, the anointing, and the bloodline form a hedge of protection that hides you from familiar spirits and all other demonic personalities, making it difficult for them to effectively track or trace you in the realm of the Spirit. There shall be no perforations or penetrations.

Scandal counterattack

Ask God to remove you from all appearance of evil and to forgive and cleanse you. Ask God to grant you the fruit of the Spirit and to wipe your image clean from the activities associated with the scandal and the residual effects in Jesus's name. Pray that God will vindicate your reputation and reengineer your character. Pray Psalm 51.

Seduction counterattack

Ask God to seduction-proof your spirit by giving you the gift of wisdom and discerning of spirits. Decree and declare that truth exposes error and that light dispels all darkness in Jesus's name.

Shame counterattack

Pray Romans 8:26–29: "Likewise the Spirit also helpeth our infirmities: for we know not what we should pray for as we ought: but the Spirit itself maketh intercession for us with groanings which cannot be uttered. And he that searcheth the hearts knoweth what is the mind of the Spirit, because he maketh intercession for the saints according to the will of God. And we know that all things work together for good to them that love God, to them who are the called according to his purpose. For whom he did foreknow, he also did predestinate to be conformed to the image of his Son, that he might be the firstborn among many brethren." "Remember ye not the former things, neither consider the things of old. Behold, I will do a new thing; now it shall spring forth; shall ye not know it? I will even make a way in the wilderness, and rivers in the desert" (Isa. 43:18–19).

Sin counterattack

Pray 1 John 1:9: "If we confess our sins, he is faithful and just to forgive us our sins, and to cleanse us from all unrighteousness."

Snares counterattack

Pray Psalm 91:3: "Surely he shall deliver thee from the snare of the fowler, and from the noisome pestilence." Remember: "Foolish and unlearned questions avoid, knowing that they do gender strifes. And the servant of the Lord must not strive; but be gentle unto all men, apt to teach, patient, in meekness instructing those that oppose themselves; if God peradventure will give them repentance to the acknowledging of the truth; and that they may recover themselves out of the snare of the devil, who are taken captive by him at his will" (2 Tim. 2:23–26).

Spirits of affinity counterattack

Read Matthew 22:36–37: "Master, which is the great commandment in the law? Jesus said unto him, Thou shalt love the Lord thy God with all thy heart, and with all thy soul, and with all thy mind."

Spiritual abortion counterattack

Bind the spirit of spiritual abortion. Decree and declare that everything that needs to be birthed through prayer and supplication will be birthed in its correct time and season. There will be no abortions and no stillbirths in Jesus's name.

Spiritual miscarriage counterattack

Decree and declare that your life is synchronized to God's original plan and purpose and that there will be no miscarriage of anything God has planned for your life.

Stigmatization counterattack

Live your life in exact contrast to the stigma. Decree and declare that God is your defense.

Strongholds counterattack

Pray according to Nahum 1:7 and 2 Corinthians 10:3–6.

Stumbling blocks counterattack

Ask God to remove all stumbling blocks and to become the light to your pathway.

Suicidal thoughts counterattack

Pray according to Isaiah 26:3 and Philippians 4:7.

Thorn in the flesh counterattack

Build prayer shields and fire walls around your life. Decree and declare according to Psalm 89:21–23: "With whom my hand shall be established: mine arm also shall strengthen him. The enemy shall not exact upon him; nor the son of wickedness afflict him. And I will beat down his foes before his face, and plague them that hate him." I am strengthened by the arm of the Lord. The enemy shall not exact himself against me. Father, weed out all who oppose me and hate me. Do not allow evil to come nigh to my dwelling. You are my hiding place. I dwell in the secret place of the Most High God.

Traditions of men counterattack

Decree and declare that the kingdom of heaven reigns and rules over the affairs of man.

Transference of spirits counterattack

Study chapter 9. Bind and loose any spirit that has been transferred in Jesus's name. Command them to loose their hold.

Unbelief counterattack

Decree and declare that the spirit of unbelief is superimposed by the spirit of faith.

Uncleanness counterattack

Decree and declare that the environment, spirit, or mind of a person is purified and cleansed by the blood, by the Spirit, and by the Word of the Lord. Command every unclean spirit to leave in the name of Jesus. Decree and declare that the former occupied space is swept clean in Jesus's name.

Underachievement counterattack

Bind the spirit of underachievement. Decree and declare that through Christ you can fulfill purpose, maximize potential, and bring glory to the name of the Lord. Set the bar of achievement higher.

Unforgiveness counterattack

Declare Matthew 6:14–15.

Unholy alliances counterattack

Ask God to assist you in discerning the spirits of those who operate around you. Bind every spirit that is diabolically assigned to you, and decree and declare that no weapon formed against you shall prosper.

Unsanctified souls counterattack

Pray the following passages: "Behold, thou desirest truth in the inward parts: and in the hidden part thou shalt make me to know wisdom. Purge me with hyssop, and I shall be clean: wash me, and I shall be whiter than snow. Make me to hear joy and gladness; that the bones which thou hast broken may rejoice. Hide thy face from my sins, and blot out all mine iniquities. Create in me a clean heart, O God; and renew a right spirit within me. Cast me not away from thy presence; and take not thy holy spirit from me" (Ps. 51:6–11); "Wherefore lay apart all filthiness and superfluity of naughtiness, and receive with meekness the engrafted word, which is able to save your souls" (James 1:21).

Vain imagination counterattack

Pray 2 Corinthians 10:4–6: "(For the weapons of our warfare are not carnal, but mighty through God to the pulling down of strong holds;) casting down imaginations, and every high thing that exalteth itself against the knowledge of God, and bringing into captivity every thought to the obedience of Christ; and having in a readiness to revenge all disobedience, when your obedience is fulfilled."

Vengeance/vindictiveness counterattack

Pray Hebrews 10:30: "For we know him that hath said, Vengeance belongeth unto me, I will recompense, saith the Lord. And again, The Lord shall judge his people." This is no light matter. God has warned us that He will hold us to account. God will judge His people. Nobody is getting by with anything, believe me. Let God be God!

Vexations counterattack

Pray the "Prayers of Activation Into Warfare" in chapter 3.

Violence counterattack

Bind the spirit of violence and decree and declare that peace, collaboration, justice, and reconciliation replace violence. Pray the "Prayers of Activation Into Warfare" in chapter 3.

Wars/conflicts counterattack

Pray the following Scriptures: Isaiah 9:6–7; 26:3, 12; Jeremiah 29:7, 11; Psalm 122:6; Isaiah 54:13; Philippians 4:7; Colossians 3:15; James 3:18

Weights counterattack

Pray this verse from Hebrews 12:1, "Wherefore seeing we also are compassed about with so great a cloud of witnesses, let us lay aside every weight, and the sin which doth so easily beset us, and let us run with patience the race that is set before us."

Works of the flesh counterattack

Pray Galatians 5:18–21. Try reading it from The Message version of the Bible.

Worldliness counterattack

Declare 1 John 2:15.

Worry counterattack

"Trust in the LORD with all thine heart; and lean not unto thine own understanding. In all thy ways acknowledge him, and he shall direct thy paths" (Prov. 3:5–6). Decree and declare that your God shall supply all your need according to His riches in glory.

Yokes counterattack

Ask God to remove the predilection to go against His will. Ask Him to grant you discipline, consistency, and a love for His Word. Decree and declare that yokes are broken and burdens are lifted by reason of the anointing in Jesus's name.

PART III

BINDING THE STRONGMAN

EIGHT

GEARING UP FOR BATTLE

What Are Your Weapons?

WHEN THE LORD initially introduced me to the concepts of intrinsic and extrinsic weapons, they were merely revelational words that were downloaded into my conscious mind by the Holy Spirit as He trained me in the art of strategic prayer and spiritual warfare. I employed these terms in my prayer vocabulary and later added them as one of the warfare declarations in chapter 3. A few months after the initial revelation, my spirit really grasped the true meaning of these terms, and the Holy Spirit once again began to reveal to me how potent the scriptural declaration "no weapon formed against me shall prosper" really was. My paradigm instantly shifted from the mere utterance of a phrase that provided me with an intellectually conceptualized arsenal, and the understanding of how the wiles of the devil are actually executed, to an understanding of how powerful intrinsic and extrinsic satanic weapons really are.

This one declaration opened my eyes to see how covert the attack of the enemy really was in my own life. I began to make inquiries of the Lord concerning the diversity and magnitude of these weapons of mass destruction. I was aware of some of them, but not all. I want to ask you two questions: Has anyone ever quoted to you the scripture taken from Isaiah 54:17: "No weapon forged against you will prevail" (NIV)? Has anyone ever explained to you what the weapons were? Well, I want you to know that you can both discern and identify how the enemy is fighting against you, the weapon(s) he has designed for your demise, and how to successfully counteract.

This chapter has been written to arm you with specific insights into the actual weapons you should use. This is not designed to alarm, but to arm you for effective battle.

YOUR ARSENAL

If a military is going to win a war, there are three important questions that must be answered:

1. Who is the enemy?
2. Where is the battle?
3. What are your weapons?

The answer to the first question is obvious. The enemy is Satan and his cohorts, as we discussed in chapter 5. Since the rebellion of Satan and one-third of the angels, this world has been in combat against demonic forces. Having elaborately established an insidious military spiritual force, Satan continues to fulfill his mission: to steal, kill, and destroy all that belongs to God and is godly. We discussed the answer to the second question in chapter 4, and now in this chapter we will unveil your arsenal of supernatural weaponry.

This arsenal is the method in which you wield counteracts to the enemy's weapons and how you release the spirits that plague you, your family, your community, and the nation. Just so you don't think I have left you hanging, I will give you the counterattacks to the enemy's weapons and how to release evil spirits from their assignments in chapter 9.

But for now, let's go over what we do know about our weapons. First, we know that the weapons we fight with are powerful and operate at their peak in the spirit realm (2 Cor. 10:3–6). The second thing we know is that none of the weapons the enemy forms against us will successfully put us out of commission and that we have a heritage of victory in God (Isa. 54:17). The most important thing we are now aware of is that we have been equipped for this battle, and there are many weapons made available to us. Let's look at them now.

Prayer

Prayer is the key to effective spiritual warfare. Prayer releases God's flow into your life so that you can defeat the enemy. It is a two-way communication system, whereby you communicate with God and God communicates with you. If we become weak during the battle, prayer links us in to God's strength, especially when we pray in the spirit. Prayer is also the surest way to receive God's instructions and commands and to lean upon His infinite wisdom. We become more sufficient through prayer, and it is during prayer that we can exchange hopelessness for divine intervention and help.

Fasting

Fasting is a spiritual discipline that increases our prayer power. It humbles the soul and gives us the ability to become laser sharp in our spiritual walk with God. It is not only an excellent means of detoxification of the body, but it is also a detoxification of the soul and spirit. Mark 9:29 tells us that sometimes gaining the victory over certain tactics of the enemy "can come forth by nothing, but by prayer and fasting."

Restricting the body from certain food also allows us to put our flesh under submission and can help us get a hold of the separation of spirit and flesh. This will enhance our ability to war in the spirit, having put the physical and carnal under subjection.

Isaiah 58:6–9 also talks about fasting being a means of loosing the bands of wickedness, oppression, heavy burdens, yokes, affliction, poverty, and sadness.

Faith

First John 5:4 and Matthew 21:22 tell us that our faith is what ensures our victory over the god of this world, and it guarantees that what we ask to be delivered from, healed of, and empowered for will be done. As we address this powerful weapon, read what E. M. Bounds said:

> In any study of the principles, and procedure of prayer, of its activities and enterprises, first place, must, of necessity, be given to faith. He *must* believe, where he cannot prove. In the ultimate issue, prayer is simply faith, claiming its natural yet marvelous prerogatives—faith taking possession of its illimitable inheritance. True godliness is just as true, steady, and persevering in the realm of faith as it is in the province of prayer. Moreover: when faith ceases to pray, it ceases to live. Faith does the impossible because it brings God to undertake for us, and nothing is impossible with God. How great—without qualification or limitation—is the power of faith! If doubt be banished from the heart, and unbelief made stranger there, what we ask of God shall surely

come to pass, and a believer hath vouchsafed to him "whatsoever he saith."[1]

The blood of Jesus

Through the shed blood of Jesus Christ, we have already won and overcome all of the forces of the enemy. Revelation 12:7–11 says:

> And there was war in heaven: Michael and his angels fought against the dragon; and the dragon fought and his angels, and prevailed not; neither was their place found any more in heaven. And the great dragon was cast out, that old serpent, called the Devil, and Satan, which deceiveth the whole world: he was cast out into the earth, and his angels were cast out with him. And I heard a loud voice saying in heaven, Now is come salvation, and strength, and the kingdom of our God, and the power of his Christ: for the accuser of our brethren is cast down, which accused them before our God day and night. And they overcame him by the blood of the Lamb, and by the word of their testimony; and they loved not their lives unto the death.

Money

According to Ecclesiastes 7:12, money is a defense against the enemy. Money in the hands of the unrighteous is used to underwrite unrighteousness, but money in the hands of the righteous can be used to underwrite the propagation of the gospel.

Wisdom

Who would know this weapon better than King Solomon? His words in Ecclesiastes 9:13–18 reveal how wisdom defeated an army greater than the one with the wisdom.

> This wisdom have I seen also under the sun, and it *seemed* great unto me: there *was* a little city, and few men within it; and there came a great king against it, and besieged it, and built great bulwarks against it: now there was found in it a poor wise man, and he by his wisdom delivered the city...Then said I, Wisdom *is*

better than strength...Wisdom *is* better than weapons of war: but one sinner destroyeth much good.

—Emphasis added

The Word of God

In Ephesians 6 we find the spiritual armor that we are to gird ourselves with. Verse 17 talks about one of the most formidable weapons we have access to—the Word of God, which is referred to in this text as the helmet of salvation and the sword of the Spirit. The sword of the Spirit enables us to quickly and keenly discern spirits, thoughts, and intents (Heb. 4:12).

The name of Jesus

The name of Jesus calls us to repentance (Acts 2:38). It is by repentance, as we have already discovered, that God gives us a change of mind, and we are then able to ward off the temptations of the enemy.

In Philippians 2:9–11 we read, "God also hath highly exalted him, and given him a name which is above every name: that at the name of Jesus every knee should bow, of things in heaven, and things in earth, and things under the earth; and that every tongue should confess that Jesus Christ *is* Lord, to the glory of God the Father" (emphasis added).

The person of Jesus

With Jesus dwelling in us, we are greater than any power at work in the world (1 John 4:4).

The anointing

According to Isaiah 10:27, every burden that is on our shoulders and every yoke around our necks will be destroyed by the power of the anointing. The anointing is the power, provisions, and presence of God manifested through the person of the Holy Spirit.

The prophetic anointing

Revelation 11:5–6 talks about the power of the prophetic in the midst of spiritual warfare: "And if any man will hurt them, fire proceedeth out of their mouth, and devoureth their enemies: and if any man will hurt them, he must in this manner be killed. These have power to shut heaven, that it rain not in the days of their prophecy: and have power over waters to turn them to blood, and to smite the earth with all plagues, as often as they will."

Spirit praying

Spirit praying, or more commonly praying in the spirit, is essential in any believer's arsenal of weapons. According to Jude 20, this weapon has the ability to strengthen the inner man. Ephesians 6:18 tells us that we must stay in the mind-set of spirit praying, being ever watchful. Praying in the spirit also helps us when we don't know what to pray or what is wrong in certain situations. It allows our spirits to pray out directly into the intercession room of the Holy Spirit, where He is able to search our hearts and intercede strategically on our behalf. (See Romans 8:26–27.)

Allow the Holy Spirit access to your prayer life and to discipline you. He is more than happy to intercede on your behalf or give you the words to utter.

Tongues of men

Sometimes, it is not always easy for us to recall Scripture word for word. When that happens, if you can just speak the principle, you will experience positive results. Learn to fill your mind with good, positive, and biblical thoughts. Since your words are the secondary conduit of your thoughts, practice meditating in the Word of God day and night so that when you speak, your speech will be automatically aligned with the Word of the Lord. (For a reference to this weapon, see 1 Corinthians 13:1.)

Tongues of angels

When I speak of tongues of angels, I am not speaking of something spooky. The "tongues of angels" is the language that angels understand. This is purely the Word of God declared. According to Psalm 103:20–21, when you speak God's Word and declare His words over your circumstances, angels respond, executing and enforcing it over your situations and circumstances. (For a reference to this weapon, see 1 Corinthians 13:1.) God hastens His Word to perform it, while giving angels charge over us (Ps. 91:11; Jer. 1:12).

Praise

We do not praise because we feel good. We praise because praise is a weapon of warfare. Psalm 149:5–9 says, "Let the saints be joyful in glory: let them sing aloud upon their beds. Let the high praises of God *be* in their mouth, and a twoedged sword in their hand; to execute vengeance upon the heathen, *and* punishments upon the people; to bind their kings with chains, and their nobles with fetters of iron; to execute upon them the judgment written: this honour have all his saints. Praise ye the LORD." Praise is also God's will for us (1 Thess. 5:18), and when we are walking in the will of God, we are assured victory.

Dance

Judges 5:18–22 shows us how the people of God used dancing in the heat of battle:

> Zebulun and Naphtali were a people that jeoparded their lives unto the death in the high places of the field. The kings came and fought, then fought the kings of Canaan in Taanach by the waters of Megiddo; they took no gain of money. They fought from heaven; the stars in their courses fought against Sisera. The river of Kishon swept them away, that ancient river, the river Kishon. O my soul, thou hast trodden down strength. Then were the horse-hoofs broken by the means of the pransings, the pransings of their mighty ones.

Clapping

For this weapon, we get a direct command from the Lord in Ezekiel 6:11: "This is what the Sovereign LORD says: Strike your hands together" (NIV).

Stomping/marching

The story of the children of Israel and the wall of Jericho is the perfect example of how effective stomping and marching is to our spiritual warfare. (See Joshua 6:1–21.)

The second part of Ezekiel 6:11 provides a complementary cross-reference, telling us to "stamp with thy foot, and say, Alas for all the evil abominations of the house of Israel! for they shall fall by the sword, by the famine, and by the pestilence."

Shouting

This weapon also has its origin in the battle of Jericho. When Joshua shouted, the walls of Jericho collapsed. (See Joshua 6:1–21.)

Music

Second Kings 3:15–19 says, "But now bring me a minstrel. And it came to pass, when the minstrel played, that the hand of the LORD came upon him. And he said, Thus saith the LORD, Make this valley full of ditches. For thus saith the LORD, Ye shall not see wind, neither shall ye see rain; yet that valley shall be filled with water, that ye may drink, both ye, and your cattle, and your beasts. And this is but a light thing in the sight of the LORD: he will deliver the Moabites also into your hand. And ye shall smite every fenced city, and every choice city, and shall fell every good tree, and stop all wells of water, and mar every good piece of land with stones."

THE GOOD FIGHT

As the enemy wages war against you, remember that you are fighting *the good fight of faith*. Your concentration should not merely rest upon what happens to you, but also upon what is happening in you and your response to what happens to you. But don't give up, and don't give in. We not only prevail; we also overcome every attack. Remember, the flip side of victory is warfare, and the flip side of warfare is victory. Either way, you win.

So, my brothers and sisters, "Gird up the loins of your mind, be sober, and hope to the end" (1 Pet. 1:13). Do not give up in this battle, and do not let the enemy wear you down. Remain "stedfast, unmoveable, always abounding in the work of the Lord, forasmuch as ye know that your labour is not in vain in the Lord" (1 Cor. 15:58).

Now we move on to the strategies and tactics of how we can effectively use the weapons we just uncovered.

NINE

ENGAGING THE FIGHT

Strategies and Tactics for Spiritual Warfare

B INDING THE STRONGMAN" is a biblical discipline taught by Jesus Christ. It is a tool Christians can use to fight against the powers of the dark kingdom. Let us examine the use of this tool in Scripture:

And he was casting out a devil, and it was dumb. And it came to pass, when the devil was gone out, the dumb spake; and the people wondered. But some of them said, He casteth out devils through Beelzebub the chief of the devils. And others, tempting him, sought of him a sign from heaven. But he, knowing their thoughts, said unto them, Every kingdom divided against itself is brought to desolation; and a house divided against a house falleth. If Satan also be divided against himself, how shall his kingdom stand? because ye say that I cast out devils through Beelzebub. And if I by Beelzebub cast out devils, by whom do your sons cast them out? therefore shall they be your judges. But if I with the finger of God cast out devils, no doubt the kingdom of God is come upon you. When a strong man armed keepeth his palace, his goods are in peace: but when a stronger than he shall come upon him, and overcome him, he taketh from him all his armour wherein he trusted, and divideth his spoils. He that is not with me is against me: and he that gathereth not with me scattereth. When the unclean spirit is gone out of a man, he walketh through dry places, seeking rest; and finding none, he saith, I will return unto my house whence I came out. And when he cometh, he findeth it swept and garnished. Then goeth he, and taketh to him seven other spirits more wicked than himself; and they enter in, and dwell there: and the last state of that man is worse than the first.

—Luke 11:14–26

When you engage in the administration of deliverance, you must ensure you are biblically correct.

Use the methods in this chapter with confidence, knowing that, according to 1 John 3:8, this was the purpose for which "the Son of God was manifested, that he might destroy the works of the devil." May the Spirit of the Lord rest upon you so that all your endeavors are initiated by and subject to the Spirit of the Lord.

> The Spirit of the Lord is upon me, because he hath anointed me to preach the gospel to the poor; he hath sent me to heal the brokenhearted, to preach deliverance to the captives, and recovering of sight to the blind, to set at liberty them that are bruised.
>
> —Luke 4:18

As you pray, you must totally rely on the Holy Spirit.

Even as the Holy Spirit led Jesus in all things, He must also lead you. Do not be presumptuous when it comes to determining who needs deliverance and who does not. The Holy Spirit operates like the sonar equipment deep-sea divers use to fathom the depths of the ocean. The Holy Spirit is He who has the ability to search and fathom the hearts of men. First Corinthians 2:10 states, "But God hath revealed them unto us by his Spirit: for the Spirit searcheth all things, yea, the deep things of God." He will help you to discern, test, resist, and reject demonic spirits and their activities.

> Likewise the Spirit also helpeth our infirmities: for we know not what we should pray for as we ought: but the Spirit itself maketh intercession for us with groanings which cannot be uttered. And he that searcheth the hearts knoweth what is the mind of the Spirit, because he maketh intercession for the saints according to the will of God.
>
> —Romans 8:26–27

Since the Holy Spirit knows the hearts of men, He can communicate His knowledge to you as a believer during your prayer and intercession. You then will be empowered by God to act in accordance with the promptings, stirrings, leading, and insight the Holy Spirit gives. Remember, one of your greatest defense mechanisms is to stay connected with the Holy Spirit as you pray.

Charge yourself up in the Holy Spirit.

Just as a car battery or a cell phone runs out of power, necessitating a recharge, the believer can recharge his spiritual battery by praying in the Holy Spirit (1 Cor. 14:4; Jude 20). This discipline should be a part of your daily prayer vigil. It is also a wonderful means by which spiritual power is accrued for prayer and during prayer.

Take dominion.

Use authority in the name of Jesus, and don't be afraid to take dominion over the strongman. Matthew 16:19 states that God has given us "the keys of the kingdom of heaven." The one who has the keys has access, which indicates authority.

When it comes to spiritual warfare, do not accept substitutes or compromises. Do not back off, back down, give up, or give in. God has given you authority over all of the devil's ability according to Luke 10:19. Ephesians 1:20–23 states that Satan is under your feet. That means that he does not have authority over you, but you have authority over him.

You must rise up and take the authority by superimposing the will of God over the will and all activity of the enemy. He is operating illegally in the earth realm. May I remind you that he is not the prince of the power of the earth, but "the prince of the power of the air" according to Ephesians 2:2. Therefore, rise up and take your rightful position as God's deputized agent. Insist that he comply with the biblically based terms issued by you.

The Bible states that in your kingly posture, you have been given power to decree a thing, and it will be established. (See Job 22:28.) When you decree a thing in Jesus's name, the enemy is aware that you are not suggesting or even giving him an option or advice. He understands that when you come in Jesus's name, he must cease and desist his illegal activities at once! Why? Because in Isaiah 45:23, God Himself states, "I have sworn by myself, the word is gone out of my mouth in righteousness, and shall not return, that unto me every knee shall bow, every tongue shall swear." It is further stated in Philippians 2:10–11, "That at the name of Jesus every knee should bow, of things in heaven, and things in earth, and things under the earth; and that every tongue should confess that Jesus Christ is Lord, to the glory of God the Father."

Become proficient in the mechanics of binding and loosing.

Binding and loosing is a way to control satanic activities. When we are born, we do not know how to do anything. Over time, we learn to roll over, sit up, crawl, walk, and run. Even if you have no experience in binding or loosing prayer and work, you can become proficient at it through practice, study, and training. Remember, you have to start crawling before you walk and run.

> Or else how can one enter into a strong man's house, and spoil his goods, except he first bind the strong man? and then he will spoil his house.
>
> —Matthew 12:29

> Verily I say unto you, Whatsoever ye shall bind on earth shall be bound in heaven: and whatsoever ye shall loose on earth shall be loosed in heaven.
>
> —Matthew 18:18

Binding and loosing is like drawing up contracts that must be adhered to in the realm of the spirit. As it relates to demonic forces and activities, binding immobilizes demonic activities by imposing or commanding adherence to a specific alternative directive. Loosing is the opposite of binding. It extricates, discharges, and releases demonic forces from specific directive or obligatory activity. Since Matthew 18:18 seems to indicate that binding and loosing are inextricably connected, then we must consider binding and loosing as a single key. If you are going to bind, you must loose; if you are going to loose, you must bind. You cannot use one without the other.

The question I'm most frequently asked is, What do I bind, and what do I loose? Simply put, you bind the activities of Satan and his cohorts; you loose any effect that their presence has had, and then you release the kingdom (God's divine rule) counterpart. The devil has no choice in the matter but to relinquish his position.

When Jesus administered deliverance to people there was evidence that not only was the strongman and spirit gone, but the effects of their presence were gone as well.

> And, behold, there was a woman which had a spirit of infirmity eighteen years, and was bowed together, and could in no wise lift

up herself. And when Jesus saw her, he called her to him, and said unto her, Woman, thou art loosed from thine infirmity. And he laid his hands on her: and immediately she was made straight, and glorified God.

—Luke 13:11–13

The following are simple principles to follow:
1. Establish your legal rights and authority in Christ Jesus.
2. Use the name of Jesus (never assume you have power in and of yourself).
3. Determine the strongman and subordinate spirits.
4. Bind their works, and make them a part of the footstool of Jesus.
5. Remind demonic spirits that they must comply because Jesus came to "destroy the works of the devil" (1 John 3:8).
6. Loose every sign, symptom, and condition associated with their presence.
7. Release the kingdom of heaven counterpart.
8. Reinforce your prayer life with fasting.
9. Remain submitted to the Spirit of the Lord.
10. Resist the devil, and he will flee.
11. Use the Word of the Lord.

Do not allow any strongholds to remain.

Declare and decree that all materials used to construct the strongholds are now demolished and utterly destroyed. Ask the Holy Spirit to demolish strongholds and to sweep all residue away.

Close doors and establish God as the new doorkeeper and gatekeeper.

Pray that God becomes the new doorkeeper and gatekeeper of your city, country, nation, personage, family, and ministry. The Bible declares that the power of our words affect change in our lives, homes, environment, communities, cities, and nations. Pray for the peace of the city so that you can have peace as well.

Lift up your head, O ye gates; and be ye lift up, ye everlasting doors; and the King of glory shall come in. Who is this King of

glory? The LORD strong and mighty, the LORD mighty in battle.
Lift up your heads, O ye gates; even lift them up, ye everlasting
doors; and the King of glory shall come in. Who is this King of
glory? The LORD of hosts, he is the King of glory. Selah.

—Psalm 24:7–10

Establish your legal right in the name of Jesus.

Using the name of Jesus means that your activities are backed up in the
power and authority of the anointed One of God, who declared the extent,
power, and magnitude of His anointing in the following verse:

And Jesus came and spake unto them, saying, All power is given
unto me in heaven and in earth. Go ye therefore, and teach all
nations, baptizing them in the name of the Father, and of the Son,
and of the Holy Ghost: teaching them to observe all things whatsoever I have commanded you: and, lo, I am with you alway, even unto
the end of the world. Amen.

—Matthew 28:18–20

Identify the strongman and the subordinate spirits.

The strongman and subordinate spirits will be exposed in the next chapter.
There I have prepared a simple manual for you to identify the strongman and
the details of subordinate spirits, their signs, symptoms, and manifestations.
My suggestion is to explore each strongman that relates to a specific spirit.
Ask God how to proceed in prayer. He might instruct you to war against one
or all of them.

Utilize a prayer journal.

A prayer journal will make your prayer time more effective. Use the "Prayers
of Activation Into Battle" from chapter 3 as you go into your prayer time.

Pray under cover.

Don't be a renegade. Make sure you stay under your pastor or prayer
leaders' covering. Stay submitted.

TEN

RECONNAISSANCE

Getting Delivered and Overcoming the Enemy

O NE REASON MANY people do not experience the kind of success they want when engaging in spiritual warfare is because of generalization or ignorance. Do not fall into the trap of making a sweeping generalization, and do not war ignorantly. Spirits are so masterful in their warfare. They engineer many deceptive activities that sometimes could fool the most skilled spiritual warrior. Flip through chapter 6, and find the spirits that you are dealing with. You will see that this list contains the main spirit or strongman and the ways in which each spirit can manifest itself in your life. These are called subordinate spirits. With this list in hand, you are facing a winning battle. As the old G. I. Joe cartoons used to say, "Knowing is half the battle."

Realize that your reliance is upon the Lord and not your skill. Therefore, as you engage in warfare, it is important to wipe out all associated spirits. Apprise yourself of the unique characteristics of the strongman. Cover yourself with the armor of the Lord, and begin to bind and loose, utilizing the authority of Jesus's name. Ask God to bring total deliverance to you, your family, your city, your ministry, and your nation.

In this chapter, I am going to expose the strongman and the subordinate spirits that can infiltrate your mind, finances, family history, health, future, and even your nation. We are going to war together for victory in all these areas. I am going to give specific scriptural references for each of these spirits, but I didn't do the work for you. You will need your sword (the Bible, the Word of God) nearby as you engage the enemy through these next two sections. We will proceed alphabetically.

SPIRIT OF ABSALOM

The spirit of Absalom is a renegade spirit that uses seduction and pretense in order to fulfill its diabolical operations. It is designed to undermine and destroy purpose, potential, and the influence and authority of men and women of God who hold strategic positions in the kingdom of God. Transferring loyalty from one person to another, it's plan is to divide and conquer. It forms a very strong alliance with the spirit of perversion and the spirit of Ahithophel in order to execute its strategies and plans. This spirit defies divine authority and attempts to deny a believer his basic human and kingdom rights. Individuals who harbor bitterness and unforgiveness are easily overtaken by this spirit and begin to move with a vengeance, forcefully and decisively sticking to the nerve center of an organization, ministry, or relationship until it is brought under their control and authority.

Scriptural reference for the spirit of Absalom
2 Samuel 13:1–19:8

Signs, symptoms, and manifestations of the spirit of Absalom		
Betrayal	Conspiracy	Cunning craftiness
Deception	Defiance	Diabolical alliance
Disrespect	Divided allegiance	Haughtiness
Hostility	Hypocrisy	Irreverence
Jealousy	Lust	Lying
Murder	Perversion	Plotting the demise of power, influence, and respect
Power struggle	Pretense	Pride
Rebellion	Sedition	Seduction
Self-exaltation	Self-righteousness	Treachery
Treason	Undermining ministry and influence	Usurping authority
Vanity		

Release

The spirit of submission, integrity, purpose, timing of the Lord, the heart of a servant, integrity, humility, apostolic anointing, wisdom, peace, truth, and prophetic intercession.

SPIRIT OF ADDICTION

An addiction is a complex illness with physical and psychological symptoms and wide-scale social ramifications. It affects not only the person but also his family, friends, and social environment. The person afflicted by this spirit lacks control over his activities and behaviors, and instead the activities and behaviors have taken control over him. In essence, an addiction is any progressive abuse of something that is difficult or impossible to control. In our natural world, the way to recovery is long and painful, and there is always the danger of relapsing. However, with God all things are possible.

Addictions can be categorized by the following:

1. Substance: alcohol, heroin, tobacco, solvents, cocaine, cannabis, caffeine, methadone, benzodiazepines, hallucinogens, amphetamines, ecstasy, painkillers, barbiturates, and steroids
2. Social: exercise, sex, sexual perversion, pornography, eating (anorexia, bulimia, overeating, binge eating, emotional eating), techno (computer games, cyber sex, Internet), work, gambling, and oniomania (an abnormal impulse for buying things)[1]

Scriptural reference for spirit of addiction

Romans 13:14; 14:23; Galatians 5:24; Philippians 3:19; 1 Timothy 3:3, 8; Titus 1:7; 2:3; 1 Peter 2:11;

Signs, symptoms, and manifestations of the spirit of addiction		
Abuse	Adultery	Afflictions
Alcoholism	Anorexia	Antagonism
Antichrist activities	Anxiety	Betrayal

Bondages	Bulimia	Carnality
Codependency	Compromise	Compulsive activities
Compulsive spending	Contaminated anointing	Crime
Crookedness	Cyber sex	Death
Deceit	Deception	Defiance
Denial	Dependency	Depression
Destruction	Dishonesty	Dishonor
Disillusion	Dreams	Drug abuse
Dysfunctions	Eating disorders	Emotional disturbance
Fear	Filthy lucre	Gambling
Greed	Gross darkness	Habits
Hallucination	Hatred	Homosexuality
Hypersensitivity	Idolatry	Independent spirit
Iniquity	Inordinate affections	Kleptomania
Lack of control	Lusts	Lying
Manipulation	Masochism	Masturbation
Mental breakdowns	Misrepresentation	Money laundering
Murder/abortion	Neurosis	Nightmares
Obsessions	Obsessive-compulsive disorder	Obstinacy
Oniomania	Oppression	Overeating
Pedophilia	Perversion	Pornography
Pride	Prostitution	Psychological bondage
Psychosis	Psychotic behavior	Railing
Riotous living	Role reversal	Sadomasochism
Secretism	Secularism	Seduction
Self-centeredness	Selfishness	Self-loathing
Shame	Sin	Slavery
Snares	Social/relational violations	Spiritual darkness
Stealing	Stubbornness	Suicide
Suspicion	Temptation	Terror
Traditional entrenchment	Uncleanness	Victimization
Violence	Vitiation of will	Voyeurism
Withdrawal	Worldliness	

Release

Salvation, healing balm of Gilead, purpose, timing of the Lord, the heart of a servant, integrity, apostolic anointing, peace, truth, fruit of the Spirit, fear of the Lord, discipline, and honesty

SPIRIT OF AFFINITY

This spirit falls into five categories: soul ties, familiar spirits, spirits of inheritance/generational curses, carnality, and unholy alliances. Although each of the aforementioned play an integral role with this strongman and form a very solid bond, we will deal with the strongman of carnality as a separate heading and soul ties, familiar spirits, inheritance/generational curse, and unholy alliances under this heading.

1. Soul ties

Soul ties have the power to attract, unite, and create forces of connectedness (covenants) between two entities or individuals for the purpose of the reinforcement of divine or diabolical intents. Concerning diabolical intents and purposes, the ultimate aim is to distract and derail an individual, thus destroying his chances of fulfilling purpose, maximizing his potential, and reaching his destiny. This spirit robs entities of their innocence, purity, sincerity, and focus, and often acts as a doorkeeper for other spirits. First Kings 11:1–13 records how Solomon had soul ties with many women. This led to the downfall of his kingdom.

But not every soul tie is diabolical, such as marriage; friendship; family; ecclesiastical; and covering, mentorship, or leadership soul ties. However, the enemy can use these God-given relationships and twist and pervert them in order to fulfill his plans and purposes. These satanic soul ties can happen through certain kinds of relationships, sexual partners, demonic influences, and organizations such as lodges, certain religions, or cults.

2. Familiar spirits

As we discussed in chapter 5, "Knowing Your Enemy," familiar spirits are demonic agents whose main assignment is to become well acquainted with a person or groups of people. They are designed to kill, steal, and destroy geographical areas, cultures, and individuals. Every city, country, family, person, and any living entity has entry points—gates and doors—that we discussed in chapter 5. To accomplish their goals, familiar spirits have the ability to use animals, talisman (any object or piece of clothing that witches and warlocks and other workers of the craft use to transfer spells and hexes), and people whose lives are characterized by demonic/satanic alliances.

These spirits are particularly effective in séances. Using deception, they attempt to hold people captive in the darkness of their underworld activities. Leviticus 19:31 clearly warns us against establishing any kind of communication with familiar spirits.

3. Spirits of inheritance and generational curses

Exodus 20:5 makes us aware of intergenerational spirits that are responsible for producing family and community peculiarities, ancestral eccentricities, idiosyncratic issues, ethnic traits, social tendencies, clannish oddities, pathological conditions of the mind and body, individualities, fundamental values, cultures, passions, motives, intentions, agendas, habits, ideologies, perceptions, temperaments, personalities, illnesses, degenerative diseases, and congenital diseases.

4. Unholy alliances: diabolical confederations and associations

These principalities and spirits identify and mobilize other principalities and spirits to form confederations. They may be configured as legions, as with the Gadarene in Mark 5:1–20, or use entire communities, nations, or individuals in order to accomplish their heinous mandates and insidious assignments such as the mob in Acts 16:12–24. Unholy alliances unite spirit to spirit, spirit to soul, spirit to body, body to body, or soul to body. This kind of satanic activity can either influence from without or take on the form of total possession when the identity, personality, and the will of a spirit being is superimposed upon the identity, personality, and will of the host. They affect humanity spiritually—mind, will, destiny, purpose, gifts, ability, conviction, belief system, value, culture, or ethics; psychologically—emotions, personality, temperament, unconscious behavior and activity, or perception; and neurologically—the nervous and limbic system.

Unholy alliances produce strongholds, vain imaginations, high things, ungodly ambitions, corrupt desires, bondages, habits, satanic soul ties, ungodly attachments and entanglements, affinities, besetting sin, snares, stumbling blocks, yokes, ungodly covenants, and a variety of intrinsic and extrinsic weapons.

Scriptural reference for the spirit of affinity

1. Soul ties: Numbers 33:55; 2 Samuel 13:1–22; 1 Kings 11:1–13; 12:6–21; 2 Kings 18:1–5; 1 Chronicles 11:1–25; Mark 5:1–10; Luke 11:52–12:3; 1 Corinthians 6:13–18; Ephesians 4:16
2. Familiar spirits: Leviticus 19:31; 20:6, 27; Deuteronomy 18:9–14; 2 Kings 21:6; 23:24; 1 Chronicles 10:13–14; 2 Chronicles 33:6; Isaiah 8:19; Matthew 9:32; 12:43–45; 15:22; 17:15–18; Mark 5:1–20; 9:17–26; Acts 16:16–18; 19:15–16
3. Spirits of inheritance and generational curses: Exodus 20:5
4. Unholy alliances: 1 Kings 11:1–5; Daniel 5:18–21; 6:1–10; 11:29–33; Nehemiah 2:17–19; 4:1–3; Psalm 83:1–8; Ezekiel 28:1–19; Matthew 28:12–15; Mark 5:1–20; Luke 9:50–56; Acts 7:54–60; 8:8–25; 16:12–24; 1 Corinthians 6:15–16; Ephesians 6:12; Revelation 16:13–14

Signs, symptoms, and manifestations of the spirit of affinity		
Accusations	Addictions	Affinities
Afflictions	Ailments	Alliances
Alterations	Assaults	Associations
Attachments (talisman, books, clothing, furniture, jewelry)	Attractions	Bands
Besetting sin	Bondages	Burdens
Calcification of the heart	Character assassinations	Concentrations/ focus
Conclusions	Confusion	Connections
Contaminations	Contentions	Covenants
Deceptions	Decisions	Defects
Denial	Depression	Deprivation
Desolation	Diabolical proclivities and appetites	Disabilities
Discouragements	Diseases	Disillusions
Disorders	Distortions	Divination
Divisions	Dreams	Dysfunctions

Enmeshments	Entanglements	Family secrets
Fantasies	Frustrations	Glass ceilings
Habits	Harassments	Hidden agendas
High things	Illusions	Impressions
Impure motives	Infections	Infirmities
Inhibitions	Inordinate affections	Insinuations
Insomnia	Insults	Interceptions
Interference	Irritations	Justifications
Knowledge blocks	Lusts	Manipulations
Misfortunes	Mishaps	Misinformation
Misrepresentations	Misunderstandings	Negotiations
Neurosis	Neurotic and psychotic behaviors and tendencies	Nightmares
Oppression	Persecutions	Perversions
Perversions of thoughts	Perverted imaginations	Prohibitions
Projections	Provocations	Psychosis
Questionable motives	Rationalizations	Relations
Repression of memories	Resistance	Resolutions
Rulings	Satanic barriers	Satanic operations
Seduction	Slanders	Snares
Speculations	Stigmas	Stirrings
Strange occurrences	Strongholds	Stumbling blocks
Subversions	Suppression of emotions	Suspicions
Temptations	Unethical behavior	Unexplainable accidents
Ungodly ambitions	Unholy desires	Vexations
Victimization	Vitiation of will	Weights
Yokes		

Release

Pursue an intimate personal relationship with the Lord (Ps. 42:1); use the declarations in the "Prayers of Activation Into Warfare" in chapter 3.

SPIRIT OF AFFLICTION

Afflictions are the pathological conditions of the body, soul, or spirit. This word comes from the Hebrew word *ra*, which literally translated means "to break into pieces or to devour." It connotes a spirit that is assigned to cause distress, disease, and to ultimately destroy. The spirit of affliction works with all major maladies and calamities. Psalm 34:19 states, "Many are the afflictions of the righteous: but the LORD delivereth him out of them all."

Scriptural reference for the spirit of affliction
Psalm 34:19

Signs, symptoms, manifestations of the spirit of affliction		
Abnormal growths on or in the body	Abuse	Aches/pains
Alienation	Anger	Arguments
Biological disorders	Bitterness	Bleeding
Competition	Debt	Depression
Deprivation	Discouragement	Disease
Disillusionment	Divorce	Emotional instability
Excessive self-analysis	Family secrets	Fatigue
Fear	Feasting/fasting syndrome	Filthy thoughts
Gambling addiction	Guilt	Guilt trips
Harassment	Incest	Inefficient recall
Infections	Insomnia	Isolation
Itching	Lack	Loneliness
Mental illness	Night terrors	Nightmares
Oppression	Phobias	Polarized emotions
Poor memory	Possession	Poverty
Prejudice	Rejection	Repression
Revenge	Shame	Suppression
Unclean fantasies	Unforgiveness	Worry
Yo-yo dieting		

Release

Healing to the mind, body, soul, and spirit; finances, prosperity, and success; alignment to biblical principles and dietary laws; miracles, signs and wonders, wisdom, budgeting, inspiration, counsel, might, patience, the will of God, hope, faith, and salvation; and forgiveness from God for sin, backsliding, misuse of tongue, resentment, pride, impenitence, mistreatment of others, hardness of the heart, idolatry, and hypocrisy

SPIRIT OF AHAB (CODEPENDENCY)

This spirit works in conjunction with the spirit of Jezebel. The individual operating under the influence of the spirit of Ahab complies with wishes, commands, and directives given by those influenced or possessed by the Jezebel spirit, even when it goes against their own personal will and conviction. This spirit undermines a person's rights and authority and totally opens them to be disrespected and to have their boundaries violated, be they territorial, personal, or psychological. This spirit is a doorkeeper, and its discretion opens doors to other principalities and strongholds.

Codependency is also a common trait of the spirit of Ahab. Codependency is when a person is so preoccupied with rescuing and helping others that they let the other person's behavior affect them. They are obsessed with controlling that person's behavior, emotions, perceptions, lifestyle, and actions by attempting to maintain balance in a highly stressful, highly addictive atmosphere. Some assume the role of hero, scapegoat, or comedian. They gain relief by diverting attention from the real problem and not attracting attention to self. Individuals caught up in this syndrome usually project themselves as "the perfect child," the "surrogate parent/ spouse," and the like. They are also clingy and smothering. When codependent children grow up, they continue to play roles until sometimes it becomes destructive.

Scriptural reference for the spirit of Ahab

1 Kings 16:33; 18:17–18

Signs, symptoms, and manifestations of the spirit of Ahab		
Alienation	Blind obedience	Compromise
Confusion	Cowardice	Demonic slavery
Dependent personality	Depression	Discouragement
Disillusionment	Excessive self-analysis	Fear of authority figures
Fear of rejection	Fear of retaliation	Guilt trips
Idolatry	Immorality upon request/force/coercion	Inefficient recall
Inertia	Insecurity	Insomnia
Intimidation	Lack of self-expression	Lost little boy/girl syndrome
Martyr syndrome	Not feeling well	Oppression
Physical weariness/fatigue	Poor me/why me?	Poor memory
Psychic manipulation	Rejection syndrome	Religious martyr
Repression	Self-blame	Suicidal tendency
Suppression	Worry/anxiety	

Release

Peace, self-control, righteousness, love, boldness, sound mind, call on Jehovah-Adonai, purpose, hope, maturity, liberty, independence, potential, and leadership

SPIRIT OF AMNON

The spirit of Amnon, through lust and the employment of devious strategies, perpetuates incest within a family line. This powerful spirit can lie dormant and go undiscovered for years. It acts as a doorkeeper to spirits of affinity, perversion, and a host of other spirits that undermine the sanctity of the family, marriage, and the home. Incest is sexual activity between nuclear and extended family members: parents with children, sexual relations between siblings, cousins, uncles, aunts, step-parents, and grandparents. The spirit of Amnon is an insidious spirit that establishes a strong confederation with the appetites of the soul, and it will stop at nothing until its lustful desires are satisfied. It does not allow the host to be constrained by convictions or internal mechanisms of right and wrong, and it will often lead its host to justify or rationalize its actions.

Scriptural reference for the spirit of Amnon
  2 Samuel 13:1–22

Signs, symptoms, and manifestation of the spirit of Amnon		
Abuse	Affinity	Alienation
Anxiety	Assault	Carnality
Coercion	Condemnation	Death
Deception	Denial	Depression
Dishonor	Disrespect	Family secrets
Fear	Guilt	Hatred
Inappropriate touching	Intimidation	Low perception of self
Lust	Manipulation	Obsession
Pedophilia	Perversion	Plotting
Rape	Seduction	Sexual addictions
Shame	Torment	Violence

Release
  Protection, purpose, forgiveness, conviction of the Holy Spirit, holiness, righteousness, love, the will of God, God- and Christ-centeredness, deliverance, and peace

SPIRIT OF ANANIAS AND SAPPHIRA (FRAUD)

This spirit lurks in the church, always ready to pounce upon the believer, especially during times of giving. Its ultimate purpose is total eradication and annihilation of individuals assigned to perpetuate the life of the church or ministry. It hides out in the anointing and disguises itself as a "willing" giver. Motivation and opportunity are the elements that generally underlie the commission of fraud. These could take the form of economic need or gain, greed, prestige or recognition (person feels that they are shrewd enough to confound and confuse others and can commit fraud and corruption without being discovered or detected), and moral superiority (person may feel that they are morally superior to those of the victim, organization, or the ministry).

It is also important to understand that very often the perpetrator of fraud rationalizes his actions. For instance an employee accused of fraud is likely to rationalize his action by saying or believing that his low pay justifies the action or that since everybody is doing it, he is also well within his right to do it.

Scriptural reference for the spirit of Ananias and Sapphira
1 Samuel 2:13–17; Acts 5:1–10

Signs, symptoms, and manifestations of the spirit of Ananias and Sapphira		
Abuse of privileges	Abuse/misuse	Abuse/misuse of organization/business property and assets
Betrayal	Breach of confidence	Bribery
Camouflage	Concealment	Conflict of interest
Corruption	Cunning craftiness	Deception
Dishonesty	Disrespect of the anointing	Disrespect of the prophetic
Embezzlement	Failure to pay tithes	Failure to pay vows
False claims	False statements	Falsification or alteration of records or documents
Favoritism	Financial fraud	Greed
Hoarding	Hypocrisy	Identity theft
Illegal financial advantages	Inducement	Insider trading
Insurance fraud	Intentional deception	Internet fraud
Lack of accountability	Loss	Lying
Manipulation	Medical fraud	Misapplication of accounting policies
Misappropriation/ misapplication of assets	Misleading actions	Misrepresentation of truth

Signs, symptoms, and manifestations of the spirit of Ananias and Sapphira		
Nepotism	Passive-aggressive behavior	Purchase for personal use
Recording of transaction without substances	Rigging	Selfishness
Stinginess	Suppression or omission of the effects of transactions from records	Surprise
Unbelief	Unfair practices	Withholding

Release

The spirit of truth, giving anointing, wisdom, loyalty, obedience, fear of God, and covenant

SPIRIT OF THE ANTICHRIST

When we speak of the spirit of the antichrist, we are speaking of this spirit operating on two dimensions: one in which the apostle Paul speaks of as the prevailing and pervasive mind-set that is dominated by a principality; and the other, the actual embodiment of Satan himself. This spirit opposes God and anything or anyone that is godly.

Scriptural reference for the spirit of the antichrist

2 Thessalonians 2:4; 1 John 2:9, 18; 4:3

Signs, symptoms, and manifestations of the spirit of the antichrist		
"Cold love"	Satanic "miracles"	Alienation
Antagonism	Astrology	Blasphemy
Carnality	Church splits	Communism
Competition	Contaminated anointing	Counterfeit anointing
Criticism	Death	Deception
Defiance	Desertion	Division
Doctrines of devils	False religion	Hate

Signs, symptoms, and manifestations of the spirit of the antichrist		
Humanism	Hypocrisy	Idolatry
Intimidation	Intolerance	Lies
Love of money	Lust	Lying wonders
Mammon	Masquerading as God or one of His ministers	Mental bondage
Murder	New Age	Occultism
Opposition to the power of God	Oppression	Oppression of believers
Persecution of the righteous	Perversion	Pride
Psychics	Rebellion	Religiosity
Religious spirit	Sabotage	Spirit of Babylon
Spirit of Jezebel	Subversion	Traditions
Unrighteousness	Witchcraft	Works of the flesh

Release

Prophetic and apostolic anointing, spirit of liberty, truth, holiness, and discerning of spirits

SPIRIT OF APATHY

This spirit causes a lack of interest or concern, especially concerning matters of importance. It also causes dullness of the spirit, blindness of the heart, and leanness of the soul. Apathy is responsible for the abortion of purpose and the undermining of potential.

Scriptural reference for the spirit of apathy

Psalm 137:1–4; Revelation 3:14–19

Signs, symptoms, and manifestations of the spirit of apathy		
Carnality	Depression	Detachment
Disillusionment	Disinterest	Disregard
Doubt	Gloom and doom	Grief

Signs, symptoms, and manifestations of the spirit of apathy		
Hopelessness	Inattentiveness	Indifference
Insensibility	Irrational thoughts	Irresponsibility
Lack of commitment	Lack of concern	Laodicean spirit
Lethargy	Listlessness	Lust
Neurotic behavior	Nonparticipation	Unsupportive
Nothing to die for	Nothing to live for	Oppression
Persecution complex	Restlessness	Sadness
Sleepiness	Slothfulness	Stubbornness
Unconcern	Unresponsiveness	Victimization
Visionless		

Release
Expedience, urgency, joy, and a sense of significance, meaning, and purpose

Spirit of Babylon

Babylon is an actual place that exists in the dimension of the spirit world. Babylon is a system of control. It has its own cosmological system, which is the exact antithesis of the kingdom of God. It has its own political system, legislative bodies, and governments, just like any other physical, natural kingdom, nation, or country. Its principles, policies, and religious practices are promoted by the doctrines of man and devils and permeate throughout the twelve systems of the universe. It is assigned to hinder, frustrate, and sabotage the fulfillment of purpose, undermine destinies, and imprison the souls of man. The spirits of behemoth, leviathan, mammon, Egypt, Pharaoh, and Herod function with the spirit of Babylon, forming a strong confederation within many nations and countries and controlling their destinies as well as the destinies of their citizenship.

Scriptural reference for the spirit of Babylon
Jeremiah 42:1–12; 51:1; Luke 22:1–5; Revelation 16:8–17:18; 18:1–12

Signs, symptoms, and manifestations of the spirit of Babylon
See "Spirits of Egypt, Pharaoh, and Herod."

SPIRITS OF BEHEMOTH AND LEVIATHAN

The Book of Job graphically depicts the spiritual powers and strength of these principalities as unconquerable by human ingenuity. I caution readers to ensure that they are fighting within their measure of rule and fighting under divine covering. Do not go head-to-head with this principality. Allow spiritual *generals* to initiate and orchestrate prayer and spiritual warfare activities concerning these spirits. Remember to pray under divine covering!

Behemoth has a dinosaur or a large, monstrous spirit. It is an oppressive, powerful, hippopotamus-like creature, known for its supernatural strength. It affects ideologies, political/military strength, and religious/cultural strongholds; involves witchcraft (control); may take years to dismantle/destroy (communication); and becomes violent when attacked. Leviathan, on the other hand, is a crocodile-like sea serpent. It is symbolic of Satan (Rev. 12) and is unconquerable by human strength or carnal weapons

We must implore Jehovah-Gibbor to divinely cause their sinews to be ripped and their bones to be crushed.

Scriptural reference for the spirit of behemoth and leviathan
Job 40:15–24; Job 41:1–34; Psalm 74:14; Psalm 104:26; Isaiah 27:1

Signs, symptoms, and manifestations for the spirit of behemoth and leviathan
See "Spirit of Oppression" and "Spirits of Egypt, Pharaoh, and Herod."

SPIRIT OF MAMMON

Mammon is the financial and economic system and currency of Babylon. It has a personality and can be made a friend or foe, a master or a slave. The word *mammon* is Chaldean in origin and is translated in English as "wealth." In the Old Testament, we are told that the wealth (mammon) of the wicked is laid up for the righteous. However, we must be very careful to remember that our priorities must be in order as we approach this particular spirit. In pursuing mammon, we must first be sold out to God. Matthew 6:24 states, "No man can serve two masters: for either he will hate the one, and love the other; or else he will hold to the one, and despise the other. Ye cannot serve God and mammon." Secondly we must make the pursuit of His kingdom our priority.

Scriptural reference for the spirit of mammon
Matthew 6:33; Luke 16:9, 11

Signs, symptoms, and manifestations for the spirit of mammon
See "Spirit of Oppression" and "Spirits of Egypt, Pharaoh, and Herod."

SPIRIT OF BALAAM

The spirit of Balaam is a spirit that causes an individual to compromise his convictions, forfeit ministry, disobey divine directives, and sell his soul for money.

Scriptural reference for the spirit of Balaam
James 1:13–16; 2 Peter 2; Jude 1–19; Revelation 2:14

Signs, symptoms, and manifestations of the spirit of Balaam		
Betrayal	Carnality	Compromise
Contaminated anointing	Filthy lucre	Fraud
Greed	Iniquity	Lust
Misrepresentation	Perversion	Self-centeredness
Selfishness	Sin	Temptation
Worldliness		

Release
Purity of heart, consecrated life, integrity, honesty

SPIRIT OF BELIAL

This outlaw spirit works in confederation with the spirit of Jezebel. It is a spirit assigned to destroy influence, sabotage ministries, undermine authority, and pilfer property. I call this spirit the spiritual mob because of its gangsterlike characteristics.

Scriptural reference for the spirit of Belial
Deuteronomy 13:13; Judges 19:22–23; 1 Samuel 1:16; 2:12; 10:27; 25:17; 30:22; 1 Kings 21:10–13

Signs, symptoms, and manifestations of the spirit of Belial		
Carnality	Character assassination	Deception
False accusation	Falsehood	Gossip
Harassment	Insubordination	Lust
Lying	Maligning character	Murder
Perversion	Pilfering	Rebellion
Riotous living	Sabotage	Selfishness
Sensuality	Slander	Treachery
Unrighteousness	Violence	Witchcraft
Works of darkness		

Release
The spirit of Jehu, the fear of the Lord, and boldness

SPIRIT OF CARNALITY

The word *carnality* comes from the Greek word *sarkikos*, which, when translated into English, connotes "rotten" flesh. Antispiritual in nature, this spirit appeals to the appetite of the soul. Isaiah 29:8 gives us greater insight, "It shall even be as when an hungry man dreameth, and, behold, he eateth; but he awaketh, and his soul is empty: or as when a thirsty man dreameth, and, behold, he drinketh; but he awaketh, and, behold, he is faint, and his soul hath appetite." Lusts are evil desires that readily express themselves in bodily activities. They are the "natural" tendency of the flesh and the soulish capacity and proclivity to gravitate toward things that are evil. Some lusts may characteristically be "refined," as in the pride of life, but they are still lusts. Desire in and of itself is not to be feared. God promises us the desires of our hearts in Psalm 37:4. Lust, however, is perverted desire that leads to sin. When lust prevails in our lives, we may get what we want, but we will lose what we have.

Scriptural reference for the spirit of carnality
Numbers 11:4–5, 31–33; Matthew 5:28; Romans 1:27; 6:12; 7:7, 24; 8:5–8; 13:14; 1 Corinthians 10:6–10; 12:7–10; Galatians 5:16–17, 19–21, 22–23; Ephesians 4:29; 5:5; Colossians 2:18; James 1:13–16; 4:1–6; 1 John 2:16

Signs, symptoms, and manifestations of carnality

Abandonment	Abusive/blasphemous language	Addictions (of all kinds)
Adultery	Alcoholism	Anarchy
Anger	Animosity	Arrogance
Bitterness	Brawling	Clamor
Comparing	Complaining	Compromises
Covetousness	Cruelty	Death
Deception	Discontentment	Dissatisfaction
Dissatisfaction with God's provisions	Doubt	Drunkenness
Effeminacy	Emulations	Envy
Error	Evil thoughts and desires	Extortion
False witness	Fault finding	Faulty perspectives
Fighting	Filthy language	Flamboyance
Formalism	Fornication	Gambling
Gluttony	Grandiosity	Greed
Grumbling	Hatred	Heresies
Historical/cultural/ generational pride	Hoarding	Idolatry
Ill will	Immorality	Ingratitude
Iniquities of the heart	Inordinate sophistication	Judgmentalism
Killing	Kleptomania	Lasciviousness
Lusts (of all kinds)	Lying	Malice
Murders	Narcissism	Perversion
Plagues/diseases	Presumptuous living	Pride
Pride of possession	Quarreling	Rage
Railing	Rebellion	Religiosity
Resentment	Reviling	Seditions
Seduction (enticing)	Selfishness	Sexual sins
Slander	Spite	Stealing
Strife	Stubbornness	Superiority
Temptations	Uncleanness	Ungratefulness
Unrighteousness	Vain glory	Variance
Witchcraft	Worldliness	Wrath

Release

Deliverance, holiness, fruit of the Spirit, and manifestations of the Spirit

SPIRIT OF COMPETITION

This spirit creates rivalry between entities that compete for the same prize or profit. This spirit is slick and covertly fulfills its mission. Competition is a door-keeping spirit. It opens doors to other stronger and more deadly spirits.

Scriptural reference for the spirit of competition

Ezra 4:19; John 9:16; 10:19

Signs, symptoms, and manifestations of the spirit of competition		
Accusations	Alienation	Antagonism
Broken relationships	Contempt	Contention
Deceit	Defiance	Detachment
Discord	Disharmony	Divorce
Emulation	Game playing	Gossip
Heresy	Hypocrisy	Ill will
Isolation	Jealousy	Opposition
Rebellion	Resentment	Retaliation
Rivalry	Sedition	Slander
Spite	Stigmatization	Strife
Territorialism	Underhandedness	Unfair practices
Withholding	Wrath	

Release

Fellowship, unity, love, forgiveness, harmony, compliance, obedience, and discernment

THE SPIRIT OF CONFUSION

The spirit of confusion causes disorder and disarray in the life and relationships of many people. It also causes an individual to live in a stunned and cluttered condition, confusing the mind, bewildering the emotions, and distressing relationships. This spirit works with the spirit of madness.

Scriptural reference for the spirit of confusion
1 Corinthians 14:33; James 3:16

Signs, symptoms, and manifestations of the spirit of confusion		
Aimlessness	Argumentativeness	Attitudes
Awkwardness	Bafflement	Bedlam
Befuddlement	Bewilderment	Clutter
Covetousness	Defensiveness	Disarray
Discomfiture	Discomposure	Disorder
Disorganization	Distraction	Double-mindedness
Embarrassment	Emotional disturbance	Envy
Feelings of discontentment and resentment	Fluster	Fretting
Furor	Humiliation	Hypnotic (stupor) state
Lack of direction	Lack of discernment/ perception	Lack of goals
Lack of purpose	Loss of memory	Loss of mental faculty
Nervousness	Pandemonium	Perplexity
Perturbation	Preoccupation	Self-conscious distress
Shame	Spite	Strife
Trancelike states	Tumult	Turmoil
Uproar	Upsets	

Release
The mind of Christ; God's original plan and purpose; and peace, love, and soundness of mind and order

SPIRIT OF DEAF AND DUMB

Although this spirit is seen through many countries and communities, it is often assigned to children and spouses of leadership. It acts as both a door and gatekeeper for other spirits and distracts the man or woman of God from fulfilling their assignment. The deaf and dumb spirit is known to target children, attaching itself to a baby while yet in the womb.

Scriptural reference for the spirit of deaf and dumb
Mark 9:25

Signs, symptoms, and manifestations of the spirit of deaf and dumb		
Addictions	Attention deficit disorders	Childish self-will
Convulsions	Daydreaming	Deafness (natural/spiritual)
Depression	Drug and alcohol abuse	Extreme immaturity
Inability to speak	Mental/psychological disorders	Physiological/emotional dysfunctions
Repression	Seizures	Sleepiness (especially while reading or hearing the Word of God)
Speech impediments	Suicidal thoughts	Sudden/involuntary body movements or sounds
Tremors		

Release
Deliverance, liberty, life, divine health, and healing

SPIRIT OF DEATH

This spirit is assigned to terminate and cause entities to become extinct. There are many kinds of death an entity can experience: physical, emotional, spiritual, relational (divorce), social (loss of influence or reputation, life-imprisonment), and financial (failure to perceive opportunities or the misappropriation of funds).

Scriptural reference for the spirit of death
Psalm 18:5; 55:15; 86:13; 116:3; Hosea 13:14; Romans 6:23

Signs, symptoms, and manifestations of the spirit of death		
Abortion	Accidents	Betrayal
Character assassination	Depression	Deprivation
Despondency	Discouragement	Disease
Disillusionment	Divorce	Emotional wounds
Fratricide	Gossip	Grief
Homicide	Homosexuality	Hopelessness
Ill-spoken words	Imprisonment	Indifference
Isolation	Jealousy	Loss
Loss of hope	Loss of vision	Lost opportunities
Maligning of character	Miscarriage	Morbidity
Murder	Oppression	Railing
Slander	Sorrow	Spiritual blindness
Stigmatization	Suicide	Terminal illnesses
Unbelief	Untimely death	Wages of sin
Gang rape	Drive-by shooting	Reprobation

Release
Divine healing, health, life, and reversal of the death cycle

SPIRIT OF DEPRESSION

Depression is a mental disease that plagues every society. Psychologically speaking, depression is a psychotic or neurotic condition characterized by inability, feelings of heaviness and melancholy, extreme sadness, hopelessness, and often insomnia.

Scriptural reference for the spirit of depression
Isaiah 61:3

Signs, symptoms, and manifestations of the spirit of depression		
Anxiety	Chronic fatigue	Confusion
Crying spells	Darkness of mind	Dejection

Signs, symptoms, and manifestations of the spirit of depression		
Dependent personality (need assistance to achieve "normal" things)	Despair	Desperation
Despondency	Distractions	Excessive sleeping
Feelings of alienation	Feelings of loneliness	Frustration
Gloominess	Homicidal tendency	Hopelessness
Increase in appetite	Insomnia	Irregular sleeping patterns/habits
Lack of focus	Listlessness	Loss of appetite
Loss of energy	Loss of focus	Melancholy
Memory loss	Need for assistance	Need for approval
Nonchalant attitude	Preoccupations	Sadness
Sleepiness	Staring into space	Strong external locus of control
Suicidal tendency	Unhappiness	

Release

The anointing, peace, the mind of Christ, and joy

SPIRIT OF DESOLATION

This spirit causes loss, abandonment, a state of anguish, and deprivation. Desolation can be manifested as a natural phenomenon, an emotional, physical, social, or psychological condition. This spirit causes loss, abandonment, a state of anguish, deprival, barrenness, and the lack of prosperity.

Scriptural reference for the spirit of desolation

Jeremiah 44:22; Matthew 12:25

Signs, symptoms, and manifestations of the spirit of desolation		
Accusation	Depression	Greed
Hardship	Hopelessness	Idolatry
Immorality	Jealousy	Morbidity

Signs, symptoms, and manifestations of the spirit of desolation		
Murder	Oppression	Pharisee/Sadducee spirit
Poverty	Religion	Sedition
Spiritual bondage	Spiritual darkness	Spiritual dryness
Subversion	Suspicion	Unrighteous mammon
Unrighteousness	Vexation	

Release

Meekness, moderation, purity of heart, a spirit of vengeance, holiness, and true and pure worship

SPIRIT OF DIVINATION

This spirit is often one of the spirits responsible for blatant anarchy of the pew and rebellion of parishioners. The spirit of rebellion is the foundation upon which Satan and the kingdom of darkness is built. The divination principality often attempts to counterfeit the work of the Holy Spirit. Rebellion is to divination as the anointing is to the Holy Spirit.

Scriptural reference for the spirit of divination

Deuteronomy 18:10–12; Acts 16:16

Signs, symptoms, and manifestations of the spirit of divination		
Anarchy fear	Accusations	Addictions
Afflictions	Ailments	Alcoholism
Alliances	Alterations	Antagonism
Assaults	Associations	Astral projection
Astrology	Attachments (talisman, books, clothing, furniture, jewelry, etc.)	Attractions
Automatic writings	Bands	Black magic
Blasphemy	Burdens	Character assassinations
Charms	Coercion	Concentrations
Conclusions	Confusion	Conjuration

Signs, symptoms, and manifestations of the spirit of divination		
Connections	Contaminations	Contentions
Control	Controlling spirit	Cultic activities/rituals
Deceptions	Decisions	Defects
Demonic activities	Denial	Depression
Deprivation	Desolation	Disabilities
Discouragements	Diseases	Disillusions
Disorders	Distortions	Divination
Diviners	Divisions	Dreamers
Dreams	Drugs	Dysfunctions
Enchanters	Entanglements	False prophets
Familiar spirits	Fantasies	Fortune telling
Frustrations	Harassments	Hexes
Horoscope	Hypnosis	Idolatry
Ill-spoken	Illuminati	Illumination
Illusions	Impressions	Impure motives
Incantations	Infections	Infirmities
Inhibitions	Inordinate affections	Insinuations
Insults	Interceptions	Interference
Irritations	Justifications	Manipulations
Masonry	Mind control	Misfortunes
Mishaps	Misinformation	Misrepresentations
Misunderstandings	Murder	Necromancy
Negotiations	Neurotic and psychotic behaviors and tendencies	Obeah
Occult	Omens	Oppression
Ouija board	Palm reading	Persecutions
Perversions	Prognostication	Prohibitions
Projections	Provocations	Psychic activities
Railing	Rationalizations	Rebellion
Relations	Resistance	Resolutions
Rulings	Satanic operations	Seduction
Slanders	Snares	Sorcery/soothsaying
Speculations	Spirit of Belial	Stigmas

Signs, symptoms, and manifestations of the spirit of divination		
Stirrings	Strange occurrences	Subversions
Suicide	Superstition	Suspicions
Tea leaf readers	Temptations	Unexplainable accidents
Unrighteous mammon	Vexation/grief	Victimization
Violence	Voodoo	Water watchers
White magic	Witchcraft	Wizardry
Words/wishes/malice	Abortion	Untimely death
Financial hardship	Desolation	Spiritual blindness
Jezebel spirit	Spirit of the antichrist	Spiritual stupor

Release

The anointing, the manifestation of the gifts of the Spirit, prophetic anointing, apostolic anointing, anointing of Elijah, anointing of Jehu

SPIRITS OF EGYPT, PHARAOH, AND HEROD

The spirit of Egypt is a spirit that oppresses groupings of people at a national or global level. On the one hand, these spirits utilize the body and souls of man to further their economic and spiritual cause, and on the other hand, they are responsible for abortion and assassination. The greatest atrocity is not becoming a physical prisoner of war, but becoming psychological prisoner of war.

TYPES OF SLAVERY TODAY

- **Bonded labor** affects millions of people around the world. People become bonded laborers by taking or being tricked into taking a loan for as little as the cost of medicine for a sick child. To repay the debt, many are forced to work long hours, seven days a week, up to 365 days a year. They receive basic food and shelter as "payment" for their work, but they may never pay off the loan, which can be passed down for generations.

- **Early and forced marriage** affects women and girls who are married without choice and are forced into lives of servitude often accompanied by physical violence.

- **Forced labor** affects people who are illegally recruited by individuals, governments, or political parties and forced to work—usually under threat of violence or other penalties.

- **Slavery by descent** is where people are either born into a slave class or are from a group that society views as suited to being used as slave labor.

- **Trafficking** involves the transport or trade of people— women, children, and men—from one area to another for the purpose of forcing them into slavery conditions, prostitution, pornography, peddling, etc.

- **Child labor** affects many children around the world who are employed in work that is harmful to their health and welfare, such as sweat shops.

- Other types of slavery include emotional slavery, psychological slavery, institutionalized religion, institutionalized slavery, and oppression.

The individuals controlled by this spirit would have to learn:

- Compassion
- To live as a free person
- Problem-solving skills
- Social skills
- Decision-making skills
- Critical thinking skills
- Values clarification
- How to budget
- Planning and goal setting
- Resource management

Scriptural reference for the spirit of Egypt, Pharaoh, and Herod
Exodus 1:7–22; 3:7; Matthew 2:16

Signs, symptoms, and manifestations of the spirits of Egypt, Pharaoh, and Herod		
Abortion	Abuse	Addictions
Affinities	Afflictions	Ailments
Alcoholism	Alienation	Alienation from the life of God
Alliances	Animalization	Antagonism
Antichrist	Antichrist activities	Anti-Semitism
Apartheid	Apathy	Arrogance
Artificial fabrication of consciousness	Assaults	Associations
Atheism	Attachments	Attractions
Backlash	Backsliding	Bands
Berating	Besetting Sin	Betrayal
Bio-chemical altering techniques (fear, etc.)	Black sheep syndrome	Blasphemy
Blind trust	Bondage	Brutalization
Burdens	Calcification of the heart	Carnality
Castigation	Castration	Catastrophication of situations
Censorship	Chattel slavery	Chemical abuse
Child abuse	Class distinction	Codependency
Coercion	Communism	Comparison
Competition	Confusion	Connections
Conspiracy	Consumerism	Contaminations
Contempt	Contracts	Corruption
Covenants	Criminal activities	Criticism
Crookedness	Crossbreeding	Crucifixion
Cruelty	Cultural entrenchment	Cultural erosion
Cultural hypnotism	Death	Debauchery
Defects	Defiance	Dehumanization
Demasculinization	Denial	Dependence

Signs, symptoms, and manifestations of the spirits of Egypt, Pharaoh, and Herod		
Depression	Deprivation	Desertion
Desolation	Destabilization of the family	Destruction
Destruction of a sense of significance/identity/direction	Devaluation	Deviant behavior
Diabolical proclivities and appetites	Dictatorship	Disabilities
Disapproval	Discouragement	Discrimination
Disdain	Disease	Disempowerment
Disenfranchisement	Disharmony	Disillusionment
Distrust	Disunity	Divide and conquer
Divination	Divisions	Doctrines of devils
Doctrines of man	Dominance	Dread
Drug addiction	Economic hardship	Economic impotence
Economic oppression	Ego gratification	Embarrassment
Emotional conditioning	Emotional deprivation	Emotional slavery
Entanglements	Envy	Eradication of personal/ethnical/national identity
Erosion and eradication of theocracy system and human rights	Erosion of self-image and worth	Error
Escapism	Family pride	Family secrets
Fantasies	Fear	Filthy lucre
Forced labor	Frustration	Genetic manipulation
Genocide	Glass ceilings	Grandiosity
Greed	Grief	Gross darkness
Guile	Habits	Hangings
Harassment	Hard-heartedness	Hardship
Harshness	Hatred	Helplessness
Herodism	High things	Hitlerism
Hopelessness	Humanism	Humiliation
Idolatry	Ignominy	Imaginations
Immaturity	Immorality	Impaired will
Imprisonment	Impure motives	Incarceration

Signs, symptoms, and manifestations of the spirits of Egypt, Pharaoh, and Herod		
Independent female/dependent male	Independent spirit	Indifference
Indifference of the oppressed to their circumstances and plight	Indignation	Infections
Infirmities	Inhuman conditions/treatment	Iniquity
Injustice	Insomnia	Institutionalize racism
Institutionalized homosexuality	Insufficiencies	Insults
Interference	Intergenerational proclivities and propensities	Intergenerational suspicions
Internal unrest	Interrelation issues	Intimidation
Invasions of personal privacy	Irrational thoughts and behaviors	Irresponsibility
Irritations	Jealousy	Judgmentalism
Justification	Knowledge blocks	Labeling
Language disintegration	Learned helplessness	Legalism
Legalization	Longing for belonging	Loss of dignity
Lust (all forms)	Lynching	Maiming
Maladaptive sets of behavior	Male castigation	Male/female role reversal
Malice	Manipulation	Martyrdom of godly leadership
Master-slave relations	Materialism	Memory loss
Mental affliction	Mental/emotional	Mind control
Miseducation	Misfortunes	Mishaps
Mistreatment	Mistrust	Misunderstandings
Money laundering	Murder	Mutilation
National degradation	Neurotic and psychotic behaviors and tendencies	Obstinacy
Oppression	Pantheism	Perplexity
Persecution complex	Perversion	Perversions of thoughts

Signs, symptoms, and manifestations of the spirits of Egypt, Pharaoh, and Herod		
Physical abuse	Political disenfranchisement	Poor nutritional habits
Poor self-perception	Pornography	Post-traumatic stress disorder
Poverty	Prejudice	Premature death
Pride	Prohibitions	Prostitution
Provocation	Psychic confusion	Psychological bondage
Psychological conditioning	Psychological games	Psychological rape
Racial cleansing	Racial profiling	Railing
Racial Profiling	Marginalization	
Rape	Rationalization	Rebellion
Rejection	Religious spirit	Repressed anger
Repression	Repression of memories	Repudiation
Resentment	Resistance	Resolutions
Ridicule	Rulings	Sabotage
Sanctions	Satanic barriers	Scorn
Secularism	Sedition	Seduction
Segregation	Self-confidence	Self-hatred
Selfishness	Sexual abuse	Sexual dysfunction
Sexual harassment	Sexual slavery	Shame
Sickness	Sin	Single parenting
Slander	Slave trade	Slavery (all forms)
Snares	Social conditioning	Social outcasts
Social rape	Social/emotional/ psychological/temporal/ spiritual/economical afflictions	Soul ties
Spiritual abortions	Spiritual abuse	Spiritual adultery
Spiritual barrenness	Spiritual bondage	Spiritual darkness
Spiritual erosion	Spiritual miscarriages	Stigmatization
Strongholds	Stubbornness	Stumbling blocks
Subliminal conditioning	Suicide	Suppression
Suppression of emotions	Suppression of expression	Suppression of genetic potential

Signs, symptoms, and manifestations of the spirits of Egypt, Pharaoh, and Herod		
Suppression of will	Surrogate parenting	Surveillance
Survival skills	Suspicion	Systemic lies
Terror	Threats	Torment
Traditional entrenchment	Traditions of man	Treachery
Tyrannical governance/control	Underemployment	Undermining of rights
Unethical behavior	Unfair practices	Ungodly ambitions
Unholy desires	Unrighteous mammon	Vexation
Victimization	Violence	Vitiation of will
Wars	Weights	White-collar crime
Whoredom	Willie lynchism	Witchcraft
Worldliness	Wrath	Yoke

Release

The hand of God, divine visitations, God's mercy, the arrows of God, righteousness to be exalted, national revival, soul-winning, the spirit of Elijah, the spirit of truth, the fear of Jehovah, salvation and deliverance, prophetic and apostolic anointing, the spirit of Jehu, the fear of the Lord, boldness, the rules of engagement, Jehovah-Gibbor, legions of heavenly angels, kingdom of God and its principles and mandates, the anointing of evangelism and teaching

SPIRIT OF FEAR AND TORMENT

The spirit of fear is released to attack the peace, courage, vision, and faith of individuals, creating a debilitating stronghold in their mind. It also has the power to abort purpose, derail divine destinies, and assassinate future hope and faith in the power of God. It is of extreme importance to comprehend the insidious nature of this spirit relative to our future, because the way we perceive or think about the future actually sculpts and contours how we handle the present. Fear comes from the root word *phobos*, which means, "that which may cause flight." This is also where we get the word *phobia*, which is a persistent irrational fear of something that is so strong that it compels us to avoid the object of the fear. It is a psychological reaction to something or someone who poses a threat to our sense of security and safety. It also denotes emotional unrest and "dis-ease" caused by uncertainty of one's ability to overcome situations and challenges in life—financial, spiritual, physical, social, material, psychological, or emotional disability. Deuteronomy 2:25 indicates that fear is experienced not only on an individual basis but also at a national level. God promises the Israelites that He will "begin to put the dread of thee and the fear of thee upon the nations that are under the whole heaven, who shall hear report of thee, and shall tremble, and be in anguish because of thee." There are different degrees of fear:

1. Alarm: initial realization of danger
2. Fright: sudden and momentary
3. Dread: stronger in intensity, dread grips the heart as it anticipates impending events that are difficult or impossible to avoid, rendering the person helpless and powerless over it.
4. Terror: overpowering, intense, and debilitating
5. Horror: a combination of fear and aversion
6. Panic: sudden, frantic fear that robs a person of reason
7. Dismay: apprehension that robs a person of courage and power to act efficiently and effectively
8. Consternation: a state of often paralyzing dismay characterized by confusion and helplessness
9. Trepidation: dread characterized by trembling

Scriptural reference for the spirit of fear and torment

Genesis 32:11; Job 3:25; Psalm 91:5; Isaiah 8:11–14; Jonah 1:10; Luke 21:21; Romans 8:15; 2 Timothy 1:7; 1 John 4:18

Signs, symptoms, and manifestations of the spirit of fear and torment		
Abuse	Acrophobia (fear of heights)	Agitation
Agoraphobia (fear of open spaces)	Alarm	Alcoholism

Signs, symptoms, and manifestations of the spirit of fear and torment		
Amathophobia (fear of dust)	Anxiety	Apiphobia (fear of bees)
Apprehension	Astrophobia (fear of lightning)	Aversion
Aviaphobia (fear of flying)	Batrachophobia (fear of reptiles)	Blennophobia (fear of slime)
Bondage	Catagelophobia (fear of ridicule)	Claustrophobia (fear of enclosed spaces)
Condemnation	Consternation	Control
Criminal activities	Crying	Cynophobia (fear of dogs)
Deception	Decidophobia (fear of making decisions)	Depression
Dismay		Doubt
Dread	Drug addiction	Electrophobia (fear of electricity)
Eremophobia (fear of being alone)	Extreme shyness	Fatalism
Fear of change	Fear of failure	Fear of people
Fear of people's opinions	Fear of success	Forgetfulness
Gamophobia (fear of marriage)	Gatophobia (fear of cats)	Gephyrophobia (fear of crossing bridges)
Gynophobia (fear of women)	Heaviness	Horror
Hostility	Hydrophobia (fear of water)	Inferiority
Insecurities	Insomnia	Intimidation by adversary
Kakorraphiaphobia (fear of failure)	Loneliness	Manipulation
Keraunophobia (fear of thunder)	Discouragement	Disillusionment
Mistrust	Musophobia (fear of mice)	Nervousness
Nightmares	Night terrors	Nyctophobia (fear of night)

Signs, symptoms, and manifestations of the spirit of fear and torment		
Ochlophobia (fear of crowds)	Odynephobia (fear of pain)	Ophidiophobia (fear of snakes)
Oppression	Oversensitivity	Panic
Phobias	Pining	Pnigerophobia (fear of smothering)
Pyrophobia (fear of fire)	Scholionophobia (fear of school)	Sciophobia (fear of shadows)
Shame	Germophobia (fear of germs)	Spheksophobia (fear of wasps)
Technophobia (fear of technology)	Tepidity	Terror
Thalassophobia (fear of the ocean)	Glossophobia (fear of performing; stage fright)	Treachery
Triskaidekaphobia (fear of the number thirteen)	Tropophobia (fear of moving or making changes)	Victimization
Witchcraft		

Release

Power, love, sound mind, boldness, peace, spiritual mindedness, liberty, and courage

SPIRIT OF IDOLATRY

One of the works of the flesh, and a master spirit used by Satan to control corporal and corporate destinies, idolatry is the substitute for God and salvation. When you place anything or anyone ahead of God, and He is preempted as the zenith of pursuits and affection, this is idolatry. Idolatry has many modi operandi, such as social, natural, historical, spiritual, and cultural. The spirit of idolatry seduces people and nations to display extravagant emotional forms of the worship of things and/or people, while establishing strongholds of traditional, cultural practices and beliefs. Idolatry can manifest itself through philosophies, education, and political activities. It also opens doors to demonic activities. According to Ezekiel, idolatry originates in the mind of Satan and is projected into the minds of mankind.

Scriptural reference for the spirit of idolatry

1 Samuel 15:23; Ezekiel 14:1–8; Habakkuk 2:18; 1 Corinthians 12:2; Galatians 5:20; Colossians 3:5

Signs, symptoms, and manifestations of the spirit of idolatry		
Astrology	Carnality	Confusion
Control	Covetousness	Cultic practices
Degradation	Doctrines of devils	Enslavement of emotion
Entanglement	Enticement	Error
Evil desires	Evil thoughts	False prophecies
False worship	Fear	Fornication
Greed	Heresies	Humanism
Immoralities	Impurities	Inordinate affection
Knowledge block	Lust	Murder
Narcissism	National/ethnical traits, tendencies, and oddities	Oppression
Perversion	Possession	Pride
Religiosity	Self-centeredness	Unbelief
Uncleanness	Witchcraft	

Release

True/pure worship (in spirit and truth), righteousness, holiness, repentance, and prophetic anointing

SPIRITS OF JEALOUSY AND ENVY

Jealousy is likened unto a raging fire that is out of control and destroys everything it touches. Jealous people are destructive people. They are also possessive people. They smother and are overly possessive of everything and everyone. Jealousy will drive man to accomplish things that are contrary to the will of God. King Saul and Nabal are two biblical examples that come to mind of how jealous people operate. (See 1 Samuel 25:1–17.)

"What about God?" you may ask. "Doesn't the Bible say that He is jealous?" While this is true, God's jealousy, simply stated, means that God owns everything and He does not want anyone to abuse what is His (Exod. 34:14; Deut.

4:24). We are mere stewards of what really belongs to God. Therefore, we do not have the right to say what another person can or cannot enjoy. We cannot dictate to God who should or should not have the right or privilege to enjoy what He allows people to enjoy.

Envy, on the other hand, is slightly different from jealousy. According to *American Heritage Dictionary*, *envy* is defined as "a feeling of discontent and resentment aroused by and in conjunction with desire for the possessions or qualities of another." Envy will convince you that other people are so much luckier, smarter, more attractive, better off, more educated, or enjoy better relationships than you do. Envy, therefore, is the desire for others' traits, possessions, status, abilities, or situations. Most people tend to use the words *envy* and *jealousy* interchangeably, but there is a difference. Envy is wanting what someone else has while jealousy is not wanting someone to have or enjoy what you have.

Scriptural reference for the spirits of jealousy and envy

1 Samuel 18:5–11; 25:1–17; Job 5:2; Proverbs 3:31; 6:34; 14:30; 23:17; 27:4; Song of Solomon 8:6; Ezekiel 8:1–12

Signs, symptoms, and manifestations of the spirits of jealousy and envy		
"Keeping up with the Joneses"	Abuse	Agony
Arrogance	Assumptions	Babylon
Begrudging attitude	Belial	Belittlement
Bullying	Character assassination	Confusion
Contention	Covetousness	Criticism
Cursing	Deception	Derision
Discord	Embezzlement	Entitlement
Extreme competition	Fear	Frustration
Gossip	Greed	Identity theft
Idolatry	Ill will	Ill wishes
Ill-spoken words	Insecurity	Jezebel
Justification	Lust	Lying
Malice	Maligning ways	Manipulation

Signs, symptoms, and manifestations of the spirits of jealousy and envy		
Misrepresentation of truth	Mocking	Murder
Obsession	Oppression	Pain
Possessiveness	Pride	Projection
Rage	Railing	Rejection
Resentment	Sabotage	Seditions
Self-centeredness	Slander	Spite
Strife	Surveillance	Taunt
Theft	Threats	Torment
Undermining (purpose)	Unsupportiveness	Violence
Witchcraft	Withholding information	

Release

Brotherly love, kindness, meekness, respect, celebration, and satisfaction

SPIRIT OF JEZEBEL
(ANARCHY, CONTROL, AND WITCHCRAFT)

The spirit of Jezebel is pious, puffed up with pride, and blatantly disregards delegated authority. It works contrary to the laws of spiritual protocol, refuses to submit, and instead, rallies for the authority and influence that rightfully belongs to God's appointed leadership. The Jezebel spirit operates through both males and females and appeals to the iniquity of the heart often utilizing those overtaken by the spirit of Ahab to fulfill its wishes and desires. Failure to oblige or obey this spirit will cause it to retaliate violently. The Jezebel spirit hates the prophetic, holiness, and righteousness, and it plots and plans the demise of delegated authority.

There are two distinct manifestations of the spirit of Jezebel spoken of in Scripture. The first, found in 1 Kings, is assigned to prophets. The other reference is found in the Book of Revelation and is assigned to masquerade as a prophet. The name *Jezebel* means "unmarried." Every child of God is "married" to Jehovah. We are His *brides*. Jezebel operates in the flesh and is guilty of fornication and harlotry. This spirit drives its host to commit spiritual fornication, consistently conceiving "bastard" children for Satan: its lover. This spirit is powerful because it can marshal satanic cohorts at a single command. (See also "Spirit of Divination.")

Scriptural reference for the spirit of Jezebel

1 Kings 18:21–25; 2 Kings 9; Revelation 2:18–29

Signs, symptoms, and manifestations of the spirit of Jezebel		
Abominations	Adultery (sexual/spiritual)	Ahab
Anarchy	Anger	Apathy
Arrogance	Belial	Bitterness
Blasphemy	Carnality	Competition
Compromise	Contention	Control
Deception	Envy	Factions
False, deceptive anointing	False doctrine (of men)	False teaching
Fornication	Frustrating growth and maturation process	Harassment
Hatred	Hatred of authority	Heresy
Hidden agenda	Idolatry	Insecurity
Insecurity protected by pride	Insubordination	Irreverence
Jealousy	Lack of faith in God	Lust for power
Lustful affections	Maligning of character	Manipulation
Mind control	Opinionated	Overconfidence
Paranoia	Persecution	Physical restraints/constraints
Prohibition of potential	Prophetic counterfeit	Railing (verbal abuse)
Rebellion	Religious holiness	Retaliation
Satanic and demonic activities	Sedition	Seduction
Self-appointment	Self-sufficiency	Sexual sins
Showing displeasure (facially, emotionally, verbally)	Slander	Spirit of control

Signs, symptoms, and manifestations of the spirit of Jezebel		
Spirit of fear	Spirit of rejection	Spiritual fornication
Spiritual whoredom	Surveillance	Suspicion
Usurping authority	Vanity	Violence
Witchcraft	Works against the prophetic	Works of the flesh
Financial hardship		

Release

Repentance, holiness, godliness, the anointing, prophetic anointing, humility, spirit of Elijah and Jehu, gift of discerning of spirits, righteousness, fire of the Lord, terror of the Lord, breaking the curse of whoredom, order the veils of curses, deception, and control to be torn down and ripped to shreds; break chains and soulish ties from current and past generations

SPIRIT OF JUDAS

This spirit is assigned to "movers and shakers" in the kingdom (those who are like Jesus) to violate allegiance to them. They give aid and information to the enemies of the one to whom they are assigned. In the military, a *sleeper* is one who has undercover, surreptitious assignments. He looks, acts, talks, and walks like "one of us," but has an assignment from another camp. This spirit can remain undercover and undetected for years before it strikes.

Scriptural reference for the spirit of Judas
Matthew 26:25

Signs, symptoms, and manifestations of the spirit of Judas		
Betrayal	Deception	Disloyalty
Double-crossing	Double-mindedness	Duplicity
Faithlessness	Falseness	Filthy lucre (love of money)
Foul play	Fraud	Infidelity
Lust	Noncommittal	Sabotage

Signs, symptoms, and manifestations of the spirit of Judas		
Sedition	Traitorship	Treachery
Treason	Unfaithfulness	Worldliness

Release

Order, protocol, humility, unity, the mind of Christ, submission, hope, faith, fidelity, trustworthiness, and faithfulness

SPIRIT OF KORAH (REBELLION)

This spirit causes insurrection to arise within the ranks of leadership. It is a spirit that forms unholy alliances and convinces leadership to rebel against divine and delegated authority (e.g., pastors, eldership). It refuses to give honor and respect to whom it is due because it causes its hosts to feel that they are equal in status, station, and call. This spirit is like a cancer that quickly spreads within a local church. In order to eliminate the contamination within the ranks of leadership, this spirit must be openly challenged, judged, and forcefully expelled.

Scriptural reference for the spirit of Korah

Numbers 16:1–19

Signs, symptoms, and manifestations of the spirit of Korah		
Accusation	Arrogance	Backsliding of parishioners
Confrontation	Corruption	Cultural curse
Deceit	Disillusionment	Disrespect
Disrespect for protocol	Divide and conquer	Fault finding
Hostility	Iniquitous hearts	Judgmental attitude
Loss of confidence in spiritual leadership	Ministerial curse	Power hunger
Power struggle	Presumption	Railing
Rebellion	Revolt against leadership	Rivalry
Sabotage	Undermining authority	

Release

Order, protocol, humility, unity, the mind of Christ, submission, hope, faith, and longsuffering

SPIRIT OF MADNESS OR MENTAL ILLNESS

I want to handle this category as sensitively as possible because there are a variety of contributing factors that may cause mental illness, such as hormonal imbalance, physical and emotional abuse, drug addiction, and so on. Inasmuch as I am aware that there are certain conditions that can be caused by spirits of oppression, I am equally aware that God does not place any form of illness upon us. In writing this section, I am not implying that the enemy has possessed everyone who displays characteristics of mental illness. I am, however, saying that we need to place the blame on the character from which these unfortunate conditions emanate: Satan himself.

Revelation 18:11–13 speaks of Satan utilizing the mental capacity of man to fulfill his plans and purposes in the earth realm. One of the ways he utilizes the minds of men is to create mental disorders and irrational, obsessive behaviors, impairing the capacity to function adequately and appropriately. The National Alliance for the Mentally Ill defines mental illness as "a group of disorders causing severe disturbances in thinking, feeling, and relating," which diminishes one's ability to cope with normal demands.[2] Common mental and emotional difficulties include anxiety disorders, substance abuse, Alzheimer's disease, and phobias.

Scriptural reference for the spirit of madness or mental illness
Mark 5:1–20

Signs, symptoms, and manifestations of the spirit of madness or mental illness		
Addictions	Alienation	Alzheimer's
Bipolar	Compulsive behavior	Confusion
Craziness	Death	Delusional projections
Dementia	Dependent disorder	Depression
Derangement	Dread	Embarrassment
Fear	Feeling down	Grandiosity

Hypersensitivity	Hysteria	Inferiority complex
Inordinate withdrawal	Insanity	Irrational thoughts
Lack of motivation	Lunacy	Magical thinking
Mania	Melancholy	Memory loss/recall
Mental illness	Mental/psychological oppression	Mistrust
Murder	Mutilation	Nervousness
Neurosis	Obsessiveness	Oppression
Overcompensation disorder	Panic disorder	Paranoia
Perfectionism	Persecutory paranoid state	Personality disorders
Phobia	Poor recall	Possessiveness
Psychosis	Psychosomatic illness	Schizophrenia
Senility	Shame	Sociopath conditions
Suppression	Terror	Uncontrolled crying
Unworthiness	Violence	Worry

Release

Love, the mind of Christ, restoration, healing, deliverance, and peace

SPIRIT OF MURDER

This spirit works with the six spirits of the underworld. It seeks to cause premature death as it unlawfully takes a person's right to live.

Scriptural reference for the spirit of murder

Psalm 10:8; Matthew 15:19

Signs, symptoms, and manifestations of the spirit of murder		
Abortion	Assassination	Character assassination
Emotional/psychological rape	Execution	Fear
Fratricide	Gossip	Homicide

Signs, symptoms, and manifestations of the spirit of murder		
Infanticide	Intimidation	Manslaughter
Mutilation	Persecution	Sabotage
Scandal	Slander	Spirit of Herod
Spirit of Pharaoh	Stigmatization	Suicide
Terror	Victimization	Violence

Release

The mind of Christ, faith, hope, love, life in Christ Jesus, the anointing, the spirit of resurrection, and the spirit of Elijah

SPIRIT OF NABAL

The name *Nabal* is literally translated as "vile, stupid, or foolish." Scripture states that he was churlish. Nabal's name in Hebrew is *Qaheh*. It literally means "cruel, impudent, and rough." You may know people who, no matter how kindly they are treated, never reciprocate with kindness. They walk around as if they have a chip on their shoulders and are mad at the whole world.

Scriptural reference for the spirit of Nabal
1 Samuel 25:2–11

Signs, symptoms, and manifestations of the spirit of Nabal		
Abuse	Apathy	Churlishness
Cruelty	Difficult personality	Dishonor
Disinterest	Disregard	Disrespect
Disrespect for authority	Grief	Harassment
Hard-heartedness	Hardness	Impudence
Indifference	Insensibility	Insubordination
Irreverence	Lethargy	Noncompliance
Obstinacy	Selfishness	Severity
Sorrowful	Stiff neck	Stinginess
Stubbornness	Vulgarity	

Release
Humility, cooperation, peace, mercy, and patience

SPIRIT OF OPPRESSION

Working in conjunction with the spirit of Pharaoh, the spirit of oppression arbitrarily exercises satanic powers to oppress and cause mental and emotional stress. It victimizes its host by taking away his rights and dignity. This spirit also creates a "slave" mentality so that even after a person is delivered from the clutches of its relentless hands, the individual must be exposed to empowering teachings in order for a paradigm shift to take place.

Scriptural reference for the spirit of oppression
Deuteronomy 24:14–15; Psalm 22:24; 25:16; 55:1–15; Proverbs 18:14; Acts 10:38

Signs, symptoms, and manifestations of the spirit of oppression		
Apathy	Behemoth	Belial
Breakdowns	Magnification of situations	Chronic weariness
Communism	Condemnation	Confusion
Creation of subcultures (social outcasts)	Defeatism	Depression
Despair	Despondency	Destruction of a sense of significance/ identity and direction
Discouragement	Disunity	Domination of will
Eating disorders	Emotional pain	Enslavement of emotions
Entrapment of perception	Eradication of personal/ ethical/national identity	Erosion of self-esteem/image
False/no expectations	Fatalism	Harassment
Heaviness	Helplessness	Herod

Signs, symptoms, and manifestations of the spirit of oppression		
Hopelessness	Inability to respond appropriately to challenges, conflict, or crises	Incarceration of motivation
Inferiority complex	Insomnia	Invasion of personal privacy
Jezebel	Knowledge block	Lack of connectedness
Lack of direction	Lack of motivation	Lack/loss of appetite
Language deterioration/ disintegration	Leviathan	Loneliness
Longing for belonging	Nervousness	Night fears/terrors
Pharaoh	Post-traumatic stress disorder	Poverty
Prohibition of fulfillment of personal purpose	Psychological enslavement	Repression
Sabotage of potential	Self-fulfilling prophecies	Slavery
Social, emotional, psychological, temporal, spiritual afflictions	Social/political disenfranchisement	Spirit of Herod
Stress	Subjugation of hope	Suppression of expression
Undermining of purpose	Victimization	Alienation
Marginalization	Exploitation	Racial profiling

Release

Deliverance, apostolic anointing, prophetic anointing, peace, healing, mercy, and liberty. For further measures of deliverance, see also the spirit of Egypt/Pharaoh/Herod.

SPIRIT OF PERVERSION

This spirit causes an individual or groups of people to deviate from what is moral, ethical, right, and good. Working with an unclean spirit, it causes its host to obstinately persist in an error or a fault. Many individuals plagued, tormented, oppressed, or possessed with this spirit will be wrongly and strongly self-willed or stubborn and marked by a disposition that opposes and contradicts. This English word comes from the Hebrew root word *aqash*, which has the connotation of being twisted and distorted; thus the English words *false*, *crooked*, *forward*, and *perverse*.

Scriptural reference for the spirit of perversion
Deuteronomy 32:5; Proverbs 28:18

Signs, symptoms, and manifestations of the spirit of perversion		
Accusation	Adultery	Bestiality
Bitterness	"Butchism"	Cannibalism
Child abuse	Chronic promiscuity	Condemnation
Control	Corruption	Cross-dressing
Cursing	Debauchery	Deceit
Deception	Dishonesty	Divination
Dogmatisms	Drag queen	Effeminacy
Exaggeration	Exhibitionism	Falsehood
Fetishism	Filthy language/thoughts	Flattery
Flirtation	Fornication	Gossip
Guile	Homosexuality	Imagination
Immorality	Impure motives	Incest
Indecency	Inflexibility	Inordinate affections
Instability	Lesbianism	Lusts of every kind
Lying	Manipulations	Masochism
Nymphomania	Paraphilia	Pedophilia
Perversions	Pornography	Profanity
Prostitution	Provocative dressing	Railing
Rape	Rebellion	Religiosity
Sadism	Seduction	Sexual perversions
Sexual violence/torture	Sexually explicit dreams	Slander
Sodomy	Stubbornness	Transvestitism
Treachery	Uncleanness	Unethical dealings
Unnatural affections	Vanity	Victimization
Vileness	Voyeurism	Witchcraft
Wrath	Zoophilic	

Release

Righteousness, holiness, self-control, deliverance, healing, the breaking of soul ties, fruit of the Spirit, and discipline

SPIRIT OF POVERTY AND FINANCIAL CURSES

This spirit creates an atmosphere of financial infertility, deficiency, lack, and an inferior quality of life.

Scriptural reference for spirit of poverty and financial curses
Nehemiah 5:1–11; Proverbs 11:24; 13:18; Malachi 3:8–12

Signs, symptoms, and manifestations of the spirit of poverty and financial curses		
Addiction	Apathy	Begrudging giving
Dearth	Debt	Defect
Defraud	Depression	Deprivation
Destitution	Drug trafficking	Embezzlement
Extravagance	Famine	Fear of lack
Financial curse	Fraud	Gambling
Greed	Hardship	Hoarding
Ignorance	Impropriety	Inability to make or keep money
Indigence	Ingratitude	Judgment
Lack	Laziness	Living above means
Not returning tithes	Oppression	Pauperism
Pestilence	Pride	Privation
Selfishness	Shame	Shortage
Sickness	Stinginess	Want
Waste		

Release

Prosperity, liberality in giving, faith, truth, and abundance

SPIRIT OF PRIDE

Pride's origin comes from the very heart of Satan. In a way, it can be said that Satan himself spawned this spirit. Pride is an inflated perception of one's own dignity and self-worth. When pride manifests itself, it often manifests as arrogance, disdainful conduct or treatment, haughtiness, and even false humility. Pride is a protector of "self." It does not betray or expose self. It is obsessed with self.

Scriptural reference for the spirit of pride
Proverbs 16:18; Ezekiel 28:13–19

Signs, symptoms, and manifestations of the spirit of pride		
Arrogance	Bitterness	Bondage
Conceit	Control	Corrupt mind
Crooked	Deception (all forms)	Defensiveness
Disobedience	Disregard of authority	Disrespect
Dominance	Egotism	False humility
Guile	Hatred	Haughtiness
Hoarding	Independence	Insolence
Insubordination	Jealousy	Loftiness
Malice	Obstinacy	Overfamiliarity
Passive-aggressive	Perverse	Perverted imagination
Perverted mind-set	Possessiveness	Poverty
Profanity	Rebellion	Resentment
Segregation	Self-absorbed	Self-centeredness
Self-importance	Selfishness	Self-promotion (often at another's expense)
Self-protection	Self-righteousness	Separatism
Stinginess	Strife	Strong delusion
Uncontrolled anger	Unteachable spirit	Vanity
Waywardness	Witchcraft	Withholding self
Wrath		

Release
True humility, submission, repentance, a spirit of giving, and faith

SPIRIT OF REBELLION

Working well with the spirit of pride, rebellion resists government and authority in all forms. It drives its hosts to blatantly disobey. It is noncompliant to protocol or order. This spirit creates a disposition that defies authority to the point of insurrection.

Scriptural reference for the spirit of rebellion
Deuteronomy 31:27; 1 Samuel 15:23

Signs, symptoms, and manifestations of the spirit of rebellion		
Arrogance	Conceit	Contempt
Defensiveness	Defiance	Disdain
Disobedience	Haughtiness	Independence
Insubordination	Loftiness	Noncompliance
Obstinacy	Pride	Rebellion
Recalcitrance	Rejection of authority	Resistance
Scorn	Segregation	Self-centeredness
Self-importance	Selfishness	Self-protection
Self-righteousness	Separatism	Strife
Unruliness	Vanity	Waywardness
Wrath		

Release
Humility, submission, repentance, love of God, and compliance

SPIRIT OF REJECTION

Rejection is the refusal of accepting a person or a thing. This spirit drives people to refuse to accept, recognize, give affection to, submit, believe, make use of, and to socially or politically ostracize another person after examination. The person that rejects usually has an unrealistic standard by which he or she measures a thing or a person. This is one spirit I believe most people have been attacked by. Depending on your response, rejection can take the wind out of your sail and cause you to drift aimlessly through life without the knowledge of your true worth and dignity. Always remember, "all things, whatsoever ye shall ask in prayer, believing, ye shall receive" (Matt. 21:22).

Scriptural reference for the spirit of rejection
   1 Samuel 15:26; 16:1, 14–23; 18:8–15

Signs, symptoms, and manifestations of the spirit of rejection		
"Nobody loves me" syndrome (self-pity)	Abandonment	Abuse of self and others
Addictions	Anger	Antisocial disorder
Anxiety	Bashfulness	Betrayal
Bitterness	Codependency	Comparison
Deception	Dejection	Denial
Depression	Disappointment and guilt	Disapproval
Discredit	Disesteem	Disgrace
Dishonor	Disrepute	Distrust
Dysfunction	Dysfunctions	Eating disorder
Emotional callousness	Emotional instability	Emotional trauma
Emotional victimization	Emotional/psychological rape	Emptiness
Eviction	Exile	False/no expectations
Favoritism	Fear of being alone	Fear of further rejection
Feelings of not being wanted	Feelings of rejection	Grandiosity
Grief	Hopelessness	Humiliation
Hysteria	Ignominy	Ignore/neglect
Inability to receive/give love	Inhibition	Insecurities
Insignificance	Intense emotional pain	Introversion
Isolation	Justification of inappropriate word/ behavior	Lack of confidence
Lashing out	Loneliness	Low self-worth

Signs, symptoms, and manifestations of the spirit of rejection		
Mistrust	Murder	Need for approval/validation
Negativism	Neurosis	Oppression
Overcompensation	Overprotection	Oversensitivity
Overweight	Passive-aggressive behavior	Perversions
Phobia	Post-traumatic stress disorder	Projection
Psychological victimization	Repression	Repudiation
Sabotage (relationships/organization/self/purpose/destinies)	Sadness/crying	Schizophrenia
Scorn	Segregation	Self-consciousness
Self-depreciation	Self-fulfilling prophecy	Sex for love
Shame	Shun	Social isolation
Suicide	Suspicions	Torment
Vexation	Workaholism	Worthlessness

Release

Love, the mind of Christ, restoration, healing, deliverance, faith, hope, and forgiveness

SPIRIT OF RELIGION

A spirit of religion portrays itself as having a very high devotion to God or a deity, but merely deceives its hosts into placing more emphasis on religious activities than a true relationship with God. In the trial of Jesus, we see another spirit called the spirit of Barabas, which seeks to make scapegoats of others. It is a spirit that assassinates and maligns.

Scriptural reference for the spirit of religion

Galatians 1:13–14; Matthew 23:17; Luke 11:37–54; 1 Timothy 4:1–2

Signs, symptoms, and manifestations of the spirit of religion		
"Holier than thou" attitude	Abortion	Ancestral worship
Antagonism	Arrogance	Blasphemy
Character assassination	Control	Cultism
Deception	Denominationalism	Disharmony
Disunity	Division	Doctrines of devils
Dogmatism	Duplicity	Emotionalism
Fables	False apostolic anointing	False evangelistic anointing
False pastoral anointing	False pedagogical (teaching) anointing	False prophetic anointing
False revelation	Falsehood	Formalism
Heresy	Hireling anointing	Hypocrisy
Idolatry	Inordinate sophistication	Institutionalized abuse
Irreverence	Judgmentalism	Libations
Negativism	Nonsubmissiveness	Obstinacy
Occultism	Phariseeism	Polarity in membership
Pride	Prosecution of truth	Religiosity
Ritualism	Sacrilege	Sadduceeism
Scapegoating	Seduction	Self-righteousness
Spirit of Barabas	Spiritism	Spiritual adultery
Superstition	Traditionalism	Treachery
Unbelief	Unholy	Unteachableness
Vain babbling	Voodoo	

Release

The Spirit of truth, prophetic anointing/utterance, discerning of spirits, and the spirit of John the Baptist. Also, declare that the Lamb of God Jesus Christ has been slain even before the foundations of the world. Apply the blood to the doorposts of your soul.

SPIRIT OF SABOTAGE

The spirit of sabotage operates as strong demonic influences that drive people to abort the progress and success of divinely ordained projects, purposes, relationships, organization, self, potential, and destinies. It stirs up jealousy, resentment, and suspicion, and is often vindictive toward the person who detects its presence. Sabotage can make you both victim and perpetrator so that even when you pronounce judgment on others, you expose and pronounce judgment upon yourself. This spirit is so skillful it will use you as a pawn and a puppet on a string, prohibiting you from detecting its hand upon you and the strings that manipulate you. Working with familiar spirits, who act as their reconnaissance, informing them of breaks in hedges of protection, strengths, weaknesses, and proclivities of both the perpetrator and victim, its works with a well-thought-out plan.

I have discovered that many agents used are not only those with malicious intent, but also those who sincerely love us and want what's best for us. Consider the incident Matthew records in Matthew 16:21–23, where Peter unwittingly was being used in an attempt to sabotage the mission of Jesus. The Book of Nehemiah also records the characteristics and behavior of this spirit.

Remember as you examine the activities of this spirit that you will discover that you are both victim and perpetrator. When the Lord gives you victory over this spirit, you will notice that a veil will be lifted and scales of deception will fall from your spiritual eyes. Everything that you thought was real will crumble before you and evaporate like a mirage. Truth will prevail and set you free from anything built upon fabrications, lies, falsehood, and untruths.

Scriptural reference for the spirit of sabotage
Nehemiah 2:10, 17–20; 4:1, 4–7, 9, 13–14; 6:1–14

Signs, symptoms, and manifestations of the spirit of sabotage		
"Cutthroat" activities	Abandonment	Abortive activities
Abuse	Accusations	Addiction

Signs, symptoms, and manifestations of the spirit of sabotage

Adultery	Alienation	Allegation
Antichrist spirit	Anxiety	Arrogance
Attachment	Backlash	Bad habits (eating, social, spending, etc.)
Bad reputation	Belligerence	Betrayal
Blaspheme	Carnality	Castigation
Censorship	Character assassination	Church splits
Competition	Compromising	Condemnation
Confusion	Conspiracy	Corruption
Covert behavior	Creating wedges in relationships	Criticism
Cruelty	Death	Deception
Demoralization	Derailment	Desertion
Desolation	Diabolical traps	Difficult personality
Disapproval	Disassociation	Disbelief
Discouragement	Disenfranchisement	Dishonor
Disloyalty	Disrespect	Disrespect of authority
Disruption	Doctrine of devils	Double-mindedness
Embezzlement	Emotional seduction	Envy
Erosion of self-worth and image	Evil	Fabrication
Faithlessness	False prophecies	Falsehood
Family secrets	Fatigue	Fault finding
Fear	Feelings of incompetence	Forgetfulness
Fornication	Fraudulence	Frustration
Gluttony	Gossip	Grandiosity
Greed	Grief	Guilt-tripping
Harassment	Hard-heartedness	Harshness
Hatred	Helplessness	Hypocrisy
Identity theft	Ignorance	Impudence
Incrimination	Indifference	Indignation
Ineffective decision-making	Iniquity	Insurrection
Irrational thinking	Irreverence	Isolation

Signs, symptoms, and manifestations of the spirit of sabotage		
Jealousy	Judgmentalism	Justification
Knowledge block	Lack of accountability	Lack of trust
Leanness of the soul	Lethargy	Loss
Loss of focus	Loss of motivation	Malicious destruction
Manipulation	Mental affliction	Misrepresentation of truth
Mockery	Murder	Noncompliance
Obstinacy	Offenses	Opposition
Oppression	Passive-aggressive	Perversion
Pilfering	Plotting and planning the demise of institutions/people	Poor nutritional habits
Prejudice	Pride	Projections
Psychological games	Rationalization	Rebellion
Recrimination	Rejection	Religiosity
Religious spirits	Resentment	Revengefulness
Ridicule	Rivalry	Rumors
Sanballat and Tobiah	Scandal	Schemes
Secretiveness	Seduction	Self-centeredness
Self-doubt	Selfishness	Self-sabotage
Severity	Shame	Silence/silent treatment
Slander	Snares	Sorrowful
Spirit of scorn	Spiritual blindness	Stealing
Stigmatization	Stinginess	Strife
Stubbornness	Subversion	Superficiality
Suppressed emotions	Surreptitious activities	Surveillance
Suspicion	Threatening	Traditions of men
Treacheries	Trouble-making	Ulterior motives
Ultimatums	Unconfessed sins	Underhandedness
Undermining activities/ cause	Undermining and destroying covenant relationships	Undermining trust
Unforgiveness	Unholy alliances	Vexation
Victimization	Violence	Vulgarity
Weariness	Witchcraft	Withholding

Release

Prayer, fasting, intercession, Jehovah-Gibbor, the Spirit of truth, discernment of spirits, repentance, the wisdom of God, and revelation of the hidden secrets of the heart

SPIRIT OF SAMARIA

According to the prophet Ezekiel, Samaria was known for its spiritual harlotry and adultery in that it promoted convenience in worship, compromise of holiness, and mediocrity in the service of the Lord, which eventually led the children of Israel to embrace carnality, sensuality, and idolatry as a way of life, possessing a form of godliness, but denying the power therein.

Scriptural reference for the spirit of Samaria
Ezekiel 23:1–20

Signs, symptoms, and manifestations of the spirit of Samaria		
"Holier than thou" attitude	Religiosity	Abortion
Ancestral worship	Antagonism	Arrogance
Blasphemy	Carnality	Character assassination
Compromise	Control	Cultism
Deception	Denominationalism	Disharmony
Disunity	Division	Doctrines of devils
Dogmatism	Duplicity	Emotionalism
Fables	False apostolic anointing	False evangelistic anointing
False pastoral anointing	False pedagogical (teaching) anointing	False prophetic anointing
False revelation	Falsehood	Formalism
Fornication	Heresy	Hireling anointing
Hypocrisy	Idolatry	Inordinate sophistication
Institutionalized abuse	Irreverence	Judgmentalism
Lewdness	Libations	Lust

Signs, symptoms, and manifestations of the spirit of Samaria		
Negativism	Nonsubmissiveness	Obstinacy
Occultism	Perversion	Phariseeism
Polarity in membership	Pride	Prosecution of truth
Rebellion	Religious spirit	Ritualism
Sacrilege	Sadduceeism	Scapegoating
Seduction	Self-righteousness	Spirit of Barabas
Spiritism	Spiritual adultery	Spiritual harlotry
Superstition	Traditionalism	Traditions of man
Treachery	Unbelief	Unholy
Unrighteousness	Unteachableness	Vain babbling
Voodoo	Whoredom	Witchcraft/sorcery
Worldliness		

Release
Jehovah-Gibbor, holiness, and the Spirit of truth

SPIRIT OF SEDUCTION

The spirit of seduction opens the gates of the soul of man, cities, and nations (natural and spiritual) to the spirit of perversion. It is a counterfeit of the anointing and an imitator of the Holy Spirit. It forms a strong confederation with the spirit of religion and is fueled by the spirit of the antichrist.

Scriptural reference for the spirit of seduction
1 Kings 11:1–8; 1 Timothy 4:1–6; Revelation 2:20–23

Signs, symptoms, and manifestations of the spirit of seduction		
Astrology	Carnality	Charmers
Deception	Divination	Doctrines of devils
Enchanters	False apostles	False prophets
False religion	False teachers	Flattery
Fornication	Homosexuality	Humanism
Hypocrisy	Idolatry	Iniquitous

Lying	Miracle workers	Perversion
Prognosticators	Psychics	Renegades
Satanic stupor	Sensuality	Spirit of Jezebel
Spiritual adultery	Spiritual idolatry	Subtlety
Warlocks	Witchcraft	

Release

The anointing of the Holy Spirit, gifts of the Spirit, discerning spirits, Spirit of truth, the wrath of God (Ezek. 13:11–15), and the prophetic anointing

SPIRIT OF SHAME

This spirit influences shame-based societies, homes, and families. It causes painful emotions, a strong sense of guilt, embarrassment, unworthiness, and disgrace. Many people who grow up in shame-based homes and communities walk through life like emotional puppets. They are easily manipulated and often use manipulation to get people to do what they want. They also walk around with feelings of unworthiness, poor self-image, and self-worth. Unconditional love, positive regard, and deep inner healing are needed for anyone plagued by this spirit. Read 2 Samuel 13 for greater understanding of shame.

Scriptural reference for the spirit of shame

Psalm 69:7

Signs, symptoms, and manifestations of the spirit of shame		
Abandonment	Abuse	Apathy
Blame	Boundary violation	Codependence
Competition	Confusion	Control
Dishonor	Distress	Dysfunction
Effeminacy	Embarrassment	Emotional deprivation
Enmeshment	Enslavement of emotions	Erosion of self-esteem
Exasperation	Excessive self-analysis	External locus of control

Signs, symptoms, and manifestations of the spirit of shame		
False humility	Faulty perspectives	Fear
Fetish behavior	Flawed view of self	Fornication
Gambling	Gossip	Grief
Guilt	Heaviness	Helplessness
Homosexuality	Hopelessness	Humiliation
Hypersensitivity	Hypochondria	Ignominy
Immaturity	Impaired will	Impropriety
Incest	Insignificance	Instability
Intimidation	Isolation	Knowledge block
Lack of connectedness	Little boy/girl syndrome	Loneliness
Loss of perception	Lust	Mental anguish
Molestation	Mourning	Mutilation
Nightmares	Ostracization	Overcompensation
Oversensitivity	Paranoid personality	Perfectionism
Perversion	Phobias	Physical abuse
Pornography	Post-traumatic stress disorder	Poverty
Projections	Prostitution	Pseudointimacy
Psychological pain	Psychosomatic illness	Reenactments
Rejection	Repetition compulsion	Sadness
Self-loathing	Sexual addictions	Shame-based homes
Shame-based relationships	Shame-based societies	Sodomy
Spirits of inheritance	Stigmatization	Substance abuse
Suspicion	Unholy alliance	Victimization
Violence		

Release

Healing, deliverance, faith, integrity, restoration, hope, and the fruit of the Spirit

SPIRIT OF SUSPICION

This spirit seduces people into forming judgments and arriving at conclusions based on what appears to be factual. It is a spirit that creates insecurities, division, and strong mistrust. Due to its nature, it often works at creating and sustaining disunity.

Scriptural reference for the spirit of suspicion
1 Samuel 18:8–15

Signs, symptoms, and manifestations of the spirit of suspicion		
Alienation	Anxiety	Apprehension
Assumption	Criticism	Discord
Disunity	Doubt	Gossip
Imagination	Isolation	Judgmentalism
Lack of trust	Misjudgment	Mistrust
Misunderstanding	Paranoia	Prejudice
Presumption	Skepticism	Speculation

Release
Faith, honesty, integrity, restoration, and harmony

SPIRIT OF TRADITION

This spirit is responsible for the passing down of elements of a culture, philosophies, behaviors, and habits from generation to generation. This spirit works with the spirit of religion and the spirit of unbelief. It forms a stronghold that facilitates the rejection of truth, thus hindering true worship and revival. This spirit is a powerful gatekeeper that prohibits the preaching of the gospel within a particular culture, region, or nation, and initiates and instigates both the persecution and martyrdom of any child of God who dares to venture into its jurisdiction with the gospel.

Scriptural reference for the spirit of tradition
Mark 7:8; Colossians 2:8

Signs, symptoms, and manifestations of the spirit of tradition		
"Holier than thou" attitude	Abortion	Ancestral worship
Antagonism	Anti-Semitism	Arguments
Arrogance	Blasphemy	Bondage
Character assassination	Condemnation	Contention
Control	Cultism	Deception
Denominationalism	Disharmony	Disunity
Division	Doctrines of devils	Doctrines of man
Dogmatism	Duplicity	Emotionalism
Fables	False apostolic anointing	False evangelistic anointing
False pastoral anointing	False pedagogical (teaching) anointing	False prophetic anointing
False revelation	Falsehood	Formalism
Harassment	Heresy	High things
Hireling anointing	Hypocrisy	Idolatry
Inordinate sophistication	Institutionalized abuse	Intellectualism
Irreverence	Judgmentalism	Legalism
Libations	Martyrdom	Negativism
Nonsubmissiveness	Obstinacy	Occultism
Persecution	Phariseeism	Polarity in membership
Pride	Prosecution of truth	Rationalization
Religiosity	Religious spirit	Resistance to moves of God
Resistance to truth	Ritualism	Sacrilege
Sadduceeism	Scapegoating	Secret sects
Seduction	Self-righteousness	Separatism
Spirit of Barabas	Spiritism	Spiritual adultery
Strongholds	Superstition	Traditionalism
Treachery	Unbelief	Unholy alliances
Unteachableness	Vain babbling	Voodoo

Release

Revival, visitation of God, apostolic, prophetic anointing, and the Spirit of truth

UNCLEAN SPIRITS

According to Revelation 16:13, this spirit has a froglike characteristic and is directly associated with idolatry, witchcraft, and vileness. This spirit works in confederation with many other spirits and is often a doorkeeper in the lives of individuals and a gatekeeper in nations, cities, and communities, such as biblical Sodom and Gomorrah. An unclean spirit entangles itself with the very essence of the person who it possesses. It is a spirit that is not always easy to identify because of its intent to seduce, influence, and eventually possess an individual. However, if you carefully listen to the contents of the host's conversations, or watch the lifestyle of the host, this spirit will eventually reveal itself through sexual innuendoes, lewd conversations, dress codes, behaviors, and filthy environments.

This spirit undermines potential, taints and contaminates the anointing, displaces individuals, and dispossesses them of both their spiritual and natural rights. In my research, I discovered that many people in the Bible who were possessed by an unclean spirit suffered from convulsions. This spirit has the power of a total ruination of a person's life because it attacks the mind, body, and spirit, corroding the foundation of moral and ethical living. Because of the nature of this spirit, very few people who live a life plagued by this spirit, whether male or female, live out half their life expectancy with a good quality of life. They generally die, martyred by their own lusts. According to Mark 1:21–26, the propensities of this spirit is to twist and pervert the very nature of its host and will be at its most violent and vile state as soon as there is a determination that its victim desires conversion and to serve God.

Scripture references for unclean spirits
Zechariah 13:2; Matthew 12:43; Mark 3:11; 1 Corinthians 10:21

Signs, symptoms, and manifestations of unclean spirits		
Abandonment	Abuse	Addictions
Adultery	Antichrist	Antichrist religions
Apathy	Bashfulness	Betrayal

Signs, symptoms, and manifestations of unclean spirits		
Blame	Boundary violation	Carnality
Cheating	Codependence	Competition
Confusion	Control	Convulsions
Cultism	Death	Deception
Demonic activities	Denial	Depravity
Disapproval	Discredit	Discrimination
Disease	Disesteem	Disgrace
Dishonor	Disillusionment	Disloyalty
Disrepute	Distress	Divination
Doctrines of devils	Dysfunction	Eating disorders
Embarrassment	Emotional callousness	Emotional deprivation
Emotional torment	Emotional trauma	Emotional victimization
Emotional/psychological rape	Emptiness	Enmeshment
Eviction	Exasperation	Excessive self-analysis
Exile	External locus of control	False/nonexpectations
Fantasies	Faulty perspectives	Fear
Feelings of rejection	Fetish behavior	Flawed view of self
Fornication	Foulness	Gambling
Gossip	Grandiosity	Grief
Guilt	Heaviness	Helplessness
Homosexuality	Hopelessness	Humiliation
Hypersensitivity	Hypochondria	Idolatry
Ignominy	Ignore/Neglect	Immaturity
Immorality	Impaired will	Impure motives
Impure thoughts	Incest	Inordinate affections
Insecurities	Insignificance	Instability
Irreverence	Isolation	Leanness of the soul
Lewdness	Loneliness	Low self-worth
Lust	Lying	Manipulation
Mental afflictions	Mental anguish	Molestation
Murder	Need for approval/ validation	Neurosis
Nightmares	Nonconformity	Obscenity

Signs, symptoms, and manifestations of unclean spirits

Oppression	Ostracization	Oversensitivity
Paranoid personality	Pedophilia	Perfectionism
Perversions	Phobia	Phobias
Physical abuse	Physiological bondage	Pornography
Post-traumatic stress disorder	Poverty	Pretense
Projections	Propaganda	Prostitution
Pseudointimacy	Psychological pain	Psychological victimization
Psychosomatic illness	Rebellion	Reenactments
Repetition compulsion	Sadness	Scorn
Seduction	Segregation	Self-consciousness
Self-fulfilling prophecy	Self-loathing	Sexual addictions
Sexual enslavement	Sexual innuendoes	Sexually explicit dreams
Shame-based homes	Shame-based relationships	Shame-based societies
Shun	Social isolation	Sodomy
Soul ties	Spirits of inheritance	Stealing
Stigmatization	Substance abuse	Suicide
Superstitions	Suspicion	Tainted anointing
Traditions of men	Uncleanness	Unholy alliance
Vexation	Victimization	Vileness
Voyeurism	Witchcraft	Worthlessness

Release

Deliverance, holiness, righteousness, and the fruit of the Spirit

VEXATION SPIRITS

This spirit changes the quality or condition of lives through constant harassment, annoyance, and irritation. It is especially assigned to those in pursuit of purpose. It creates feelings or exasperation, often driving the victim to give up.

Scriptural reference for vexation spirits:

Numbers 25:17–18; 33:55; Ezra 4:1–6; Ecclesiastes 4:6; Acts 12:1

Signs, symptoms, and manifestations of vexation spirits		
Accusation	Addiction	Aggravation
Annoyance	Antagonism	Anxiety
Bitterness	Confusion	Delirium
Despondency	Discouragement	Disgust
Disillusionment	Distraction	Distress
Dread	Emotional instability	Exasperation
Frustration	Hostility	Hounding
Hyperactivity	Indecision	Irritation
Knowledge block	Mental agitation	Oppression
Painful thoughts	Paranoia	Provocation
Repression	Restlessness	Stress
Subversion	Tension	Undermining purpose
Victimization	Weariness	Worry

Release

Prophetic anointing, favor of God, discerning of spirits, and a hedge of protection

CONCLUSION

FORWARD MARCH!

I N THESE LAST days, God is marshalling prayer warriors who are anointed to gain jurisdictional authority over the powers of darkness so that families, communities, governments, ministries, corporations, countries, kingdoms, and nations are brought back into divine alignment and individuals fulfill purpose and maximize their personal potential. This is to be done by effectively superimposing the plans and purposes of God over the plans and purposes of the enemy through the effective use of the Word of God. The Holy Spirit will become a type of *drill sergeant* whose responsibility is to train you in the art of strategic prayer and spiritual warfare. He will also train you to become a sniper in the realm of the spirit and enable you to hit the swiftest of moving satanic and demonic targets. As with David, He will also train you to conquer the proverbial demonic bear, lion, and giant. It is my prayer that you have learned the principles and strategies contained in this book and that God will raise you up as an End Time spiritual warrior and prophetic sniper.

During your prayer time, the Lord may even place the spirit of a watchman upon you, and you may perceive either activities that are a part of God's divine will or those that are diabolical in nature. (See Ezekiel 3:17.) If divine, prevail in prayer according to what is perceived, saying, "Thy kingdom come. Thy will be done" (Matt. 6:10). If the activity is of a diabolical origin, pray against it using the tools, weapons, strategies, and tactics contained in this manual.

The Bible, indicating that there is power in numbers, clearly states that if two touch and agree on anything that is asked, "it shall be done" and that "one [can] chase a thousand, and two [can] put ten thousand to flight" (Matt. 18:19; Deut. 32:30). Praying with others increases your power base. However, one of the reasons we do not get the kinds of prayer breakthroughs we desire when we pray in groups, and with others, is because many times individuals in the group may be at different levels of spiritual maturity and cannot pull their weight, or we are using different prayer strategies, tactical approaches, and vocabulary.

I have even witnessed times when individuals gather together to pray and the individual prayer agenda is a different prayer agenda from the group. The devil, knowing that God commends His blessings in the midst of unity (Ps. 133), will attempt to sabotage the spirit of unity so that although we are in one place, we are not one in mind, intent, or language. True unity is when we are one and in agreement on all levels of warfare. I strongly recommend that when a church calls a prayer meeting, the entire prayer group should be praying from the same stance, using the same language, and agreeing on the same agenda. This book is written to accommodate this, so that even young Christians can pray at the same level of effectiveness and intensity as seasoned and veteran saints. This book is intended to facilitate this level of unity as we "touch and agree" in Jesus's name.

When praying for specific things concerning the church, ministry, or organizations, it is important that any and all spiritual activities be accurately recorded and submitted to the chief prayer warrior, prayer team, and your pastor so that your insight may be accurately judged and that you may receive full support and reinforcement in prayer.

As you pray and war in the spirit, remember to use your legal right and spiritual authority. God has placed the enemies under your feet and given you power to tread on serpents and scorpions, and over all the power of the enemy; nothing shall by any means hurt you. "Notwithstanding in this...the spirits are subject unto you" (Luke 10:20). Show no mercy to the enemy as you employ these strategies and tactics. According to 2 Corinthians 2:14, God will cause you to triumph. Remember that you are not fighting with the flesh and blood, but against spiritual beings who use human agents to fulfill their purpose in the earth realm. Since your weapons are not carnal, but mighty through God (2 Cor. 10:4), then "No weapon that is formed against [you] shall prosper; and every tongue that shall rise against [you] in judgment [you] shalt condemn. This is the heritage *of the servants of the LORD, and their righteousness is of me, saith the LORD*" (Isa. 54:17, emphasis added).

GLOSSARY

annihilate—to decisively defeat; to nullify or render void

arrest—to subjugate, bring under subjection, and cause to cease

bind—to irrevocably place under legal obligation. It means to prohibit undesirable spiritual activities (as you would if you were to issue a restraining order). Satan is legally obligated to observe all terms and agreements as outlined by you, the issuer, within your prayer.

confederate—an ally (person, groups of persons, country) or accomplice who assists in a plot or supports a criminal act

contention—a state marked by conflict, discord, division, strife, and hostile encounters. Satan employs demonic spirits to create discord in our relationships, especially those who have a divine assignment for its existence

covert operations—covered, hidden, not easily detected activities

deception/illusion—the intentional act of cheating, misleading, or the willful act of misrepresentation of facts and truth. Paul warns us to judge nothing before its time. He also exhorts us to walk after the Spirit so that we may overcome the lust of the flesh (Gal. 5:16).

declare—to state emphatically and authoritatively

decree—an authoritative order, directive, or command enforced by law. In our kingdom role, we must accept our God-given jurisdictional authority and effectively utilize our power through the spoken word

disallow—to forbid and refuse to allow

disapprove—to refuse to approve, or to reject

DNA—a self-replicating nucleic acid that carries genetic information in cells and is responsible for the synthesis of RNA. DNA consists of two long chains of nucleotides twisted into a double helix (a spiral form or structure) and joined by hydrogen bonds, the sequence of which determines individual hereditary characteristics. It is postulated that demonic spirits (known as spirits of inheritance) attach themselves to the DNA and are passed down as proclivities, idiosyncratic behaviors, family traits, and peculiarities.

domicile—a dwelling place, home, or residence

employ—to utilize the service or assistance of another

enforce—to compel observance of or obedience to; to impose and compel

establish—to enact, institute, and firmly secure

execute—to take action in accordance with specific divine requirements

forbid—to refuse to allow

Goshen—a prophetic spiritual place in God that protects believers from judgment and diabolical activities imposed upon specific persons, residing in specific geographical regents and special locations harassment—an exasperating, disturbing annoyance or irritation that threatens or undermines personal peace and tranquility. Satan's ultimate plan is to oppress and victimize the person he is harassing.

illusion—an erroneous perception of reality

impression—conception, notion, idea, or feeling projected upon a person by an outside spiritual source

inhibitions—intrinsic or extrinsic things that prevent, restrain, block, or suppress appropriate reactions and responses

injunction—an obligatory directive, command, mandate, or order intended to ensure compliance

interference—a satanic act or instance of hindering, impeding, or obstructing God's work and the fulfillment of destiny and purpose

interception—to stop, reroute, or interrupt progress or an intended course

limitations—anything that restricts, constrains, restrains, controls, confines, or curbs

loose—to emancipate or release from an assignment, contracted activities/post, or undesirable state of confinement or imprisonment. As believers, we have the power to release demonic spirits from any and all diabolical assignments given by Satan that ultimately will be contrary to the will of God.

negotiations—the skill and ability to reach an agreement through the act of bargaining. As a believer, never, never negotiate with the enemy.

obliterate—to destroy completely so as to leave no evidence of prior existence

overt operation—the antithesis of covert operations, in that the works of the enemy are obvious and easily detected

overthrow—to cause destruction and downfall through the use of strategic maneuvers and decisive tactics

prohibition—a law, order, or decree that forbids, restricts, or stops something from occurring

projections—attitudes, feelings, or suppositions attributed to and imposed upon another

provocation—a perturbing stimulus that intentionally incites or rouses you to action. In the case of Satan, actions and activities are always diametrically opposed to the will of God for your life.

rebuke—to denunciate, condemn, and censure

resist—to defiantly and courageously withstand and remain firm against the actions, effects, or force of another

rules of engagement—a directive issued by a competent military authority that delineates (describes, relates, reviews) the limitations and circumstances under which forces will initiate and execute combat engagement with other forces encountered

ruling—a decree, proclamation, judgment, command, authoritative decision, or regulation announced by a lawful or unlawful authority after considerable deliberation. In this instance, we overthrow any ruling released by Satan because his authority has been usurped and is both illegal and unlawful.

satanic alliance—allied union instigated and held together by spirits, formed to advance the interests and causes of Satan

satanic concentration—the total focus of satanic powers upon individuals, organizations, governments, ministries, etc. Satan often focuses on one person in a family, church, territory, or group of people at the exclusion of others. Usually this person or group of people have a divine purpose that threatens Satan, and that he seeks to abort (e.g., Joseph, the nation of Israel, Esther, Daniel, and Jesus).

satanic database—using modern-day computer vernacular, Satan downloads information that he uses to accuse the saints before God. He also uses information to derail and destroy, undermine and sabotage a believer as well.

satanic wombs—spiritual dimensions where satanic plots, plans, and schemes are incubated, waiting for the most opportune time for their manifestation

spirit—a supernatural being

spiritual abortion—as in the natural, so it is in the spirit. The enemy seeks to apprehend and arrest wombs of the spirit in order to terminate that which is divine so that his plans and purpose can be manifested, thus superimposing itself over and against the plans and purpose of God.

spiritual incubation—the act of being held in a spiritual location designed to provide the optimal environment for divine or diabolical plans and purposes to be manifested at a future date

spiritual miscarriages—spontaneous, spiritual, and diabolically initiated loss of divine purpose and destiny

spiritual womb—a spiritual/physical dimension or location where something is generated and incubated awaiting the proper time and season for its manifestation

stigma—discredit or disgrace designed to undermine reputation, integrity, influence, or spiritual authority

stirring—an agent, an action, or a condition that elicits or accelerates a physiological or psychological activity or response

strategy—the science and art of military command as applied to the overall planning and conduct of large-scale combat operations

strongman—a principality of high rank and order assigned as a gatekeeper to a person, people, or geographical region. This entity is responsible for protecting that which Satan deems his possession.

subordinate—that which is subject to the authority or control of another

subversion—organized opposition intended to overthrow authority

suggestions—warnings, hints, or clues that subtly signal the existence of something that you may have overlooked or have been unaware of

superimpose—to lay or place something on or over something else, thus prohibiting or overruling the effect of the thing it replaces

NOTES

ONE

YOU—REDEFINED: TRUE DOMINION STARTS WITH KNOWING WHO YOU ARE

1. E. M. Bounds, "The Weapon of Prayer: God's Need of People Who Pray," http://www.cbn.com/spirituallife/prayerandcounseling/intercession/weapon_prayer_0303d.aspx (accessed May 19, 2008).

2. "Spurgeon's Boilerroom," http://www.christian-prayer-quotes.christian-attorney.net/ (accessed May 19, 2008).

3. Eternal Perspective Ministries, "Great Quotes on Prayer," http://www.epm.org/articles/prayer_quotes.html (accessed May 20, 2008).

FOUR

THE BATTLEFIELD *IS* YOUR MIND: WHERE ALL IS WON OR LOST

1. Francis Frangipane, *The House of the Lord* (n.p.: New Wine Ministries, 1996).

2. Cindy Jacobs, *Deliver Us From Evil* (n.p.: Regal Books, 2001).

3. Ibid.

4. Ibid.

5. Frangipane, *The House of the Lord*.

SIX

WEAPONS OF MASS DESTRUCTION: HIROSHIMA OF THE SPIRIT

1. *Strong's Greek and Hebrew Dictionary* (Nashville, TN: Crusade Bible Publishers, 1980).

2. Salvador Minuchin, MD, *Psychosomatic Families: Anorexia Nervosa in Context* (Cambridge, MA: Howard University Press, 1978).

3. Melody Beattie, *Codependant No More* (Center City, MN: Hazelden, 1986).

4. ThinkExist.com, "Elie Wiesel Quotes," http://thinkexist.com/quotation/the_opposite_of_love_is_not_hate-it-s/204711.html (accessed May 23, 2008).

5. www.thememoryhole.org/edu/schoomission (accessed March 1, 2006).

EIGHT

GEARING UP FOR BATTLE: WHAT ARE YOUR WEAPONS?

1. E. M. Bounds, *The Necessity of Prayer* (n.p.: Baker Book House, 1976), http://www.whatsaiththescripture.com/Voice/Necessity.of.Prayer.html (accessed May 19, 2008).

TEN

RECONNAISSANCE: GETTING DELIVERED AND OVERCOMING THE ENEMY

1. Merriam-Webster Online, "Oniomania," Merriam-Webster's Medical Dictionary, http://medical.merriam-webster.com/medical/oniomania (accessed April 11, 2008).

2. National Alliance on Mental Illness, "Understanding Mental Illnesses," http://www.naminc.org/understanding_MI.htm (accessed May 19, 2008).

INDEX

T

U

TO CONTACT CINDY TRIMM:

Cindy Trimm International

242 Medical Boulevard

Stockbridge, GA 30281

Tel: 678-565-9888 Fax: 678-565-8899

Email: info@cindytrimm.com

Web site: www.cindytrimm.com

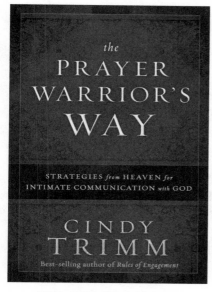
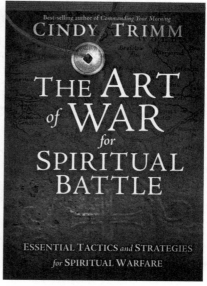

FREE NEWSLETTERS
TO HELP EMPOWER YOUR LIFE

Why subscribe today?

☐ **DELIVERED DIRECTLY TO YOU.** All you have to do is open your inbox and read.

☐ **EXCLUSIVE CONTENT.** We cover the news overlooked by the mainstream press.

☐ **STAY CURRENT.** Find the latest court rulings, revivals, and cultural trends.

☐ **UPDATE OTHERS.** Easy to forward to friends and family with the click of your mouse.

CHOOSE THE E-NEWSLETTER THAT INTERESTS YOU MOST:

- Christian news
- Daily devotionals
- Spiritual empowerment
- And much, much more

SIGN UP AT: **http://freenewsletters.charismamag.com**

8178